T0358352

TOWARD RESPONSIBLE INNOVATION

Responsibility and Philosophy for a Humanely Sustainable Future

TOWARD RESPONSIBLE INNOVATION

Responsibility and Philosophy for a Humanely Sustainable Future

Xavier Pavie

ESSEC Business School, Singapore

World Scientific

NEW JERSEY · LONDON · SINGAPORE · BEIJING · SHANGHAI · HONG KONG · TAIPEI · CHENNAI · TOKYO

Published by

World Scientific Publishing Co. Pte. Ltd.
5 Toh Tuck Link, Singapore 596224
USA office: 27 Warren Street, Suite 401-402, Hackensack, NJ 07601
UK office: 57 Shelton Street, Covent Garden, London WC2H 9HE

Library of Congress Control Number: 2021040976

British Library Cataloguing-in-Publication Data
A catalogue record for this book is available from the British Library.

TOWARD RESPONSIBLE INNOVATION
Responsibility and Philosophy for a Humanely Sustainable Future

ISBN 978-981-124-322-6 (hardcover)
ISBN 978-981-124-323-3 (ebook for institutions)
ISBN 978-981-124-324-0 (ebook for individuals)

For any available supplementary material, please visit
https://www.worldscientific.com/worldscibooks/10.1142/12440#t=suppl

Desk Editors: Balamurugan Rajendran/Thaheera Althaf

Typeset by Stallion Press
Email: enquiries@stallionpress.com

Printed in Singapore

Some other books by the same author

- *Imaginer son futur* (editorial director), L'Harmattan, 2021.
- *Imaginer le monde de demain* (editorial director), Maxima, 2021.
- *Critical Philosophy of Innovation and Innovator*, Wiley, 2020.
- *Innovation, Imagination and Creativity* (editorial director), World Scientific, 2019.
- *Le Choix d'exister*, Les Belles Lettres, 2015.
- *Le Design Thinking au service de l'innovation responsable* (co-author), Maxima, 2015.
- Pierre Hadot, *Discours et mode de vie philosophique* (editor), Les Belles Lettres, 2014.
- *L'Innovation, élan du xxie siècle* (co-author), L'Harmattan, 2014.
- *Responsible Innovation: From Concept to Practice* (co-author), World Scientific, 2014.
- *Exercices spirituels, leçons de la philosophie contemporaine*, Les Belles Lettres, 2013.
- *Exercices spirituels, leçons de la philosophie antique*, Les Belles Lettres, 2012.
- *La Méditation philosophique*, Eyrolles, 2010.
- *L'Apprentissage de soi*, Eyrolles, 2009.
- *Exercices spirituels dans la phénoménologie de Husserl*, L'Harmattan, 2008.
- *L'Influence du dialogue sur les relations et l'expérience client* (co-author), L'Harmattan, 2013.
- *Innovation responsable – Stratégie et levier de croissance des organisations*, Eyrolles, 2012.
- *Valuing People to Create Value: an Innovative Approach to Leveraging Motivation at Work* (co-author), World Scientific, 2011.
- *Management stratégique des services et innovation: complexités et nécessité* (editorial director), L'Harmattan, 2010.

***

The French version of this book was awarded the 2019 Management Book of the Year by the FNEGE (French national foundation for the education in business management), *L'innovation à l'épreuve de la philosophie*, Presses Universitaires de France.

Translated by Ròisein Kelly

About the Author

 **Xavier Pavie** is a Philosopher, Professor at ESSEC Business School, Academic Director Master in Management Asia Pacific, Director of the iMagination Center, Director of Management of Responsible Innovation advanced program for executives and Research Associate at the IRePh (Research Institute in Philosophy) University Paris Nanterre.

His research activities addresses the notion of responsible innovation through philosophy and spiritual exercises. In 2011, he was in charge of defining responsible innovation with the support of an international network of universities (sponsored by the European Commission). In 2014, he was appointed President of the evaluation commission "Innovation-Regulation-Governance" of the French National Agency for Research (ANR). Xavier Pavie has published numerous articles and books in philosophy of spiritual exercises and philosophy for responsible innovation.

Xavier Pavie has been recognized as one of the most influential personalities in the Education category in the world (LinkedIn Top Voices n°5).

Acknowledgements

I would like to express my thanks to the various people who influenced, in one way or another, this work which seeks to combine innovation and philosophy. First of all, thanks to the various academic institutions, particularly the philosophy department of the University of Paris Nanterre and to my colleagues at ESSEC Business School. In addition, thanks to the students I was lucky enough to have in class with whom I was able to engage on the different aspects of this research, especially those concerning responsible innovation and philosophy of spiritual exercises.

I would also like to thank Ròisein Kelly for her great translation work.

Contents

Introduction

Philosophy is not a body of doctrine but an activity.

Ludwig Wittgenstein
Tractatus logico-philosophicus

The purpose of this book is twofold. We hope to demonstrate not only why a philosophical approach to innovation is needed, but also how this can be achieved. To that end, we will analyse innovation through the lens of philosophy, challenge it from a philosophical standpoint, and in so doing, put the very concept of innovation to the test. To put to the test for a thing means using it; for a person it means to put them through their paces. It means to experience in some way what or whom is being tested. It means evaluating how resistant they are, their endurance over time when put under constraint, or when dealing with a specific environment. One way to test something, for example, is to submit it to difficult circumstances and observe whether or not it remains the same, and measure any alteration it suffers.

Before going into space, new materials are tested under extreme conditions so as to verify whether they can withstand Archimedes' principle, even under high pressure. The same applies to individuals. Testing schoolchildren or students by means of exams, or testing military personnel in complex situations is about testing their resilience, and assessing their abilities. Testing something or someone is a necessity because that is what guarantees the effectiveness, proper functioning and durability of what is being tested. Doing otherwise means taking a gamble, it is to take risks – sometimes unnecessary – possibly jeopardizing the object or individual whose suitability has not been evaluated.

It is easy enough to test something or someone and, in fact, ideas and concepts can also be put to the test. A political proposal can be submitted to the people as a way of verifying its relevance, measured by its acceptance or refusal. Whenever what is tested fails, whenever it is met with a refusal, the proposal must be reworked, taking account of the lessons learned thanks to the test. Just as for an object which does not pass a stress test, or an individual who fails an exam, ideas, too, the proposal needs to be reworked to try and make it successful. Therein lies the very essence of testing: to enable what is put to the test to evolve, to bring about an improvement in order to obtain something accepted and acceptable. Whether talking about an object that needs modifying, an individual who needs training or a proposal that needs reviewing, testing is just as much about improving, as it is about understanding.

This does, however, pose the question: "improvement" according to what perspective? A test which results in failure in a given context will not necessarily result in a similar negative outcome in a different situation. Moreover, success in one particular circumstance quite often makes us forget about previous or subsequent failures. So, when a test results in failure, it may be a matter of improving the idea, or the proposal, or the individual; but it might also be about testing again in a new environment. For example, a soldier who has vertigo and has to do a parachuting test can either work on his condition, or change army corps.

Putting innovation to the test through the lens of philosophy means that the tool we are choosing to test innovation is wisdom. This is the ambitious task this book sets itself. The proposal we are to evaluate is innovation, and to do so we need to have a clear definition and understanding of what it means. Equally, by choosing philosophy as the way to evaluate it, we must also have a clear definition and understanding of this concept.

In the light of what has just been said, putting innovation to the test of philosophy is wrought with challenges. When our examination, our test, our experiment is completed, will innovation have to be slightly modified, improved, or maybe undergo a profound transformation? If so, in what way and to what end? This, in turn, will raise other, no less fundamental, questions: why should innovation be tested through philosophy? How is this relevant, considering broaching this issue from the opposite point of view could have been equally valid? Throughout its very long history, philosophy itself has been a breeding ground for innovation. It has not been submitted to many innovative approaches – some conceptual, some not – concerning its mode of dissemination, but also in its organisation.

If we consider innovation from a purely commercial perspective, spontaneously it seems far removed from questions related to wisdom. If, however, innovation is seen as a propositional modality, then philosophy – like science and technology – can be a subject which can be analysed through wisdom, just as politics or sociology, history or psychoanalysis.

The challenge we are setting ourselves is to question innovation from a philosophical perspective, or more precisely, we are to examine innovation through this perspective. Of course, this will be in as much as it is a proposal, but also in as much as it relates to objects or individuals. To submit innovation to examination is to test it, which seems to be a pressing need in our contemporary world, even if this examination is to be done by means of a unusual discipline not traditionally associated with it. The categories of philosophy, with their titles such as evil, good, responsibility, respect, ethics, morality, etc., are not those such of profit, creativity, or performance which are usually applied to innovation. However, if the need for this evaluation seems so pressing, it is because innovation seems to have undergone a paradigm shift. Over the past half century, innovation has taken on a new dimension: the Internet; DNA sequencing; genomic manipulation; advances in transhumanist technology; nanotechnologies, etc. These are only some of the many recent innovations all of which raise new issues whose consequences are as significant as they are irreversible.

Innovation seem to have been liberated from two major constraints. The first is technical and scientific: in a relatively short time scale, everything has become possible, and anywhere on the planet. The second limitation is that of institutional moral constraints. The strength of moral persuasion which Churches used to wield, especially related to questions of human life, has completely dissipated. All this is taking place in a liberal world where each of the continents and almost all countries have launched themselves into varying degrees innovation, generally perceiving it purely from the perspective of growth. The growth dimension goes hand in hand with recent evolutions in the funding of innovation, where increasingly this is being developed by private structures. There is still some public funding devoted to innovation, but this, too, is driven by the perspective of financially profitable investments, thereby adopting the same attitude as private organisations, the same as any company looking to secure profit, rather than to advance the common good in a genuinely altruistic way.

Philosophy constitutes the perfect tool to put innovation to the test because it is profoundly human in nature. In a way, innovation, too, is primarily human: in its proposal – the idea of doing; in its mechanism – the notion of implementing; and in its purpose – a desire to improve life. Despite this, we can still ask might innovation have become too human? In other words, to what extent has it sought to go beyond its limits, sometimes even unintentionally, or without being aware of doing so? Innovation would thus find itself trapped in a system whereby it no longer had the necessary critical distance and perspective that the evolution of the world actually requires. In fact, we are really talking about the innovator, the person behind innovation, who now has at their disposal great technical possibilities, is free from any ethical or moral constraints, in an environment where states are subject to the diktat of the market, and is the sole person in command. They are an *Übermensch* whose nature ranks as divine. They are above other humans, beyond the common person. Consequently, we might ask ourselves: is it innovation or the innovator which we are to put to the test of philosophy? What are the real actions, goals and motivations of the innovator? How can the innovator assume the fundamental issues of responsibility that lie upon them? This is all the more relevant in the face of recent advances which are disrupting both humankind and our ecosystem. People are capable of innovating. They do know how meet the demands of innovation and how to implement it; but do they know how to deal with the consequences and grasp all that is at stake? If the triad of technical possibility, lack of morality and liberalism is the angle from which innovation is analysed, is the only frame of reference, the only perspective, then unbridled innovation will continue to make its way along the highway which perhaps leads nowhere.

However, the innovator is not condemned to be the prisoner of such a fixed identity, trapped in this triad, as long as they are able to think about innovation or know how to think about it. It is not impossible that the innovator themselves could be educated to engage in such analysis, could work on themselves, develop their knowledge in adjacent fields which would enable him to approach innovating in a new way. Philosophy, as it always has, could serve as the stimulus for this to happen. Philosophy has always sought, in fact, to help humankind control its passions, to help us be able to control ourselves. Of course, philosophy concerns itself with understanding the world, but it is first and foremost about enabling people to live better, or suffer as little as possible, in the face of the uncertainties of life, the suffering, obstacles and worries which it brings with it. Stoicism, Epicureanism, Cynicism all developed "spiritual exercises" to precisely this end. These exercises, designed to work on our own self-improvement, sought to help people reflect about themselves, to make them work on themselves in order to change, transform themselves, and to act wisely. It would be far from useless, and even very salutary to make it possible for the innovator to practice spiritual exercises, so that they could formulate a critical response to this triad in which they are immersed. It would seem that it has become indispensable to educate the innovator so that they are no longer crushed by the environment in which they operate, but rather become the source of critical insights on this same environment thanks to their innovative work.

Innovation – and with it the Innovator – stands at a fork in the road, a road which splits in two, a *bivium*. On the one hand, there is a simple, easy, straight, but short path. This path is that of continuing to innovate as before, as we have always done, without careful examination, without scrutiny. This path perpetuates the triad, the path of unbridled innovations, where innovation goes unchecked, where innovators themselves are surpassed by themselves and their innovations. The other path is narrower, winding and complex, but it goes further, higher, and its destination is wisdom. Given that a new context has emerged in which it is not so much a matter of questioning our *ability* to do, but rather *whether or not* we should do, this path which must be taken, is a philosophical journey. This is the path which responsible and benevolent innovators should take. It is not just about what is right and what is wrong; the innovator needs to build an inner citadel for the necessary reflection on *what* he does and *why* he does it.

In order for us to truly test innovation, we must first understand exactly what it is that we are testing. Understanding innovation with all its complexities is an important part of this project because it enables us to cut through the mythical notions this term evokes. It will also, for example, enable us to avoid confusing innovation with invention. Not least, by delving into the mechanisms which give birth to innovation, we will be able to pinpoint precisely where these processes could be improved.

In parallel, philosophy needs to be examined with the same attention. It is a question of understanding philosophy not so much in terms of its history, its genealogy, its chronology, but rather in terms of the effects it has consistently sought to produce since Ancient philosophy. We will also see that philosophy has always been, even from its outset, a way of living, behaving and acting. Against this background, it will become clear that innovation, which pervades every aspect of our daily lives, is an object on which philosophy must reflect, on which it must comment, and in so doing evaluate the way in which innovation is implemented. Contemporary philosophy has not yet fully understood that its focus must be on the daily lives of individuals, what they experience, what they do, how they act. In ancient times, the *raison d'être* of philosophy was to be a discipline of action, to produce a discourse, *theōria*, but was always unequivocally in perspective of a matching *praxis*. The ordinary person evolves in an environment composed of organisations, companies, communities, and their involvement in these areas of life occupies the greater part of their existence. It is on this existence that philosophy must reflect, even if it happens to be called management or organisation. By opening up these activities to philosophical examination, they are now not perceived exclusively as organs of productivity, devices whose sole purpose is to ensure the organisation's performance. Philosophy, by seeking to maintain its purity of thought, finds itself caught in its own trap, and ends up relegated to the background in those areas where the vast majority of human activity takes place. Innovation is a major component of these activities – in fact we will argue it is the most decisive. That is why it must be subject to philosophical analysis. The development of innovations, together with the investments it requires, its omnipresence in the everyday life of non-profit organisations, of political parties, of companies, in education, all compel us to stop relegating this to an afterthought, and on the contrary, thanks to philosophy, to bring it to the forefront.

Chapter 1

What Is Innovation?

"The only constant in life is change, continuing change, inevitable change, that is the dominant factor in society today. No sensible decision can be made any longer without taking into account not only the world as it is, but the world as it will be ..."

Isaac Asimov
Asimov on Science Fiction

Why Do We Innovate?

Innovation precedes its conceptualisation. The latter emerged in the Middle Ages, but innovation *per se* predates this, and is inherent to any organism, organisation or organ striving to survive. In fact, we ourselves innovate to survive. Consequently, we must change from within, evolve, transform – in short, do all that is possible in order to ensure our survival. Etymologically, this is the meaning of the word: the need for self-transformation. It comes from the Latin word *novare* (to change) and *in* (inside), i.e. from within something or someone. The "inside" to which we refer can be anything ranging from an organisational structure to an actual physical body. Whenever change is necessary for survival it is for one reason and one reason only: the environment. The evolving character of our environment requires we, too, undergo evolutions and changes. If the context never evolved, innovation would cease to be. The gradual disap-pearance of the third molars, also called "wisdom teeth", is a perfect illus-tration of this. Teeth first appeared several hundred million years ago, with

1

the first jawed vertebrates. In mammals, differentiated teeth appeared due to the need to catch certain species with shells for sustenance. Mammals thus acquired a differentiated dentition – incisors, canines, premolars, molars, etc. – for crushing these shells and feeding themselves. In such a context, we can easily understand the importance of the third molars which enabled our carnivorous ancestors to cut flesh, tear off certain skins, shred roots, etc. However, the evolution of the human environment over the past several thousand years means we no longer require such a dental apparatus for food, and therefore for our survival. Today, everything is more or less within reach. Livestock and production systems provide a "flexible" diet, rendering our "wisdom teeth" obsolete. In some instances, it is even medically recommended to have them extracted in order to prevent the development of health issues, sometimes severe – cysts, infection, damage to the jawbone, etc. As a result, nowadays it is better for our survival to have our wisdom teeth removed than to keep them. Over the last several hundred years, scientists have observed the gradual disappearance of these third molars in the human body. We are not all born with wisdom teeth, and sometimes we only need one or two out of the four removed. Of course, this can vary from one individual to another, but there is a definitive trend in the population as a whole toward people no longer having wisdom teeth. These now useless, or sometimes even problematic, atrophied organs – which play no role in chewing – are disappearing. This illustrates just how fundamental, ingrained and recognised evolutionism is, and just how vital adaptability is. It is because the body is able to adapt that it is capable of surviving and developing. This does not mean that all organisations, organisms or bodies are capable of such adaptation, nor that they adapt regularly. The history of the evolution of species is concrete evidence of this fact: those who survive are not necessarily the "strongest"[1] but the most adaptable. The human body has had to innovate in the Latin sense of the word: it has "changed from within" in order to ensure its continued survival in an ever-evolving environment.

To innovate is to change

What holds true for the body holds equally true for all living and shifting organisations which find themselves in an ever-evolving context. In the

---

[1] Charles Darwin, *On the Origin of Species* (the complete title of the original edition is *On the Origin of Species by Means of Natural Selection, or the Preservation of Favoured Races in the Struggle for Life*), 1859.

face of the arrival of a new competitor, a company has no choice but to undergo change, to transform itself, in order to survive. Of course, this competitive aspect is not the only driver of change. This can come in the form of new legislation, for example, which reshapes a company's environment, and so force it to change. Non-profit organisations are equally concerned: if legislation is passed changing the statutes on which it depends, or if its funding changes in one way or another, it must consider how to adapt in order to ensure its continued existence. We often seek protection in one form or another, shy away from change; change is something we tend to avoid at all costs because it projects us into the unknown, which is full of fears, risks and uncertainties. When our environment does not change, there is no need for us to change, and it is often easier to fight to ensure that our context does not change rather than to question how we should adapt to a new reality. This is what drives society to call on governments to provide protection in the way of statutes and laws. In a way, we are calling upon something from a transcendent order for protection. The reverse is equally true, a government will be harshly criticised if it tries to change a context which will force an organisation to adapt. A range of factors have put all sorts of organisations (profit-driven companies, NGOs, charitable organisations, political parties) under pressure: the opening up of borders in recent decades – whether physical or economic, the intensity of globalisation and the acceleration of trade – whether commercial, material or data – the unprecedented development of techniques and technologies – profit-driven companies, NGOs, charitable organisations, political parties – have under pressure. The same applies to the human body, profoundly transformed by the growing emergence of techniques with more and more devices being implanted or replacing our flesh, organs and limbs and which question our relationship to our human nature. In recent decades, all of our environments have changed drastically. Every single aspect of our lives is different from that of previous generations, even those of our parents or grandparents. The ways in which we eat, travel, learn, move, communicate, work, act as citizens have been disrupted, sometimes profoundly, over a very short period of time. This is particularly true for communication, for example, where technical advances over the past two decades alone have generated a paradigm shift in the way we interact with one another.

The more radical and fast-paced the changes, the greater the fear and rejection they cause. It is not so much an opposition to change, but rather to change insofar as it affects "me". It is conceivable that we would all be in favour of change, including when it impacts us, if we were able to evaluate its benefits positively and immediately. Clearly, change is more easily accepted when it does not directly impact us or when it is favourable to us. For example, a deregulation which is in our favour as consumers is considered necessary, but if it forces us to transform our organisation, to change the way we do things, our spontaneous reaction is to reject or criticise it.

Indeed, it is much more comfortable to be protected by a state, a monopoly, a father figure, to be chaperoned by an environment than to have to modify ourselves, to change who we are, especially since we know nothing about the effects and consequences of these transformations. Without going so far as sharing Kant's conclusion that an individual's intelligence can be measured by the quantity of uncertainty they are is able to bear, it goes without saying that those who have the capacity to accept change despite the absence of security, protection, clear and distinct future results, have a clear advantage which ultimately enables them to be one step ahead of those who cling obstinately to a past that will inexorably change.

Everything is innovation

Innovation is the way the world advances. It is not a question of interpreting this statement positively or negatively, it is a simple observation. The world and its evolution are nothing more than a sum of permanent innovations. Since the beginning of existence, we have been nothing but simultaneously the product and the parents of innovation. We may even entertain somewhat of an incestuous relationship with innovation because we sometimes generate innovations which become our masters, making us so dependent on them that they end up inhabiting us and, in turn, generate new innovations.

Doctors who develop new reproductive methods such as medically assisted procreation, surrogate pregnancies – what we might call the "descendants" of the first "test-tube baby" – are developing innovations which generate a dependence from which there is no escaping. Only a few decades ago, the "natural" way and adoption were the only methods available for having a child; today there are multiple techniques and options. Whatever your sexual orientation, whatever condition may have made you sterile, today there are many possibilities available for becoming a parent. In other words, the "product" of innovation (in this case, the new-born), gives its parents – through the intermediary of the innovator-doctor – love, passion and affection. Without medical innovations in this field, prospective parents would not have experienced this dependency on their child. Innovation is what put them in this situation, one which they clearly appreciate as much as they depend on it.

This example also illustrates an interesting point: there is no such thing as creating needs. It is a fallacy to believe that one can create needs. It is not for lack of trying, and a good number of companies have paid the price. Despite product launches built on extensive research and communication campaigns, 76% of all new products fail in their first year.[2] It is impossible to create a need, as we are amply reminded by examples of famous failures such as Apple's NewtonPad, France Telecom's Bi-bop, Google Glass or the Kodak Digital camera. The same holds true for luxury items, such as watches from major brands, for example, which are obviously not sold to display the time but to "nourish" a social stature. A designer handbag is not intended to be practical, but rather to showcase the owner's social "success", just as owning a racing car is not about driving at high speed but rather highlighting one's social "status". Such needs to display social success with a watch, purse or luxury car may be considered ridiculous, useless, superfluous for some; but it is not necessarily the case for others. "Nurturing" a social status is a need that can be quite obsessive, and can even become a way of life for some.[3]

Viewing innovation as the world's way forward is to understand that systematically something is being produced, made, manufactured, added, modified or amended through this process, whether in terms of products/services or intellectual production. Everything around us is innovation, just as we ourselves are the product of innovations, in at least three ways: how they impact us; the innovations we introduce into society; and through our own innovative developments – thoughts, physiological changes, etc. This does not prevent us from disparaging certain innovations which we do not consider "positive" because they seem harmful, ineffective or useless to us. The fact remains, whether we like these innovations or not, they are none the less innovative. A pesticide, a genetically modified organism or a machine gun: these are all innovations in their own right, on a par with a vaccine or a process that makes water fit for human consumption.

---

[2] Nielsen Breakthrough Innovation Report 2014.
[3] Michel Pinçon, Monique Pinçon-Charlot, *Voyage en grande bourgeoisie*, PUF, 2005.

Everything is innovation. This is the only possible conclusion that we can draw from the thorough observation of our environment. All living beings have inexorably continued to innovate throughout their history, and it is the lack of innovation for certain species which, at one point, led to their disappearance. Their lack of adaptation and evolution doomed them to extinction. For the rest, continuity, i.e. survival, has only been achieved through continuous innovation. From the first living organisms until the beginning of humanity, the variations, selections, and struggles to survive have systematically adopted different forms. From cavemen to contemporary man through modern man, the continued existence of humanity was ensured solely by the innovations we developed, whether they concern housing, urban planning, food, medicine, protection. If the human species had disappeared between its emergence and our contemporary times, this would have been because of a lack of innovation, an inability adapt; and if it were to disappear, it would, again, be because of our failure to innovate. To put it simply, the bleak environmental situation in which we find ourselves today demands that we innovate in the coming decades. It is imperative we transform ourselves, we change our lifestyles, in order to fight global warming and survive. Otherwise, the human species will go extinct in the more or less long term. Alternatively, our survival could stem from a techno-scientific process to increase or modify the ozone layer so that we would no longer be dependent on it. Another solution would be to leave this tired, dried up planet to live on a planet which would enable us to prolong the human species. Last but not least, the human body too adapt to a polluted environment, to climatic change. Perhaps our skin will become more airtight, our lungs will change shape, or maybe our entire respiratory system will be radically transformed to adapt to these new conditions. If we do not change our lifestyles, if we do not find a way not to be constrained by the ozone layer, if we cannot live on another planet or if our bodies do not adapt, then the human species will eventually disappear.

Innovating, Inventing, Discovering

Innovating is not the same as inventing

As mentioned earlier, it is the context, the environment and changing situations which force organisations to innovate in order to survive. It is because other players offer a better proposal for their customers that some companies have no choice but to offer something even more attractive. The environment changes, so too must we. However, simply offering a new proposal is not enough in order to ensure survival. The proposal needs to be relevant, garner interest and generate value in some form. No matter how "brilliant" the proposal, if it does not enable survival, the organisation in question will ultimately perish. This is yet another of the complexities in understanding innovation.

Innovation and invention are often conflated. The key difference lies the output innovation simply must generate. An invention is an idea, a proposal, sometimes it can even be a prototype. If a company launches a product or service which has required significant investments in terms of financial and human resources, and that it fails to generate value, profit, even if this product is "fantastic", it will not enable the organisation to survive. In these circumstances, the product or service is nothing more than an idea, an invention, or even just an intention. Austrian economist Joseph Schumpeter expressed this clearly in 1911 by stressing that innovation is the industrial exploitation of inventions, their dissemination, and their economic significance.[4] This definition of innovation, which is still relevant today, clearly explains that while there may be an invention at the origin of the innovation, this invention is not, *de facto*, an innovation. In order for an invention to become an innovation, it needs to be exploited in industrially, in other words it must be more than a prototype, an idea or a model. However, industrial production in itself is not sufficient. In order to be considered an innovation, the invention then needs to be distributed, produced on a relatively large scale. Lastly, and most importantly, one of the most fundamental aspects is that, in order for an invention to be called an innovation, in reference to an organisation, it must yield economic value. This economic performance will not be measured in terms of turnover alone – however significant it may be – but rather in terms of the profit it generates. Profit is what enables organisations to survive; without profit, organisations will ultimately go under. Such an understanding of innovation perfectly highlights the importance of identifying three phases in the life of a product or service. The first is upstream, and concerns its development. The following two take place downstream, which is divided into

---

[4]Joseph Schumpeter, *Theorie der wirtschaftlichen Entwicklung*, revised edition, 1925. Translation to English by Redvers Opie, *The Theory of Economic Development: An Inquiry into Profits, Capital, Credit, Interest, and the Business Cycle*, New Brunswick, Transaction Books (1938) 2008.

two phases: the moment when the product or service is put on the market, i.e. when it is offered for purchase and generates its first sales, generates turnover; and a second phase when the offer attracts a significant enough number of customers to generate sufficient income to offset the investments required for its development. The transition from this second to third phase takes place when you cross what is referred to as the "Moore chasm".[5] Crossing this chasm is a necessary transition in order for a new product or service to be considered as an innovation. Prior to this transition, we can speak of "candidates for innovation", but not innovation in and of itself, because it does not yet permit the survival of the organisation. When a new offer reaches this point by securing a significant number of buyers, and by corollary, the product or service generates more revenues than costs, then the "candidate for innovation" does effectively become an innovation.

Innovation, therefore, is fraught with uncertainty because it is impossible to know ahead of time whether or not the proposed product or service will cross this chasm successfully. The organisation will do its best to communicate, distribute and position the offer, but the fact remains that only consumers can turn an invention into innovation. This principle sheds light on why innovation must be understood first and foremost as failure. As a direct corollary to the very existence of this chasm, this unknown, uncontrolled phase, the organisation proposing an invention needs to amplify, as much as possible, the upstream phase of development of its new idea. Indeed, the more inventions there are, the more likely it is that an innovation is hiding among them. In other words, with only one invention, the risk of total failure is almost assured.

Discovering is not the same as innovating

In order to fully understand the entire innovation process, we must first understand the upstream phase of the process. This phase covers what happens before the launch, within the organisation itself. It is during this phase that new ideas are developed, that they emerge, that they are tested, that they are created. This can be achieved in a number of ways: by collecting information from prospects, by asking them for their opinion or by

---

[5] Geoffrey Moore, *Crossing the Chasm: Marketing and Selling High-Tech Products to Mainstream Customers*, second edition, Harvard Business, August 2006.

observing them. This can also be achieved by using internal or external R&D structures. As we have already pointed out, ideas do not automatically result in innovations; nor is R&D a guarantee of innovation. R&D departments can offer a product, a very original and unique piece of technology, but if, once on the market, this proposal does not find enough buyers and does not succeed in generating more profits than the costs invested, then it will have done nothing to ensure the survival of the organisation. In 2016, the top seven companies in terms of R&D spending were[6]: Volkswagen, with $13.2 billion; Samsung, with $12.7 billion; Amazon, with $12.5 billion; Alphabet, with $12.3 billion; Intel, with $12.1 billion; Microsoft, with $12 billion; and Roche with $10 billion. However, on the list of the most innovative companies, the top seven were: Apple, which spends "only" $8.1 billion on R&D; followed by Alphabet; 3M; Tesla; Amazon; Samsung; and Facebook. In other words, few companies succeed in being both on the list of those that spend most on R&D and those that enjoy economic success thanks to their launches. The Apple case is particularly telling, because the Cupertino firm spends 3.1% of its revenue on R&D, i.e. half as much as its competitors, and yet it is at the top of the list of most innovative companies.

This illustrates the importance of distinguishing both between invention and innovation and between R&D and innovation. There is often confusion among these terms, but clearly, they are in no way identical. They can interact and complement one another, but in no way replace one another. In all events, what organisations strive for is innovation.

The Breeding Ground of Innovation

What has been presented so far is partly based on the foundational concepts about innovation set out by Schumpeter. This, however, should not obscure the fact that a great many economists, and sociologists and philosophers, have also worked on developing the concept of innovation, some of whom have shed light on the particular context which fosters innovation.[7]

---

[6]Strategy & 2016 Global Innovation 1000 Survey data and analysis.
[7]Godin, Benoît (2008). *Innovation: The history of a category*. Working Paper. Institut national de la recherche scientifique, Centre Urbanisation Culture Société, Montréal.

The term "innovation" first appeared in the Middle Ages, and in its early stages, innovation was related more to the notion of change than to that of creativity. This notion first emerged in the field of law to signify a contract for a new debtor. Before the 20th century, the term was only very rarely used in the arts and sciences, where the term "novelty" was preferred, as was "creation" and particularly "invention". It was Nicolas Machiavelli, in *The Prince* (1513), and Francis Bacon, in *Of Innovations* (1625), who were the first to devote pages to innovation, more specifically to discuss – particularly in the religious context of the 17th century – people who were resistant to innovation and change. At the time, literary productions and debates around innovation always focused on the notion of change, rather than creativity. Until the 18th century, innovation was, in fact, a pejorative concept. A "novator" was a person which ought not be trusted, of whom one should be wary. This was the case in the political domain, where political change was perceived negatively, as well as in religious spheres, where, because of orthodoxy, innovation was regarded as heresy. This pejorative connotation persisted until the 18th century, at which time inventors began to earn money from their inventions.

We owe the first theory of innovation to French sociologist Gabriel Tarde, at the end of the 19th century. His work distinguished the core notions of static versus dynamic, and focused on explaining the various social changes of his time, whether in grammar, linguistics, religion, the law, the Constitution, the economic system, industry and the arts. His work promoted the notion of innovation as something new, however, he did not offer an explicit definition of this idea.[8]

In the economic sphere, and again before Schumpeter, Adam Smith is of particular interest. The Scottish economist whose work does not focus on innovation as such, or even technological progress for that matter, but he does explain the means necessary for nations to be competitive in an environment which was – already in the 18th century – highly competitive. Smith highlights the link between a nation's increased production and its increased ability to consume and therefore to meet needs. However, such an increase in production can only come from an increase in labour productivity. According to Smith, this productivity can be achieved through the division of labour, which, in turn, generates a growth process based on increased productivity and developing trade. To explain his point, he uses the now famous example of the pin factory, and in so doing

---

[8]Gabriel Tarde, *Les lois de l'imitation*, Paris Seuil, 2001.

underlines the increase in productivity due to a thorough division of elementary tasks and the need for people to specialise in these tasks: *In the progress of the division of labour, the employment of the far greater part of those who live by labour, that is, of the great body of the people, comes to be confined to a few very simple operations, frequently to one or two. But the understandings of the greater part of men are necessarily formed by their ordinary employments. The man whose whole life is spent in performing a few simple operations, of which the effects are perhaps always the same, or very nearly the same, has no occasion to exert his understanding or to exercise his invention in finding out expedients for removing difficulties which never occur. He naturally loses, therefore, the habit of such exertion, and generally becomes as stupid and ignorant as it is possible for a human creature to become.*[9]

It is interesting to note that although Adam Smith initiated the reflection on the need for innovation in order to be competitive with other nations, his proposal ultimately shaped a typology of innovation which is called process innovation.

Between Adam Smith and Joseph Schumpeter, there was the English economist David Ricardo, who deserves mention David Ricardo, especially since he is one of the first economists to have formalised the concept of innovation and its role in the economy, without, however, generalising it. He was also interested in the importance for nations to specialise, and more particularly to do so in a field where they already have a competitive advantage. The most prosperous and wealthiest national economies, he tells us, always have one or more economic activity that gives them a competitive advantage over other nations. Consequently, they should position themselves within the international market, where they will become a key player. If a country successfully specialises in a given economic activity, it will dominate its market and gain a decisive advantage. It will even be free to set the reference price on important markets. Germany, for example, opted to specialise in the high-end car segment, chemicals and machine tools. For the first sector, German brands do indeed set the benchmark – whether it is in terms of price, performance or quality – and this benchmark against which French and Italian brands, for example, seek to position themselves. In another

---

[9] Adam Smith, *An Enquiry into the Nature and Causes of the Wealth of Nations*, New York, Random House, 1937; Adam Smith, *Recherches sur la nature et la cause des richesses des nations* (1776), Paris, Flammarion, 1991 (trad. G. Granger), L. II, p. 406.

context, the United States is a leader in the arms and entertainment indus-tries as well as information technologies and everything related to digital technology in the broadest sense. Whatever the organisation, all seek to secure a dominant position on the market, whether in terms of the operat-ing system, the hardware itself or the search engine. Paradoxically, the United States advocates ultra-liberalism and complete deregulation, and yet, only a small group of organisations have a virtual monopoly in each of their respective fields. So, each country needs to secure this specialised competitive advantage for which it will be chosen over all others. Other examples include: the luxury sector – perfumes, wine and haute couture – for France; electronics for Japan; or high-tech for South Korea. This advantage on the scale of a country, designed to generate a monopoly in a given sector, is strictly equivalent to what happens within organisations: all seek to secure a monopoly, whether it is exceptional coffee that can be made at home, the most hegemonic social network for all segments of the population, a social network for professionals or even electric vehicles, and so on. Monopoly, as Schumpeter points out, ought to be the ultimate goal of any organisation; and it is through their innovations that this can be achieved. In essence, this monopoly is systematically redefined according to how relevant the supply is to the demand. For example, the company which held the monopoly on high-quality ground coffee was edged out by Nespresso, which offered a different way of making coffee which earned the preference of consumers, thereby totally deconstructing the existing monopoly.

Politics and innovation, innovation policies

If, as posited, nations need to identify the innovative sector which will sustain them, then this in turn means that there is a crucial link between politics and innovation, in at least two ways. On the one hand, as outlined above: a more liberal government will encourage competi-tion among organisations which, in order to survive, will be driven by the obsession to develop new products or services. By contrast, a socialist policy which protects the status quo in terms of positioning and players, and tends to curb competition will not produce innova-tion, which, due to this specific political context, is not necessary. This is one of the explanations – in addition to demographics and economic development – for the large number of innovations proposed by the North American continent.

When the Mayflower arrived in what would become New England, the Puritan English were not necessarily welcome on this inhabited land. Although they were initially helped by Squanto, a famous native American from the Wampanoag tribe, their survival could only be achieved by exploiting the land, growing cereals and developing crops thanks to the tools and know-how (many of the passengers on the boat were farmers[10]) they had brought from their home country. Over time, these techniques were adopted, deployed and used by all the inhabitants of the American territory, with a transition from communal to privatised agriculture. This marked the beginning of American entrepreneurship, the importance of exploitation in order to create value. Native Americans had their own know-how. However, English pilgrims used well-proven developments from their home country to take possession of land. This conquest was achieved through wars and by confiscating land belonging to the local indigenous populations, but also through the implementation of crop production techniques. The conquest from east to west in the 17th century in the United States was also a technical conquest. This historical moment definitely fostered a pioneering, conquering spirit, which could also be qualified as individualistic, in the Emersonian sense of the term.

Contrary to popular belief, individualism does not mean selfishness. Emerson's idea of individualism does not pit the individual against the community, but rather calls for the individual to become the expression of both self and the community.[11] The ultimate goal is to attain self-improvement, but through an iterative construction with others. This improvement of the self is at the heart of Emerson's argument, according to which each and every one of us develop our self in order to exist, to live, to create, to do. This requires what Emmerson calls self-reliance. Emerson proclaims that *The virtue in most request is conformity. Self-reliance is its aversion,*[12] thereby standing against conformism which destroys the individual. For Emerson, society is responsible for this conformism in its abhorrence of

---

[10] Bernard Vincent (dir.), *Histoire des États-Unis*, Paris, Flammarion, 1997. It should be noted that some theories question the extent of the help which the pilgrims received.

[11] Sandra Laugier, "Emerson, la voix, le perfectionnisme et la démocratie", in Sandra Laugier (dir.), *La voix et la vertu*, PUF, 2010, p. 368.

[12] Ralph W. Emerson, "Self-Reliance" in *Essays: First Series (1841). The Collected Works of Ralph Waldo Emerson*, Vol. 2, R.E. Springer, A. R. Ferguson, J. Slater, D. E. Wilson. J. F. Carr, W. E. Williams, P. Nicoloff, R. E. Burkholder, B. L. Packer, Cambridge M.A., Harvard University Press, 1971–2003, p. 29.

self-reliance. For conformity turns men into mere bedbugs, small fry, rabble. Emmerson regularly points out in his essays and conferences that through conformity, individuals do not exist; they join dead churches and vote for major political parties.[13]

In order to eschew conformity, we must become self-reliant, without, however, relying solely on ourselves, because that is what makes us "small fry".[14] We must stand up against conformity, that is, undertake a conversion which steers us away from conformity, shedding our conformity, as if "we were born again".[15] For Emerson, we must create, imagine what does not yet exist and it is in doing so that we oppose everything that is conformity. In order to achieve this, we must dismiss anything which is usually deemed of value because it is rational, homogeneous or coherent. Instead, Emerson tells us: "I hope in these days we have heard the last of conformity and consistency",[16] adding that "With consistency a great soul has simply has nothing to do. He may as well concern himself with his shadow on the wall".[17]

Emerson is considered to be the first true philosopher born on American soil, whose influence on the American way of thinking, whether academic, political or civic, is considerable, and his proposals around individualism and self-reliance became pillars of American history. The founding beliefs of American society, conveyed through phrases such as the "self-made-man", "the American dream", the recurring idea that an individual can start from nothing in life, have no money or education, and become wealthy and successful, is in fact the legacy of the first settlers who, in a way, managed to conquer this new continent. For example, for settlers, land exploitation is what defined land ownership. Close to Lockian theories, the person who owns a piece of land is not necessarily the person who lives there – as was the case for the native Indians – but rather the one who exploits it. Consequently, the person who is capable of making the land fruitful by growing and cultivating cereals becomes the "owner" of the cultivated plot rather than the person who only lives on it.

---

[13] *Ibid.*, p. 32.

[14] Stanley Cavell, *Qu'est-ce que la philosophie américaine?*, translated by Sandra Laugier, Gallimard, 2009, p. 284.

[15] Ralph W. Emerson, *The Collected Works of Ralph Waldo Emerson*, Vol. 3, *Op. cit.*, p. 41.

[16] Ralph W. Emerson, "Self-Reliance", in *Essays: First Series (1841). The Collected Works of Ralph Waldo Emerson*, Vol. 2, *Op. cit.*

[17] *Ibid.*, p. 33.

There is, then, a dominant theme in the American way of thinking to the effect that one must do something, develop, use, exploit or test something or be enterprising. Entrepreneurs are always revered, seen as pioneers, adventurers – just like the first settlers. The history of the United States continues to portray as heroes those who have "done something", its great inventors and innovators such as: Cornelius Vanderbilt; John Morgan; Alexander Bell; Nikola Tesla; Andrew Carnegie; John Rockefeller; Thomas Edison; etc.

The evolution of American history has never disavowed these foundations. It is not surprising to see that, according to a study conducted by the Library of Congress and the Book of the Month Club, the book that has most influenced American history – after the Bible – is *Atlas Shrugged*.[18] This novel is a must-read for anyone who wants to understand American thought, past and present. Ayn Rand, the book's author, explains that the challenge of the book is to make people understand "the *role* of man's mind in existence", more precisely the minds of those who "produce", pioneers, creators, those who contribute something to society whether they are scientists, entrepreneurs, artists, workers, etc. These individuals bring value to society and for Ayn Rand they must be protected from state interventionism, from those who do nothing and from parasites, from those who take advantage of the system. For, she asks, what would become of society without men of spirit, without intellectuals, without people to develop ideas, proposals, concepts? This book, which has consistently been a best-seller since the late 1950s, has been read and studied at length by teenagers in most American high schools, in politics classes; her thinking is studied in university courses across the United States; and the Ayn Rand Institute regularly offers internships.[19] It has become the bible of American entrepreneurs, and has been the subject of numerous studies and research projects, and sometimes even at the heart of debates during presidential election campaigns.

In this impressive novel, two entrepreneurs find themselves having to manage both their company and the fight against governments which continuously hinder investment and development through their incompetence. The philosophy which permeates the book questions the role of each person in society and the compensation that can be expected, whether symbolic, financial or moral. In other words, it shows that there

---

[18] 1991 Survey by the Library of Congress and *The Book of the Month Club*.
[19] Link to Ayn Rand Institute website: https://ari.aynrand.org.

is nothing to be ashamed about for having succeeded thanks to your own ideas and not those of others, for amassing wealth without exploiting others, for being proud to be recognised for what you have achieved without having relied on society, its aid and handouts. It is easy to understand how this philosophy resonates particularly well with the American history of the pioneers, and is still as appealing today to entrepreneurs, who, even though they are the product of new generations, are still fervent defenders of liberal or even libertarian ideas.

American policies, whether Democratic or Republican, are both liberal-inspired. The difference is only a matter of degrees, because there is no socialism/capitalism opposition as may still be the case in countries of the old continent. As a country with a free market economy based on an entrepreneurial history, the United States has naturally developed innovative behaviour. Whether in the deployment of large organisations or start-ups, innovation is a guiding principle for this country and never seems to run dry.

This history of the development of the United States with entrepreneurship and innovation from the middle of the 19th century needs to be analysed in the light of the emergence of communist policies, particularly in the then-USSR. On the one hand, there was the Emersonian philosophy convinced that society develops through the sum of "individualists" who comprise it, that everyone must create their own work, educate themselves, play an active role in the development of society and that all these actions will ultimately pave the way for a prosperous society. In stark contrast, communist society at that time advocated for the exact opposite, particularly through Marx's ideas, where society is represented by a State whose role is to organise and govern society on behalf of the individuals who comprise it.[20] As a result, all citizens should receive the same education, have access to similar diets, live in identical housing with a relatively similar salary. It is easy to identify the benefits of this philosophy, the ultimate goal of which is to bring about a fully egalitarian society where all individuals can, together, live a relatively decent and similar life. These theoretical ideas, however, largely failed in the face of the impossibility of implementing such a system, wide open to the weaknesses of human nature and where issues of power and corruption work against such an ideal society. While the American philosophy prevailed, it did bring with

---

[20]Marx/Engels Selected Works, Vol. 1, Progress Publishers, Moscow, 1969, pp. 98–137; Translated: Samuel Moore in cooperation with Frederick Engels, first edition 1848.

it a great many inequalities. We simply cannot ignore that the gap between the richest and the poorest is constantly widening and inequalities exist across the system, namely in terms of access to healthcare, to property, to education, etc. It should be noted that in his work, Amartya Sen showed that certain categories of individuals born in the United States have a lower life expectancy than people born in China or in the state of Kerala in India.[21] Sexually transmitted diseases, drug addiction, daily violence, the cost of healthcare, the lack of an employment system which protects employees all widen the inequality and injustice among American citizens.

If, however, we look at the United States from the sole perspective of innovation as defined previously, it is clear that it prioritised innovation over invention; which, throughout its history, has consistently focused on the profitability of its developments, and on ensuring the success of whatever it proposes. For example, NASA has always set itself the objective of establishing links between technical and technological developments on the one hand and civil society on the other. For Americans, therefore, it is not only a question of conquering space, but of seeing how space exploration can contribute to the economic success of all its citizens. The development of computers, programming languages and embedded systems owes much to space exploration, and to the first manned flights, and in particular the Apollo program in the 1960s. The same is true of the survival blanket, which was initially developed in the 1960s, using a mylar aluminised plastic film to reflect radio waves on the Echo 1 balloon satellite. Fire retardant fabric, the flameproof textile made of Kevlar fibre that protects against the effects of thermal radiation, is yet another innovation resulting from space exploration. The airbag is yet another system invented and developed as part of the development of space accelerometers at a time when automotive manufacturers were engaged in parallel research. In medicine, space imaging has contributed to the evolution of medical imaging, such as MRIs. Disposable diapers were initially designed for the first astronauts whose suits included absorbent materials so they could perform their bodily functions. The coating on the pans we use today comes from materials originally designed to protect satellites from shocks in space.

---

[21] Amartya Sen, "Health in Development", Keynote address to the 52nd World Health Assembly, Geneva, May 18, 1999, in *Bulletin of the World Health Organization* 77 (1999a).

These ties between scientific discoveries and civil society stem back to a principle that had been developed in the 18th and 19th centuries by American John Kay.[22] It is easy to understand the importance of establishing systematic links between R&D and civil society, because this is what will drive profit from these initial investments and therefore enable scientists to develop new ones. Without economic success, the only alternative sources of investment for funding the continued development of innovation for a country is through taxes of one kind or another. When there are no financial resources from profit through commercial success, nor through taxes, then development for space conquest, for example, is carried out by private organisations. This is what we are currently witnessing in these early decades of the 21st century.[23]

NASA's objective was to develop practical applications in civil society of the innovations it was developing. This was clearly less of an obsession for the Russians, where the Soviet leaders had first and foremost understood the international stakes as well as the benefits that the regime could derive from the successes of its space program. Consequently, the USSR is at the origin of several significant advances in space exploration: the first artificial object in space with Sputnik in 1957; the first living being in space with the dog Laïka that same year; the first lunar probe with Luna in 1959; the first man in space with Yuri Gagarin in 1961; the first woman with Valentina Terechkova in 1963; and the first spacewalk with Alexei Leonov in 1965. However, these advances have not really benefited Russian economic development.

This highlights the extent to which it is impossible to unravel the connection between innovation and politics (in the broad sense). The context and the environment play a decisive role. Silicon Valley is what it is today simply because it is the result of situations which have fostered innovation. The economic boom this area has enjoyed can be attributed to William Hewlett and David Packard, who set up their company in the vicinity of Stanford at the instigation of their Professor Frederick Terman. However, it is mainly related to the war in the Pacific during World War II. The 1940s led the United States government to establish a large number of military contingents on the west coast, armed forces who

---

[22]Paul Mantoux, *La Révolution industrielle au XVIIIᵉ siècle*, Société nouvelle de librairie et d'édition, 1906.

[23]The most prominent initiatives are: Space X by Elon Musk; Blue Origin by Jeff Bezos; and Virgin Galactic by Richard Branson.

deployed from California and from Hawaii, mainly to Japan. Very quickly, partnerships were formed with researchers and engineers from Stanford University. Over time, this became the place where the children of the military families pursued their studies, who together started founding small businesses – what we now call start-ups. Companies flocked to benefit from the unique ecosystem and from the research facilities, to the extent that the population of Palo Alto doubled in the 1950s. This interplay between businesses and research in universities has continued to grow with Stanford but also with Caltech and Berkeley and the fledgling organisations in Silicon Valley – notably the famous Honors Cooperative Program established in 1955, again by Terman – which gave engineers from companies in the area access to university programs.

This evolution shows the extent to which innovation and the breeding ground in which it operates are interrelated. Today's contemporary world is driven generally by capitalistic ideology; however, some nations are "more" capitalistic (or freer) than others, as a result of which some nations are structurally better equipped to launch innovations which are greater in number and in importance. Whenever a government prevents or hinders a certain innovation, whether the reason is social, ethical, political, financial or environmental, there is an absolutely certain consequence: in other parts of the world, where governments might authorise the development in question, this innovation will come into being. This includes extremely sensitive developments such as human cloning, for example. From the moment a technical or technological advance is achieved, it cannot be undone, so while some countries, such as France, prohibit this type of research, a country less concerned about the ethical aspect of this advance will authorise its development. Even if public organisations were not to authorise this type of research, many private powers would invest in research into this potential innovation. Just as the saying goes, "once the genie is out of the bottle, you can't put it back in". When a new idea emerges, it is impossible to pretend that it never happened. Even though a new idea can be banned, it will never remain in the shadows for long, it will re-emerge, later or elsewhere. Assisted death, for example, is banned in France; and yet in Brussels, only an hour and a half away from Paris, it is completely legal.

All the proposals which emerged from the so-called new economy at the beginning of this century perfectly illustrate this situation. Some governments tried to slow down, if not prohibit, developments that called into question monopolies, whether in the mobility, in rental or services industries in general. This did not prevent alternative models from developing and eventually, the proposals resurfaced. Moreover, the inclination to ban an innovation in order to favour the continuity of a monopoly has consequences which go beyond the simple protection of existing players. What might a 7-year-old think in front of their television set observing strikes, the violence perpetrated by a fringe group within the population to protect its monopoly, which ends by the government giving in and legislating to prohibit opening up of to competition? To what extent might this child wonder whether it is the government who decides on innovations rather than them or key players? If innovation is in the "DNA" of young Americans, it is thanks to the fertile ground of innovation the nation has cultivated. Liberalised markets, intense competition and almost complete freedom to pursue new endeavours expects everyone to reinvent themselves constantly, so as to propose new solutions, new products or new services, to create their own jobs rather than looking for one. That is not to say that this is an ideal or even desirable situation, but looking solely through the lens of innovation, it is undeniable that this allows for the emergence of more proposals than in other contexts, such as in Europe, and in France in particular. However, in the current context of globalisation, in which everyone can become each other's customer and supplier, the areas where innovations can be generated and developed *en masse* overpower those which tend to stifle, hinder or slow down innovation. This does not mean, however, that we should believe the current hegemony enjoyed the United States in this respect has always existed, nor that it is a *fait accompli* which we are obliged to accept when faced with such an aggressive country in this domain.

One century ago, France was the equivalent of Silicon Valley and revered as such. It was the time of great scientists, Louis Pasteur; Pierre and Marie Curie; and Henri Poincaré, to name just a few; great inventors, such as Clément Adler or the Lumière brothers; and great entrepreneurs, such as Édouard Michelin, Louis Renault or André Citroën. Nor should we overlook the political advances with the 1905 law on the separation of Church and State, a proposal which was quite radical for the time, and particularly ahead of its time. Philosophy was just as prolific, this was the era of great minds such as Henri Bergson, Jean Wahl, Alain or Gaston Bachelard. These leading figures concentrated the entire French intellectual wealth in a remarkable 30-year period. At the European level, the intellectual and scientific power of the region were all the more significant if we add Einstein, Freud or Nietzsche, among many others.

It could be expected that within Europe, cooperation among countries would be easier, that they would be able to work better together, to make common advances in terms of discoveries and technological progress. The countries of this zone have shown incomparable power and leadership in all fields thanks to their history, their experience and their diversity. But what has become of the audacity which used to characterise them? What has become of the entrepreneurs of the last century? Its inventors? The philosophies which marked a certain pioneering spirit? Today, in Europe as in France, a large number of schools, universities, research centres and institutes are staffed by some of the greatest researchers, the most respected and renowned Nobel Prize winners. How does this knowledge translate into innovation?

In other words, you can never presume that the favourable context which fosters innovation will endure. The changing nature of this environment means that at the national scale, we must constantly monitor the conditions to ensure we allow for the emergence of innovative proposals. If we take the example of France, since the time it was a "French Silicon Valley", the two intervening world wars have considerably reduced research, the focus on innovation, invention and discoveries. In addition, France and other European countries only belatedly understood the phenomenon of globalisation. This enabled a large number of countries – most notably the United States and China – to take the lead, because from the early 1980s onwards they understood the new global and liberal rules which were taking shape.

The Ways of Innovation

The different types of innovation

If we want to understand innovation, we must first understand its many variants. Too often, innovation is reduced to the most recent product on the market, products which are trendy or which offer new technological features. This is only one fifth of what innovation actually is. In his *Theory of Economic Development*, Schumpeter identifies five categories of "new combinations of knowledge",[24] which is how innovation was described at that time.

---

[24]Joseph Schumpeter, Theorie der wirtschaftlichen Entwicklung, *Op. cit.*

The first of these categories is the introduction of new goods, which he calls creation of new products. This refers to a new object or technology with which consumers are not yet familiar. This is the most widely-known category because it is naturally the most visible and significant; it covers the launch of a new or slightly improved product or service. This definition includes enhancements to technical products, to components and hardware, to software as well as user- friendliness or any other functional characteristics. To cite but two examples illustrating what product and service innovations are, the two major organisations of the last 30 years – Apple for products and Microsoft for services – are particularly representative.

The second category is the introduction of a new production method, coined the creation of new methods of production. This refers to a new method not yet used in a given sector. This does not refer to a scientific discovery, but rather to a new way of doing things. This type of innovation, therefore, essentially concerns the creation or improvement of a production or distribution method. The computer technology company Dell is a very good example of this type of innovation. The company's microcomputers (microchip, screen, hard drive, etc.) have never been recognised as being particularly innovative in terms of product. However, where Michael Dell did innovate was in the brand's manufacturing and delivery process. It was based on the observation that Moore's law – which observes that every 18 months, components are halved in size while simultaneously doubling in computing power – meant that they were systematically offering technologically outdated microcomputers. Indeed, between the time of design of the microcomputer in the company's offices, selling it to intermediaries – wholesalers, resellers, distributors – it can take between a year and a year and a half for a microcomputer to reach the market, just when new, smaller, more efficient, and sometimes less expensive components are available. This means that each new PC reaches the market at the very moment at which it becomes outdated. The company was also facing stock issues: by the time the computers matching what customers had ordered were ready, it was the new components for building the newer versions that were in their warehouse. Michael Dell solved both these constraints by innovating the computer manufacturing process: he designed an on-demand service, whereby customers could procure their computers directly at their assembly centres and without intermediaries. Dell is in direct contact with its customers, who order the type of computer they want – hard disk storage, screen size, keyboard format, processor speed – which is then assembled by the company, and sent directly to the customers without any intermediaries. This process enabled the company: to save a considerable amount of time between the design of the computer and its delivery to its customers; to offer computers that were not necessarily technologically innovative, but that were not outdated either; and to control its stock flow of components for the different generations of computers. This offers an excellent illustration of the fact that innovation can enable an organisation to be more efficient without developing new products. Simply by changing its way of doing things, i.e. its process, this company was able to take a different approach from its competitors and develop a competitive advantage which enabled it to survive, in an era when key IT players were merging or being bought over, or simply went out of business.

The third type of innovation concerns entering into new markets, what is sometimes referred to as business model innovation. This type of innovation proposes a new way of selling, buying or using a product or service. This may involve the arrival of an industry in a new country, whether or not that market already existed. It could also be creating a new sales process which implies significant changes in the way the product or service is made available for sale.

Two examples illustrate this form of innovation. Amazon has completely revolutionised book buying, not so much through its remote distribution model, but through its ability to build a very large network of partners, enabling it to offer products, in this case books, in a way no one else had ever done before. The brand's proposal, called "marketplace", means anybody can become a potential bookseller, ranging from normal individuals by advertising the books we have on our bookshelves on its platform, to small or large independent book shops, who can do the same with their stock of books. By creating this new marketing mode by pooling together stocks which it does not own, Amazon created an ecosystem in which players sustain each other. At the same time, it developed an essential hub which compels everyone to go through Amazon whenever they want to be assured of finding what they are looking for.

As indicated previously, this type of innovation also applies to the business model. To a large extent, this concerns mainly industrial organisations which, faced with increasingly intense price competition, are beginning to innovate in the way they market their goods. The scene for this was set in the 1980s when the then leader on the photocopying market, Xerox, was facing emerging competitors such as Minolta, Canon,

IBM. These new rivals offered almost identical machines at lower prices. Since Xerox had already developed its R&D, all the new entrants had to do was copy it. It was impossible for the leader to align its prices given the level of their investment in R+D. The only option it had, therefore, was to completely redesign its business model. By deciding to lease rather than selling its equipment, Xerox initiated what would later be called the functional economy. It was no longer a question of selling the machine itself, but of proposing to provide a photocopier and deliver it to the premises of the customer company and charge a fee for usage i.e. for each photocopy or every time it is used. The customer is then invoiced on a per unit basis. This innovation offers many benefits, both for the customer and for Xerox. Since the 1980s, this model has continued to develop in a large number of sectors, including Michelin with its Fleet solutions, Safran with its Aircelle subsidiary, which specialises in landing gear, IBM with the move towards IBM Business Services, and many others.

Market innovations cover a wide range of specific activities, from a new way of marketing a product or a service to a solution which completely reshapes the business model for both customers and suppliers. The functional economy is a perfect example of this.

The fourth type of innovation according to Schumpeter is "organisational" innovation, that is, the development of new forms of business organisation, which consists in implementing a new organisational method, whether in processes, in the operation of the workplace or even in the company's external links. Initially, Google developed a "70/20/10" model, according to which, the work of employees was divided as follows: 70% devoted to their core competency, i.e. the reason for which they were initially hired by the company; 20% on adjacent projects, i.e. the project of a colleague; and the remaining 10% on side projects, on projects not related to the company. Understandably, employees ought to be spending most of their time on their own tasks. However, the remaining 30% of relative freedom is significant enough, and generates a large number of advantages. First of all, by promoting collaboration among teams and employees, no innovations are ever the work of one single individual, but are the product of a collective process. This fosters a natural sense of ownership of the innovation within the organisation because each and every one could have contributed to it. Conversely, each Google employee receives support and ideas from many colleagues, and which also ensures projects are not limited by the individual abilities of each employee. This form of organisation calls into question the natural relationship of filiation each person has with innovation, with their ideas – a relationship which is not always healthy. It can be difficult for a person to detach themselves from an idea, not to see themselves as its father, its creator. Yet the survival of an idea, its development within organisations and its deployment outside of them, can only be achieved through a psychological detachment from this idea. By its nature, this proposal imposes such a detachment. In other words, ideas are proposed within an ecosystem which can potentially be nourished by all employees; and this idea can, in turn, directly or indirectly, nourish other projects. The remaining 10% represents only a modest portion of employees' time, but is enough to be impactful nonetheless. Employees are encouraged to devote this time to charities, to invest in social causes for example; this could also be involvement in sports clubs or school centres. Google obviously understands the importance its employees being invested in civil society, not to enhance its own image, but rather to identify future needs, to understand what the needs of society are and how they can meet these in the more or less long term.

Organisational innovation, therefore, is the permanent quest for the best way to work within an organisation, but also with its external network. This is also the case with "open innovation"[25] techniques, the essence of which is to thwart traditional innovation methods which consist in developing strictly within the confined environment of the company. Open innovation, on the contrary, strives for the utmost openness towards the outside world, in order to capture the needs of individuals, to establish relationships with suppliers who can participate in the development of ideas, to establish links with distributors, to disseminate the latest launches as quickly as possible. In other words, organisational innovation serves to weave a dense internal and external network which enables the company to avoid the pitfall of self-interest and which, on the contrary, encourages the pooling of skills, ideas and proposals aimed at making its innovation policy more successful.

The last category of innovation concerns the introduction of new materials and sources. This is a category of innovation which is no longer as relevant as it once was, partly because there are not really any new emerging raw materials and partly because current sources are clearly

---

[25] Henry Chesbrough, *Open Innovation: The New Imperative for Creating and Profiting from Technology*, Harvard Business School Press, 2003.

exhaustible – particularly fossil energy sources. That is why we more commonly use the first four forms of innovation.

Degrees of innovation

The four major innovation categories enable companies to define the type of innovation in which they wish to invest. It is clearly not a matter of preferring one type of innovation over another, but rather of knowing how to choose the right type of innovation in order to activate the corresponding resources for its implementation. The type of innovation, however, is not the only criteria to be considered; companies also have to consider the degree of innovation they want to implement. There are three degrees of innovation: incremental; radical (or disruptive); and paradigmatic.

Incremental innovation focuses on improving existing products or services. These minor changes may include: increasing the number of pixels in the camera of a smartphone; the ability to access your bank account online; the size difference between the sedan or station wagon version of a vehicle; etc. These innovations are sometimes marginal. However, they enable companies to keep offering solutions continuously that are in line with the daily evolution of consumers. Such innovations are regularly proposed by organisations which did not propose the original idea or product, who copy existing products, and improve them only marginally in order to be as close as possible to customer needs without having to invest in surveys, testing and R&D.

Radical or disruptive innovation is often based on emerging technologies, or existing technologies but used in a novel way. Behind the notion of "disruptive" lies the idea of a break from the existing way of doing things. Consequently, this degree of innovation significantly disrupts existing models, whether in reference to the product itself, or the service made possible thanks to a given product or technology. For instance, the iPhone is considered a radical innovation insofar as it offered, via its touch screen, a new way of using a phone. To be more exact, the introduction of these devices reshaped the contours of communication by associating different uses within the same accessory. The iPod is less of a radical innovation than the iTunes platform. When this device was introduced, MP3 players already existed: the first MP3 player with a hard drive was developed by the French brand Archos. The iTunes platform, on the other hand, was a radical innovation, both from a technological view point and a service view point. The idea of "disrupting" what already exists was an integral part of this innovation introduced by Apple in 2003; iTunes marked a before and an after in the way music is marketed, purchased, downloaded and listened to. This radical innovation hinged on three axes: making music as cheap as possible – the first titles were less than $1; making buying, downloading and listening to music very simple – which iTunes achieved whereas the Archos Jukebox was not very user friendly; and to have an solid ecosystem, which Steve Jobs' firm set out to build by forging strategic partnerships with record labels.

The combination of these three elements – namely, costs, user-friendliness and ecosystem – is often the triad required to disrupt a market. Ryanair radically innovated in the air transport sector applying the same principles: a low-cost offering; simplicity in the booking experience – one single segmentation, limited and easily identifiable options; and a unique ecosystem with the establishment of its own airports in partnership with the regions in which they are located. Both Apple and Ryanair leveraged the ecosystem in order to revolutionise the business model as a whole.

It should be noted that radical innovation, as with the other innovation degrees, is not limited to business organisations. Sport provides a perfect example of radical innovation, as demonstrated by high jumper Dick Fosbury. In 1968, at the Mexico City Olympic Games, he decided to use a new technique, now known as the Fosbury Flop, jumping over the high bar by swinging his shoulders backwards over the bar first – unlike the straddle method where athletes go over the bar facing down and arms first – so that his pelvis could rise higher than with the traditional method. He did not invent this jump: Bruce Quande had used it 5 years prior. However, Fosbury is the innovator, because he is the one who introduced it during a competition, and he derived a direct benefit from this in the form of the Olympic gold medal. In this example, it is obviously not a question of financial profit, yet there is undeniable value creation through radical innovation. If Fosbury had achieved his jump thanks to a physical advantage, say for example a physical malformation which might have enabled him to jump higher but which could not have been reproduced by any of his opponents who did not have this particular physical trait, then there would have been no value creation, and the "Fosbury flop" would have remained a mere invention.

In politics, the suffragette movement in the United Kingdom in the 1910s can also be considered a disruptive innovation. These women were not calling for a change in voting methods, nor for it to be improved, which would have constituted an incremental innovation. Their goal was to radically change voting by including 50% more voters, i.e. women. This example is also relevant for understanding that innovation is not necessarily profit-driven, but rather focuses on creating value, in this case in the social context. The major social innovations achieved in France in the 19th century in favour of social solidarity – progressive taxation, the right to work or social security[26] – are other examples of just such a perspective.

The third degree of innovation, paradigmatic innovation, also referred to as transformational innovation, is concerned with primarily historical scientific innovations and historical techniques. Close in essence to the work of fundamental research, R&D centres and laboratories, paradigmatic innovations are ones which fundamentally and irreversibly change our way of life. This was the case with the steam engine or vaccinations. More recently, the Internet is a paradigmatic innovation and it seems that 3D printing is taking a similar path. Paradigmatic innovation is characterised by being very expensive and in needing an extremely long time for invention, exploration and research. This is rarely a path that companies venture down on their own. They often rely on institutions or research centres, such as the French National Centre for Scientific Research and the French *National Institute for Agricultural Research* in France, or the National Aeronautics and Space Administration for the United States. These state bodies can work for a longer period of time without the pressure of delivering profitability since they are financed by public funds. This is a luxury private companies to which luxury private companies can seldom commit. Paradigmatic innovation is, in a way, the grail to which all inventors aspire, with Leonardo da Vinci as their paragon. He advanced knowledge in the fields of anatomy, optics and hydrodynamics but he never innovated in the strict sense, since he "only" made proposals for planes, helicopters and submarines. Paradigmatic innovation is not limited to the domains of science and technology, nevertheless, it is often through one or other of these that the uniqueness of the paradigm an emerges, sometimes it can even link these disciplines, as is happening currently at the beginning of the 21st century. The famous "great convergence" of NBIC (Nanotechnologies, Biotechnologies, Information technologies and Cognitive Sciences) is an example. The paradigmatic innovations resulting from this convergence seem to be gathering momentum in an

---

[26]Juliette Grange, "Au XIXᵉ siècle. La république sociale et ses critiques", *L'idée de République*, Paris, Pocket, 2008, pp. 137–148.

unprecedented way. By combining the infinitely small, manufacturing living matter, thinking machines and the study of the human brain, many new proposals have emerged, such as brain implants to help people with disabilities to restore certain functions or to stimulate certain muscles. This convergence is ushering humanity into a paradigm moment hitherto unknown and which – as did the Internet – will become a part of our daily lives, and will lead to the spontaneous adoption in our everyday lives of all its various its forms.

Combining the different innovation types on the one hand – product/ service; process; marketing and organisation – with the various innovation degrees – incremental, radical and paradigmatic – offers 12 different and equally important ways of innovating. It is not a question of considering that incremental process innovation is less relevant than paradigmatic product innovation, for example. All innovations can have relevance depending on the strategy of an organisation and the means at its disposal.

The innovation process

For a complete understanding of innovation, it is important to be aware that innovation in organisations is structured around five main phases: ideation; feasibility; capability; launch; and post-launch. The management of the innovation process should constitute the driving force behind internal innovation within the organisation. This process can be summarised as follows. The first phase is to use the three axes for finding ideas: insight, ideation and R&D; the second is to measure the technical and financial feasibility of projects, both internally – does the company have the means to make this project a reality? – and externally – if the company does not have the means to bring about this idea, can it obtain them with outside help? Then comes the phase called capability. The challenge here is to ensure that the human, financial and technical skills are in place to develop the idea: measure the structural impacts, is there a need to develop a new plant or production line? what is the level of debt if this idea is implemented? The second, and equally important, part of the capability phase is the process of accurately measuring financial risks and considering the consequences on the rest of the organisation. The launch phase deals with marketing issues, communication campaigns, price positioning, distribution channels, and also the organisation needed to ensure fluidity between production and users. The last phase of the process is the post-launch phase. The challenge here is to measure the development of the idea on the market, evaluate its success or failure and potential changes that need to be effected.

Understanding and Accepting Innovation

The multiplicity of types and degrees of innovation underline just how omnipresent innovation is, always has been, and always will be. Many people spontaneously consider innovation as something technological or as pertaining exclusively to the economic sphere. Etymologically and historically, however, the concept of innovation is much broader.[27] Everyone is or can be, in a certain way, innovative: artists are innovative, scientists are innovative, as is an organisation in its everyday life.

Innovation has always existed, even if its conceptualisation emerged only a few centuries ago. Innovation can be anecdotal, but can also cover aspects that fundamentally change the history of humanity and contribute to the discovery of the world. Analysing innovation is never about making a value judgment about it, but rather of understanding why it came about. It is not a matter of qualifying an innovation as useful or useless. These are not the terms in which to think about innovation. The real question is whether or not an invention has been successful in meeting a given need. If the technology, product, service or method responds to an unmet need and enables an organisation to survive by meeting that need, then there is innovation. Whether in the field of art or economics, literature or sports, innovation is everywhere. We already quoted the example of Fosbury to illustrate radical innovation in sport. Innovation is no less relevant in art. Claude Monet innovated with impressionism, which in its early days was characterised by relatively small paintings, visible brush strokes, open composition, the use of original angles of view and the expression of meteorological phenomena. Monet was not an inventor, but he contributed to creating an artistic value which is characterised by the development of this new "school" with Pissarro, of course, or Sisley and Renoir, among many others. The same happened in music, with the emergence of rap music in the 1970s, which then became a musical innovation in its own right in the 1980s when it was commercialised by labels such as

---

[27] For the history of the concept of innovation, refer to the excellent article by Godin, Benoît (2008). *Innovation: the history of a category* Working Paper. *Op. cit.*

Public Enemy or Run-DMC. In literature, we can say that the *nouveau roman* is an innovation. This self-reflexive art form constantly challenges the position of the narrator – their place in the story – and relegates the plot and the main characters to the background. It is a literary movement in its own right, not initiated by any one specific author, but by several, including Claude Simon, Michel Butor, Alain Robbe–Grillet, Samuel Beckett, Nathalie Sarraute, etc. Together, they created unprecedented literary value. Their collective work far surpassed the stage of invention, as would be the case for a first book which struggles to find its readership. On the contrary, their proposal rapidly won over a readership and so became a major literary movement that would develop thanks to new authors such as Claude Ollier, Jean Ricardou, Suzanne Prou, and thanks to its ever-increasing number of readers.

It is irrelevant to ask whether or not the innovative techniques developed in sport, music or literature are useful. The fact that they meet a need, however, is beyond doubt, whether this is a need to survive in a competition, a need to enjoy a new musical or reading experience.

It is very important to have an informed understanding of what innovation is, which may involve delving into detail some technical explanations, in order to clearly define the scope of our discussion, and so able to express a critical perspective. Opposing innovation is pointless, given it has been intrinsic to human development, since their very beginnings and even before humans appeared 3 million years ago. The real question is: what types of innovations do we want to design for what type of world? Indeed, it is not just about questioning the needs of individuals and formulating an answer in response to these needs. Another very important question is: should we always meet the needs of individuals with a new product or service? This is a question which innovators should regularly keep in mind. What underlies this question concerns the consequences of innovation. Are there any known or unknown adverse consequences following the emergence of an innovation? Innovation always brings with it a number of questions, but these should be not addressed from the stance of value judgment that we might naturally make about an innovation founded on not seeing its interest, usefulness or any personal need for it. However, a proposal that does not make sense for us does not mean that it does not make sense for others, depending on their age, gender, place of residence, religion, culture, history, experiences, etc. Equally, an innovation developed to meet a specific need with a particular target might have an impact on other populations, and as such its development and relevance ought to be questioned. In other words, innovation necessarily generates a great many questions for the person to whom the innovation is directed, to those who develop it and to those on whom it will have an indirect consequence – all questions which often are not addressed. As a result, commercial organisations too often fail to measure the consequences of their innovations, as if overwhelmed by the challenge of a demand that promises survival through profit. It would seem, however, that in the course of recent decades we have no longer been able to innovate as we did before: we can no longer develop solutions without ourselves about their potential consequences. Innovations that can potentially profoundly alter human nature need to be measured differently from some banal packaging innovation, or a new phone.

Perhaps today there is a need to question innovation not in terms of its economic relevance – the market will be the judge of that, but on the gain it offers. This can be formulated ontologically, where it is a question of thinking about innovation as an innovation. Etymologically, the proposal of innovation is to *in-novare,* to change within. However, are the changes which result always the intended changes, and only those changes, or do they also provoke other changes? Ought we not question the role of innovation today, if only to remain in control of it, and not be taken over by it? This might already be happening with the exponential development of artificial intelligence which is interfering in our everyday lives. On another level, have we not become dependent on and overtaken by innovations such as fertilisers and pesticides that inundate our fields and crops? Has innovation not already taken precedence over those people who are struggling to survive in today's world without an Internet connection on their phone? Has not innovation already surpassed its master when the nanotechnologies we use in technical products are discharged into wastewater and we are unable to recover them to destroy or recycling them?

In a way, the innovator sets up an idea which they can no longer control. Innovators believe themselves to be endowed with a strength superior to that of innovation, but in fact, it is innovation which masters them. Much like Victor Frankenstein who was overpowered by his creature, the innovator takes flight to escape toward other creations, leaving it to someone else to solve the problem they created.

Chapter 2

Creative Destruction and The Innovator, The Hero and Their Myth

All creators break with the norm. All innovation is abnormal.

Boris Cyrulnik
L'Ensorcellement du monde

Innovation is a proposal made by an individual which is so completely necessary to this person that it becomes absolute. Eschewing criticism, innovation is seldom if ever analysed in terms of its potential harmful impact. From the moment an innovation is proposed, it is held up as a positive symbol, and its consequences, no matter how significant, ultimately gain acceptance over time. There was unanimous outrage when the founder of Facebook declared that the social norm on data protection needed to evolve, i.e. that personal data, hitherto reserved exclusively for the private sphere, could be used by commercial organisations, in this case, his own. Over and above the importance of being able to market data in order to generate profit, what is at stake is much more complex. To seek to change a social norm is to set yourself up as herald of an evolution, claiming this to be necessary for society as a whole, regardless of the consequences. To put it another way, the innovator sees only their creation, but not its inherent destructive consequences even if they are actually aware of these. There is no innovation without disobedience.

Creation and Destruction, Mythological Roots

Creation and destruction in economic cycles

Contrary to what is commonly believed, the expression "creative destruction" was not coined by Joseph Schumpeter but by Werner Sombart.[1] The overall idea of this expression is that creation and destruction are intimately linked. Destruction bears within itself the fruits and attributes of creation. One of the complexities lies in the fact that while creation and destruction are linked, they are often orchestrated by different actors.

From a general perspective, when we look at the Kondratieff economic cycles since 1800, we can see that there has been a succession of waves of growth and decay.[2] For instance, there was significant world economic growth between approximately 1785 and 1815, which was followed by major economic decline until around 1845. A new wave of growth emerged between 1850 and 1880, before economy collapsed again until the 1900s. In 1905, once again, the economy grew strong for another 30 years, after which it experienced another recession. A new positive wave began in the 1950s and carried on to the 1980s, a time at which the economy experienced a major decline, and bounced back some 20 years later, until the recession we have been experiencing globally since approximately 2005–2007. Looking at these waves, Schumpeter observed that the development of periods of growth occurs concurrently with the development of major innovations. For the first wave of the 18th century, the innovations concerned the techniques of water control, the beginning of the structured production of textiles, as well as major advances in iron-making. For the period around 1850, the innovations were rail, steelmaking, and the steam engine. The growth at the beginning of the 20th century was triggered by the emergence of electricity, combustible energy and the beginnings of industrial chemistry. This was followed by other

---

[1]André Lapied et Sophie Swaton, "Sélection naturelle ou volonté de puissance: comment interpréter le processus de destruction créatrice", *Revue de philosophie économique* 14(2) 2013, 45. W. Sombart, Krieg und Kapatalismus, Munich, Duncker & Humbolt, 1913.

[2]Andrey Korotayev, Leonid Grinin, "Kondratieff Waves in the World System Perspective", in *Kondratieff Waves. Dimensions and Perspectives at the Dawn of the 21st Century,* Leonid E. Grinin, Tessaleno C. Devezas, and Andrey V. Korotayev (eds.), Volgograd, Uchitel, 2012, pp. 23–64.

innovations for the 1950s, such as aviation, but also electronics and petrochemicals. The latest wave is eminently linked to the advent of the Internet and other digital developments.

For Schumpeter, the organisations which propose these great paradigmatic innovations earn a de facto monopoly. This monopoly, however, collapses as soon as competitors start copying their innovation, which leads to a banalisation of progress which gradually drags the economy into a phase of recession. This highlights the existence of an interrelation between creativity and destruction. When the destruction of the economy occurs, it is followed – more or less closely – by a wave of creativity. What is remarkable is that these new developments do not build on what was destroyed, but rather offer something completely new. It is also important to note how these cycles have grown increasingly shorter. In the past, these Kondratieff waves could last as long 60 years; as from the 18th century, they tended to last 50 years; then 40 years and now they last around 30 or even 20 years. This can be explained by the development of globalisation. Two centuries ago, it could take several decades for an emerging innovation to reach the entire world population, something which can now happen on the very day of its release. Globalised production and trading systems provide innovators with the opportunity to launch their new product or service on the same day, all over the world. When a new smartphone is launched, it is available in New York, Paris, Beijing, Singapore, Perth, Rio or Mexico City on the same day. If a delay does occur, this is by choice, prompted by a strategic business decision, but not because of constraints stemming from difficulties in commercial expansion or production.

The brain: Object of the next creative destruction?

Appreciating the existence of creative destruction is easy when observing how new innovations appear and disappear. However, we must bear in mind that creative destruction can also operate in different ways, across all layers of existence, including for individuals themselves, and more particularly, for their brains. The latest wave of major innovations is that of the Internet and digital tools. There is evidence that the brains of those born in this environment have developed new abilities, possessed by neither their parents nor grandparents. The brain is malleable, and has evolved continuously since the appearance of living beings. Depending on the environment with which it is confronted, the brain transforms itself, innovates, so to speak, in order to adapt and survive. The brains of individuals born in the late 1980s and early 1990s has adapted to life in the age of screens, or rather, to be more exact, to the characteristics of which screens are a medium. Video games are a striking example of this. When someone is playing a video game, their repeated manipulation of the virtual character or the fictitious car they are driving, for example, develops their speed and agility. While they are having fun, each time they earn points or move on to a new, more challenging level their brain system is stimulated by reward system. The reward stimulus releases dopamine, a natural stimulant which feeds the player's prefrontal cortex. Over time, the player becomes accustomed to this simplified gratification system, and his or her behaviour changes accordingly. For example, digital natives have developed wonderful multitasking skills and are extremely apt at switching quickly from one website to another, from reading about one topic to another, or similarly from one discussion to another. However, it is not that the brain acquires a new ability in addition to existing ones; it adapts, and consequently no longer works on other important qualitative aspects. When the brain develops superficial memory by scanning information, or simply looking for information on search engines, it does so at the expense of not developing a more linear literary intelligence, which is what enables the brain to retain in-depth information thanks to a cognitive synthesis carried out by the prefrontal cortex.[3] If individuals do not resist the cognitive automatisms generated by screens – something which concerns not only gamers but also all intensive and regular users of screens – they act more and more by impulse, by reflex, with all the consequences this entails. Susceptibility to manipulation of thoughts or beliefs, and the lack of coherent or structured reasoning are among the direct effects on a brain which has been subjected to superficial learning focusing on reflex and automatisms rather than having been exposed to in-depth research, reading lengthy texts, and exercises relying more on reasoning than on instinct and speed.

Once more, it is not a matter of passing judgment on the evolution of the brain, and certainly not of questioning whether or not people should

---

[3]See the research by Prof. Olivier Houdé, Laboratory for the Psychology of Child Development and Education, laboratory of the French CNRS, Paris-Descartes University and Caen University. https://www.lapsyde.com/.

moderate their passion for video games. The brain evolves. This is a fact, and there is nothing exceptional about it. The brain has changed continuously to adapt both to its environment and to the innovations to which it has been exposed. This is what happened, for example, with the advent of the mass production of books, as a result of Gutenberg's invention, and therefore to the massification of literacy. Today a "new gen" brain is in the making, and – unless the use of screens is called into question in a lasting way – will replace the brain of previous generations. Those born at the end of the 1980s have already joined the workforce, but few are in senior decision-making roles, apart from in a few very young and very innovative organisations. When cohorts of "new gen" brains assume responsibility for organisations – whether these are businesses, charities or political organisations – this will mark the beginning of a new creative wave. The destruction of previous brains will give way to a new form of thinking, because their learning processes were radically different. Yet again, it is not a question of making a value judgment on the "quality" of these brains but of accepting and taking account of the consequences of one type of brain being replaced by another. Here is another way of looking at this. In a presidential election in the 2010s, voters had to choose between two political programs, between two personalities, but also between two very different ways of functioning depending on the candidates' education and the environment in which they developed. This is because the brain of candidate who was born in the 1940s is structurally different from another candidate who was born 30 years later in a thoroughly digital economy. As a result, it is two opposing forms of governance which are on offer: the former candidate might be more precise, reasoned with linear thinking; whereas the latter might be faster in decision-making, be somewhat more dynamic and be a multitasker. However, the question cannot be reduced to a preference for one or the other "form" of brain. Rather, the question is: what kind of brain does the country need in order to face up to its competitors, partners and allies? And who the leaders of other countries with whom the elected candidate will have to work, and consequently, which brain type would be more beneficial for the country?

What seems valid on the scale of a nation is no less valid at the level of an organisation, or a company, which has to consider the how the brain of its leader operates in a globalised, ever-more competitive world, where the leader's speed of decision-making must match the urgency with which decisions need to be taken.

The Origin of Creative Destruction

Werner Sombart developed the notion of creative destruction[4] by setting his own economic theories, as well as evolutionary theories[5] within the perspective of Nietzschean philosophy by which he was particularly influenced.[6] Creative destruction, as explained earlier in this chapter, is intimately linked to the environment of an individual or organisation, and more particularly, to the intensity of competition in this environment. The more competition develops, the more structured it is, then the more likely it is to lead to destruction, for the simple reason that resources are scarce. This is also the very reason that there is creative destruction: because resources are finite. When the number of customers for any given product or service is limited, then suppliers must battle to curry favour with consumers. This is true in all circumstances: if the only way to survive is to obtain access to a very limited water supply, competition, perhaps maybe even war, will ensue between the thirsty protagonists. In other words, scarcity is what drives some to want to destroy others in order to secure the coveted goods. This can be skills, techniques which an organisation would like to possess. Football clubs, for example, go to great lengths and huge expense to transfer a player with rare qualities into their teams. The same goes for an exceptional researcher which a laboratory wants to recruit.[7] The rare resource in question can be secured through money (possibly also strategy or positioning), or through the annihilation of competition (those interested in acquiring the same goods). It is understandable that when ride sharing companies emerged, taxi drivers tried to do everything in their power to annihilate them, with government and sometimes even by using physical force. The key factor which drove them to act in this way was the lack of unlimited resources. If there had been an

---

[4]Werner Sombart, *Krieg und Kapitalismus,* Munich, Duncker & Humblot, 1913.
[5]André Lapied and S. Swaton, "Sélection naturelle ou volonté de puissance: comment interpréter le processus de destruction créatrice", *Op. cit.*
[6]Hugo Reinert and Erik Reinert, "Creative destruction in economics", in *Friedrich Nietzsche (1844–1900), Economy and Society,* J. G. Backhaus and W. Drechsler (eds.), New York, Springer, 2006, pp. 55–85.
[7]Professor Luc Montagnier, co-discoverer of the AIDS virus in 1983 and winner of the 2008 Nobel Prize in Medicine, was recruited by Shanghai's prestigious Jiaotong University at the age of 78. He had been forced to retire by the CNRS. He described this indignantly as "A wicked, scandalous measure, which risks provoking a French brain drain" (*Le Monde*, December 6, 2010).

unlimited number of clients, it would not even have been an issue, everyone could have had the share of the customers they needed to make a living. However, faced with a limited number of customers, the traditional players found themselves facing direct competition with others and had to fight back to try and safeguard their revenues and sustain their livelihood. The dwindling number of competitors, or even their complete disappearance is what renders the availability of resources clearer and easier. Destruction and creation go hand in hand, because creation does not emerge out of nowhere, it emerges in an existing market, in a sector, in which there were already players, who end up in danger of being destroyed. Similarly, the military contingent which has access to the only water supply will be able to continue to fight, to advance, to grow, whereas its opponents will be unable to continue because they cannot meet their basic physiological needs.

The notion of creative destruction which Werner Sombart applies to economic theory is, in fact, age old, and is in fact omnipresent in ancient myths. According to Greek mythology, the cosmos, the universe, was formed by the Gods who created – out of the most complete destruction – the first primordial entity: chaos. Then came Gaia, Mother Earth, and Eros, the creative power and also the God of Love. The development continued with Erebus (darkness) and Nyx (night), who together gave birth to Aether (light) and Hemera (day). Gaia gave birth to Uranus (the sky), Pontos (the sea), and Ourea (the mountains). Other pairings gave birth to Titans, Titanids, Cyclops, etc. A similar notion can be found in Egyptian myths with the famous Phoenix rising from its ashes.

Creative destruction is at the origin of humanity and runs through history. It also lies at the heart of many religious beliefs, as is the case for Hinduism where three deities coexist: Shiva, who destroys the universe so it can be reconstructed by Brahma, as well as by Vishnu, whose role is to provide for the needs of human beings. For Christians, the Son of God is executed, destroyed, then rises from the dead to deliver a message of re-creation and hope. The destruction–creation from Indian mythology inspired German the poet Herder, the author Goethe, as well as the philosopher Nietzsche.[8] This is particularly true for the latter, who built on these notions to develop the notion of "will to power".[9] This famous

---

[8] Hugo Reinert and Erik Reinert, "Creative destruction in economics", 2006, *Op. cit.*
[9] Friedrich Nietzsche, *Fragments posthumes sur l'éternel retour*, Allia, 2003, p. 87. Published in English as *The Will to Power*.

phrase refers to an individual's desire to rise above others, above the masses, above the crowd in order to surpass their condition. This is what can be found in *Thus Spoke Zarathustra*. With this expression, the philosopher does not refer to a desire for power, but rather a desire for life-long growth. This is something incumbent on each of us to bear that in mind and to act upon accordingly, so that we may grow:

> *When Zarathustra came into the nearest town lying on the edge of the forest, he found many people gathered in the market place, for it had been promised that a tightrope walker would perform. And Zarathustra spoke thus to the people:*
>
> "I teach you the overman. *Human being is something that must be overcome. What have you done to overcome him?*
>
> *All creatures so far created something beyond themselves; and you want to be the ebb of this great flood and would even rather go back to the animal than overcome humans?*
>
> *What is the ape to a human? A laughing stock or a painful embarrassment. And that is precisely what the human shall be to the overman: a laughing stock or a painful embarrassment.*
>
> *You have made your way from worm to human, and much in you is still worm. Once you were apes, and even now a human is still more ape than any ape.*
>
> *But whoever is the wisest among you is only just a conflict and a cross between plant and ghost. But do I implore you to become ghost or plant?*
>
> Behold, I teach you the overman!"[10]

This extract perfectly summarises the message Nietzsche wants to convey with the idea of the underlying "will to power". It is about becoming aware of who we are, what we are doing and where we are going. Zarathustra's questions challenge each individual in the crowd, as well as

---

[10]Friedrich Nietzsche, *Thus Spoke Zarathustra*, Translated to English by A. del Caro, ed. A, Del Caro and R. B. Pippin, Cambridge, Cambridge University Press, 2006, pp. 5–6. A translator's note explains his choice of "Overman" for *Übermensch*: "Overman is preferred to superhuman for two basic reasons; first it preserves the word play Nietzsche intends with his constant references to going under and going over, and secondly, the comic book association called to mind by 'superman' and super-heroes generally tend to reflect negatively, and frivolously, on the term superhuman", *Op. cit.*, p. 5, note 3.

his readers. In the style of Socrates, Nietzsche asks us: what are we going to do about the state in which we currently find ourselves? We have been plankton, amphibians, apes and now that we have become human, what is the next step? If there is no advancement, no growth, no progress, then is it not a step backwards? Is this not a return to our bestial condition? There is no doubt that what is being envisaged here is self-development, the development of our human condition, what Nietzsche calls "overman". The will to power is thus intimately linked to the act of creating, to the surpassing of a given condition, and Zarathustra provokes the crowd by asking them to take action, and to create, instead of passively accepting. Therefore, it is about no longer being subject to the various rules and laws imposed by others, but rather of creating one's own laws.

Schumpeter found in Nietzsche's proposal the answer to the will for power he had intuited in the behaviour of entrepreneurs,[11] Schumpeter sees this will to power as being the temperament which drives a person to be an entrepreneur: someone who emerges from the mass of people, from the crowd; someone for whom existing laws, rules and conventions do not necessarily have the relevance that others, that society, seems to grant them. The motivations of the entrepreneur may be founded on the desire to accomplish something, an appreciation for complexity, discomfort, or an ambition to break down resistance, they are not necessarily limited to that. The innovator is also driven by a set of irrational motives: the will to power; victory; success against the established order.

The entrepreneur, who exists only through innovation, is that extra-ordinary person whose purpose – consciously or unconsciously – is to overcome a series of obstacles which they encounter on their way.[12] The organisation the innovator sets up has for its sole purpose breaking down this resistance. This is precisely why the entrepreneur is not a "manager", an administrator, nor do they concern themselves with legal, accounting, IT or human resources issues. Their proposal is "over", goes far beyond these considerations. The challenge to which they seek to respond is how to resolve the issue which they have determined to resolve by surpassing the restrictions of classical structures. This does not mean that at a certain point in the development of their innovation or organisation the

---

[11] Yoshiki. Shionoya, *Schumpeter and the Idea of Social Sciences*, Cambridge, Cambridge University Press, 1997.

[12] François Perroux, *La pensée économique de Joseph Schumpeter: les dynamiques du capitalisme*, Genève, Librairie Droz, 1965.

entrepreneur will not behave like a manager, but in so doing they will no longer be acting in their capacity as the innovator fighting against resistance which they once were. In fact, it is not uncommon to see multi-entrepreneurs, people who are driven more by the various issues they want to solve so as to bring about new proposals than by the prospect of managing of an organisation.

From Nietzsche to Ayn Rand, protecting the weakest from the strongest

When in 2005, Mark Zuckerberg declared that social norms needed to evolve, in other words that private data should no longer be considered, analysed or protected in the same way as it had been in the past, he was, in fact, doing nothing less than setting up his own rules on the management of private data, not only for his social network but more globally for the management of databases as a whole. This ability to create one's own rules of play is utterly characteristic of individuals who are intrinsically self-reliant, who do not let conventions they consider outdated get in their way. In other words, whereas the weakest are content to go along with the status quo, complacently stuck in stagnant passivity, the strongest – morally, spiritually – emerge with proposals which first and foremost serve their own personal interests. A perfect example of this can be found in entrepreneurs such as Xavier Niel, who presented his proposals as laws, standards and references, which his competitors first observed, criticised but ultimately accepted and fell into compliance Although the weak exist complacently in a wait-and-see attitude, they do not stand idly by; they revolt against those who want to change the system in place. Here again, Nietzsche can serve as a relevant illustration when he offers the seemingly counter-intuitive statement that we must *protect the strong against the weak*.[13] This is because the weakest, the mass of people, is greater in number than those who create, and will do anything to stop anybody who is trying to change the system. Whether it was Travis Kalanick (founder of Uber) who suffered the scorn of the mass of taxi drivers, whether it was Brian Chesky (founder of AirBnB) who faced the wrath of the hospitality industry as a whole, or Édouard Leclerc (founder of the French chain of

---

[13]Friedrich Nietzsche, *On the Geneaology of Morals*, IIIBykeith Ansell-Pearson (ed.), p. 14 [Translated to English by Carol Diethe].

hypermarkets E. Leclerc), who was slammed by pharmacists,[14] the entrepreneur who changes the rules of a profession ends up having a target on their back, figuratively and sometimes even literally. The events surrounding the debate around ride-sharing companies have clearly shown that the desire to destroy a new competitor can be physical. The strong must be protected against the weak so that they can bring about a potentially innovative, new proposal, despite the risks. Indeed, the act of creating is intimately linked to the risks which only the strongest, most exceptional men and women are willing to take in their pursuit of both power and glory. However, risk-taking in and of itself is no guarantee of success. Whereas the weakest want to protect themselves at all costs, innovators are impervious to the notion of protection and so take risks even if this could ultimately lead to their demise.

The excellent man and the mass man according to Ortega y Gasset

"Acting and doing" becomes reality through the "excellent man", he who is a minority within society, who is not part of the mass of the weak who want nothing other than stagnation. The idea of the "excellent man" (as distinguished from "mass man" or "common man") – which we owe to Spanish philosopher José Ortega y Gasset – is a person, irrespective of gender, a "universal" man, who makes great demands on himself and who aspires to difficulty.[15] This universal man, aware that he will never achieve perfection, nevertheless strives for perfection unceasingly and consequently redoubles his efforts to overcome his doubts and uncertainties. This minority of excellent men are inventors, creators, people who "do", whatever the chances of success and outcome. They are inhabited by a pioneering spirit, driven by the need to do something which no one has ever done before. The "mass man", on the other hand, is nothing but a common man, as Ortega says, the mass is *the assemblage of persons not*

---

[14]In 1988 Édouard Leclerc launched a para-pharmacy, selling over the counter, non-prescription medicines at prices some 25–30% cheaper than in conventional pharmacies who until then had a monopoly on the selling of all medicines.

[15]José Ortega y Gasset, *The Revolt of the Masses*, W. W. Norton & Company Inc., 1932. English translation authorised by Sr. Ortega y Gasset, the translator remains anonymous at the translator's request.

specially qualified. He is the average man, the one who does not differen-tiate himself from the others, who resembles everyone, who is generic. The Spanish philosopher carefully avoids qualifying the excellent man as coming from the bourgeoisie, the aristocracy, or with a higher education. The strong man is he whose nature cannot be inherited, cannot be bought, his efforts are expressed through his willingness to go beyond the "vulgar-ity" in which the mass man indulges.

Pindar's philosophy, and his expression *become who you are*,[16] which was also found in Nietzsche, is probably the closest to Ortega's philoso-phy. While elements of this notion can be found in Sartrean existentialism, Ortega's proposal is much more radical because human life transcends natural life: for Ortega, man must invent himself. When some philoso-phers, from pseudo-Demosthenes to Foucault, including Oscar Wilde and others, recommend making one's life a work of art, for the class of individuals with which we are concerned, this is achieved through entrepreneurship.

In a way, Ortega y Gasset's proposal is somewhat anti-democratic. The fact that one voice counts as much as another in the public space, in his opinion, has a devastating effect, because the mass man will not sur-render to the excellent man, to the superior man, and will ceaselessly cre-ate debates, confrontations and conflicts that will only set back the good decisions the excellent man brings forth. For the Spanish philosopher, who was recognised by Aron and Camus, this is particularly true for cul-ture. For Ortega y Gasset, democracy is incompatible with "high culture", as are good manners and morals, because *There is no culture where there is no acceptance of certain final intellectual positions to which a dispute may be referred*.[17] He argues that questions pertaining to morality, truth, aesthetics or the good are not discussed according to known frames of reference provided by science and philosophy, but subject to democratic consensus. Consequently, high culture can no longer address the general public, it can only move in smaller and often selective circles.

What Ortega denounces through the example of culture (although he uses others), is the oppression which the masses inflict on the cultivated, intelligent, deserving minorities, those who want to create something and against whom the minorities stand. What is more, Ortega argues that pub-lic space should be reserved for these minorities, these elites who are the

---

[16] Pindare, *Pythian* 2, line 72.
[17] José Ortega y Gasset, *The Revolt of the Masses, Op. cit.*

sole legitimate producers of ideas, works and performances. As a practical example, for Ortega, letting the mass man take over "culture" or "entertainment" is what, in our contemporary space, has led to the emergence of reality TV, the production of songs which call for violence, or the irruption of senseless websites. In other words, if we allow the masses or certain masses to take the reins of culture, it should come as no surprise that street art and other popular art forms which are easily accessible, art forms which can be understood or appreciated without effort and without work, are popularised. As a result, high culture, whether classical music, paintings by the great masters or a body of philosophical knowledge, for example, is relegated to the background or restricted to a minority and inherently elitist population. It will always be easier to promote, organise and gain public acceptance for a photo exhibition than for a reading of *Being and Nothingness*; a new blockbuster will be more popular than a lecture on Flemish painters; and a street-art performance will certainly be much more widely accepted than listening to a symphony, even if it's Brahms. High culture is not at all popular because its role is to not be easily understood, or to lower itself to the level of the masses, but on the contrary, that people have to work to understand it, they have to learn and elevate themselves to this culture. It is therefore incumbent upon those who are cultured, intelligent and educated, who have undertaken this work of self-betterment to disseminate and promote culture, as opposed to those who strive to reach as many people as possible in an easily accessible and effortless way. The seduction of the masses does not represent success. The majority will never want anything else than something simple and easily accessible, within their reach. Undeniably, reality TV is a success in terms of ratings; the same cannot be said of the qualitative aspect which it has brought to millions of viewers. The same can be said about certain music styles, or artistic creations. We must always bear in mind that simply because something has been produced, it does not mean it is qualitative. New, emerging artistic styles are not qualitative simply because they are commercially successful, and the role of the media is key in this process.

The task of the minority man is never to build success, but rather to help the masses reach elevation, even if this goes against ambition and success. It is in this respect that Ortega sees in the minority man a hero: someone deserving who, in spite of the oppositions, in spite of the mass man standing in his path, will unfailingly seek to promote intelligence, reason and high culture.

More generally, democracy does not uphold the truth, it upholds the sovereignty of the people, no matter how absurd that may be. We can imagine that what the select man experiences with the common people is what the Innovator experiences when dealing with the masses. The Innovator to develop in such an environment where they regularly find themselves alone against a popular mass which fails to see them as the provider of solutions for the future, and who identify them as the person attempting to sabotage the status quo, the one who is bringing into society new behaviours, new habits, in other words, changes to which the people do not wish to submit.

The Innovator is the excellent man, the Innovator is the one who refuses to take the world for what it is and proposes to change it. Such a position is anti-democratic because it is not a decision of the people, it is an individual position based on work, effort, reasoning, research which the masses will not have accomplished, and who will therefore reject the proposed advancement. Intrinsically, then, the Innovator cannot be democratic because they exist outside of the space in which everyone has agreed to live, or rather endure. In other words, the Innovator "despises" the mass, which is entrenched in stagnation, does not rise up against a bleak society, against problems which can be solved and which they themselves proposes to solve. The Innovator somehow embodies a division, a rift, between those who do and those who do nothing, as Ayn Rand points out with as much force as provocation.

Ayn Rand, paragon of the innovator of the 20th century

The Russian-born American author Ayn Rand, whom we have already briefly mentioned in our previous chapter, was an avid reader of Ortega and her work is influenced by the radical ideas he defends. Rand, however, takes the ideas of the philosopher even further in this dichotomy between the "strong" versus "weak" man, with a particularly strong inclination for liberalism where "laissez-faire" and individualistic capitalism reign supreme. Close to libertarian movements, Rand, whose real name was Alissa Zinovievna, developed an extensive body of work such as *The Living Source* or *The Virtue of Selfishness*, an objectivist concept which she summarises as follows: *My philosophy, in essence, is the concept of man as a heroic being, with his own happiness as the moral purpose of his life, with productive achievement as his noblest activity, and reason as his only absolute*.[18] From this concept emerges what Rand calls "rational selfishness"[19] or "concern with one's own interests".[20] Rand argues that the foundation of morality ought not be the collective, but rather the individual, which is why *man must live for his own sake*[21] and never sacrifice himself for others, nor sacrifice others for himself.[22] This unconditional promotion of the individual led her, as she herself acknowledges in no uncertain way, to adhere in part to Nietzschean philosophy, and in particular, to the notion of the Overman which is omnipresent in her philosophical production.

None was more perfect to illustrate this philosophy than the figure of the entrepreneur, the innovator, the man who has ideas and seeks to implement them, and which features prominently in her seminal book *Atlas Shrugged*. It is not surprising that many personalities such as Ronald Reagan, Jimmy Wales, Alan Greespan or Pieter Thiel among many others, acknowledge to have been highly influenced by her work.

This novel pits a society in which there are men of spirit, entrepreneurs, independent scientists, or to put it in simpler terms, men who create value, who create wealth, i.e. "strong" men; against the State, the administrators, the nay-sayers and those who do nothing, i.e. the "weak", but who nevertheless hinder the deployment of other people's ideas and set out to create obstacles. These are undeserving, "plunderers" to use Randian terms, who, in the name of an alleged general interest, despoil, ruin and prevent the development of great innovative minds. Not surprisingly, many entrepreneurs recognised themselves in the story of *Atlas Shrugged*. Rand's words echo the everyday life of those entrepreneurs who try to develop their idea and who find themselves confronted with a discouraging number of administrative obstacles to set up their business, who see their first income hollowed out by an excessive tax grab, who find themselves legally trapped by employees perceived as incompetent but protected by law, who have to spend more time dealing with regulations than in developing their idea.

---

[18] Ayn Rand, in *Atlas Shrugged*, Random House, New York City, 1957.
[19] Ayn Rand, "Introduction", *The Virtue of Selfishness*, A. Signet book, 1964.
[20] Ayn Rand, "The Objectivist Ethics", *ibid*, p. 31.
[21] *Idem*.
[22] *Idem*.

The famous novel written in 1957 focuses on a critique of the state, depicted as "parasites" who hinder the success of others. However, other key themes of the novel are the promotion of the noble man "who does", and of scientific progress. The fear of progress is presented here in the sense of the risk it represents for society, citizens and users, which is primarily underpinned by the fear of competition. In the novel, innovations such as the metal alloy invented by Hank Rearden, or the engine imagined by John Galt, are condemned both in light of their success – and therefore the honorary and financial repercussions this success affords their creators –, and because of the repercussions these inventions had on the traditional players in these markets, who were thus at risk of disappearing due to their lack of willingness to take action.

When Hank Rearden, John Galt, and many other "people of mind" understand the power of the "weak", those who do nothing but prevent them from existing, from developing their ideas for the benefit of all, they decide to go on strike. They refuse to continue to work for the government, to share their inventions, their ingenuity, their entrepreneurial spirit, their scientific research with the rest of the world if they do not receive the recognition and remuneration they deserve. By deciding to make her characters go on strike, Rand wants to prove the morality of rational selfishness. If entrepreneurs no longer propose anything, if they no longer develop their ideas, if they stop innovating, then the world stops working: this would put a stop to value creation, to job creation, to taxes, to meeting citizens' needs.

Rand's goal is not to turn "people of mind" into heroes, but rather to highlight that, at the very least, there should be no impediment to their willingness to "do". "Laissez-faire" is the fundamental pillar of Randian philosophy, advocating there should be no intervention whatsoever, from whomsoever, whatever the subject. This idea is vividly expressed in a sentence from the novel, in the motto of these entrepreneurs who decide to take action by no longer "doing": *I swear by my life and my love of it that I will never live for the sake of another man, nor ask another man to live for mine.*[23]

Rand's work is in no way recondite and her philosophy has had a considerable influence as we have already pointed out.[24] Although this

---

[23] Ayn Rand, *La Grève*, trad. Sophie Bastide-Foltz, Les Belles Lettres, 2011, p. 1068. Ayn Rand, *Atlas Shrugged*, Random House, New York City, 1957.
[24] See page 46 of this book.

novel is criticised in the United States, its philosophical, literary and commercial success is undeniable, and American readers see how her proposals echo Emersonian individualism or build on the legacy of industrial heroes such as Vanderbilt, Edison, Ford, among others, pioneering entrepreneurs who made the glory and fortune of the United States.

Creative Destruction, A Contemporary Demonstration

As presented above, creative destruction finds its roots in mythology and religious systems, and theoreticians of economic systems have long taken up this theme to explain the vagaries of growth but also to explain competitive systems, that is, the competitive mechanisms which make or break organisations, whatever the environment in which they operate. Moreover, in keeping with the idea of creative destruction, those who benefit from this, i.e. creators, are not those who were destroyed. Schumpeter summarises this eloquently when he explains that the new *does not grow out of the old, but appears alongside of it, and eliminates it.*[25]

In our recent and contemporary era, generally speaking since the 2000s and the rapid development of the Internet, creative destruction has already been set in motion in a number of sectors, and it is by seeing the damage this movement can cause that we can become fully aware of its brutality, its speed and its force. Traditional telecommunications companies were perhaps the first and most savagely affected by this new wave, starting in the late 1990s. By deregulating the communications market, which until then had been owned by a single player, the sector saw the emergence of several new companies in an already more than mature market. The only way to survive was to take market shares – in other words, customers – from the historical, most important player. The problem was that the long-standing player in France was not at all ready. Its staff was highly protected under statutory regulations, with very competitive salaries, and therefore represented a very high labour cost.

---

[25] Joseph Schumpeter, *Capitalisme, socialisme, démocratie*, trad. Gaël Fain, éd. Payot, 1951, p. 40. Joseph Schumpeter, *The Theory of Economic Development: An Inquiry into Profits, Capitals, Credits, Interest, and the Business Cycle*, Transaction Publishers, 2004, p. 2016 [Translated to English by Redvers Opie].

Its competitors, however, had very low costs, and were therefore able to offer aggressive, highly preferential rates. The consequences were catastrophic: loss of markets, reduced turnover and profit, changes in working conditions and disastrous repercussions on employees. This resulted in a virtual destruction of the historical player along with value creation for new participants in the sector.

In such a situation, the dominant players end up losing their leading position, and are ultimately crushed by non-specialists, who are much smaller than they were when they started out. This is also the case with bookshops whose business has been destroyed by a non-book specialist, in this case Amazon. Driving schools are being replaced by organisations such as Ornikar,[26] which are in no way specialists in driving. Traditional hotels are constantly losing nights to a non-hotelier, Airbnb. The same goes for car rentals; the small French start-up BlaBlaCar[27] has succeeded in taking away rental customers from traditional players which have been established for decades. Of course, this is also the case for taxis, with the development of ride sharing companies. In New York City in January 2004, a taxi licence cost around $250,000. Over time, this increased steadily, and by March 2013 it had reached $1,250,000. In November 2014, Uber came to New York City, with 10,000 drivers. As a result of this new competition, the price of a taxi licence dropped to around $800,000 in April 2015. This is an illustration of the creative destruction movement at work, with the financial destruction of the value of the taxi licence in New York alongside the simultaneous financial success of Travis Kalanick's company.[28] These examples are only a small illustration of what the "new economy" is implementing through what is commonly referred to as "uberisation". In the next few years, this will affect pharmacies – which are already starting to disappear – then medical analysis laboratories, opticians, notaries and banks as well. It is not so much the profession itself which will disappear, it is that it will be profoundly transformed, and it is unlikely the current players will benefit from this, and less likely still that they will keep their dominant position. Medication will be delivered by Amazon or its equivalent, medical tests will be available on our mobile phones, glasses are already available on the Internet, online banks have

---

[26]A French driving school marketplace: https://www.ornikar.com/.

[27]https://www.blablacar.com/.

[28]New York City Taxi and Limousine Commission: http://www.nyc.gov/html/tlc/html/about/statistics.shtml.

already been taking a large share of new accounts for many years. And each time, in each sector, it is a different player, a new player, who corners the market, when the more traditional players struggle to protect whatever is left of their domain, and attempt to defend what they consider to be their rightful place, their "rights", by haranguing the new entrants.

Of all sectors, the most affected is undoubtedly education. The traditional actors of education, universities, business schools but also high schools and secondary schools, teach in much the same way as they did at the beginning of the 20th century. One century ago, education was imparted by an all-powerful teacher, who stood at the front of the class, taught a lesson. Opposite this authoritative, knowledgeable figure, students sat quietly jotting down what the teacher was saying. If we look at education today, at the beginning of the 21st century, what has changed apart from a few computer presentations and the occasional group projects? Still today, professors dispense the so-called knowledge to pupils, who are sitting at their desks, taking notes, albeit with a modern medium as opposed to the traditional pen and pencil, but they are still required to learn these teachings off by heart. It would seem then, that over the last century, education has not undergone a profound change. Ought not education, like other sectors, also transform itself so as not to disappear? Is it not missing out on the opportunity of opening itself up to greater learning opportunities than mere digital applications? The future of education might lie in examples such as the Khan Academy, which broadcasts thousands of hours of qualitative educational content in the form of tutorials, which last just a few minutes and cover subjects such as mathematics, history, finance and physics. The future of education could build on proposals such as the French école42, the essence of which is to offer a singular pedagogy, whereby learners are no longer evaluated by "educators" but by their peers. Another example could be Coursera, a digital platform offering online courses open to all. Today, several million courses are delivered throughout the world, 24/7 in all languages. Education no longer takes place within the four walls of the traditional school, it takes place any time, everywhere, for everyone and by everyone. If traditional players fail to understand the evolution that is necessary for their survival, just as pharmacists with connected e-health, taxis with innovative services, booksellers, record stores and others, they will not survive and education will still happen, but without them.

All this raises the question of the inevitability of destruction: is destruction something we always *endure*? Should we accept it by resigning ourselves to it? Do pharmacies have no choice but to witness, powerless, their dispensaries closing down one after the other? Have engineering schools no other choice than to experience a "brain drain" and see their best talents move on to more disruptive education models? Have taxis no other choice but to count the bankruptcies in the sector? Are all these players, who are disappearing one after the other while their own sector is booming – medication consumption is at its highest, there is considerable demand for education, and mobility is a major axis of economic growth – condemned to be spectators of their own demise? Or might the solution lie in a form of "creative self-destruction"? This would require awareness of the evolution of one's environment, its changes, its unavoidable evolution, and, in response to this, to self-destruct in order to rebuild anew. Pharmacists are under increasing competitive pressure from supermarkets and Internet vendors; they are also under the increasing pressure of calls for reforms from both European and French governments; they are facing more and more urgent demands from "patients". Questioning the current model is a matter of survival Destruction is inevitable and it is certainly preferable to engage proactively in this destruction, as with creation, rather than to suffer it through the arrival of new actors or laws which force one's destiny.

Creative self-destruction

What is true for companies is just as true for individuals. An employee who has been in the same company for several decades and who has not had regular and rigorous training over time, who has evolved little by little without ever fundamentally questioning themselves, cannot but fear the arrival of new people, who may have less experience but more recent and relevant education which is extremely effective for the challenges of the present. Such a traditional employee has every reason to fear possible organisational changes if they have never questioned themselves, if they have never been prepared for the current environment. Over the last 20 years, the world of work has been dramatically changed by the combined effect of the advent of the Internet, globalisation, robotisation, highly intense competition and new communication tools. A person who is in their forties in 2020 has had no formal education on the techniques which constitute the reality of their clients, and still has at least 20 years left to work, as has the Teacher and their students. Such an employee lives in fear of potential organisational changes carried out by the company, which has to adapt to its environment, perhaps without this individual, who has been loyal for 20 years. This fear must, in fact, come from the inertia in which we are all entrenched, and the only way forward is self-examination, so that we can "destroy" ourselves in some way in order to create a new version of ourselves, relearn and develop ourselves. Sometimes we must forget what we have learned because it is no longer relevant to the situation in which we live. We must question again and again who we are, personally and professionally, and start the process of creative destruction of our own accord, and in so doing, control it. If we are the masters of our own destruction, by corollary, we are also the masters of our own creation, and therefore do not leave any room for others to decide on our behalf. The question, then, is how this creative destruction should be set in motion or when it should be triggered, because the risk is that we become aware of this necessity when it is already too late. In other words, we only change for better when we are already doing well. The challenge is to put ourselves in this position of change even when everything is fine. The crux of the matter lies in identifying this moment: being able to "destroy" oneself when all is well – so as not to risk being destroyed by others –, while at the same time already devising the creation we want to bring about. The value of self-destruction in such a context is that this process can only be positive, since "all is well", or rather, "still" well. The same applies to businesses. They must understand that they can and must change only when they are doing well, when their finances allow it, when management is stable, supportive and constructive, because change necessarily causes upheavals and disruption. But all of this is more desirable than changing when you are already in the throes of a crisis, and when the business is struggling because of an aggressive environment, a new competitor for example. Change at that stage is often more difficult, more costly, more complex, unless it leads to absolute destruction and the business starts from scratch, with the ensuing collateral damage: downgrading, unemployment, bankruptcy, etc.

Innovation, Political Revolution and Power

Mainly driven by the Internet (but not only), the early 2000s saw the emergence of a new use of innovation: innovation applied to the political sphere. It was not so much about promoting a new regime or party, even if this was also the case, but rather of developing new proposals for redesigning, as it were, both value creation and its redistribution.

More than 30 years ago, French philosopher Michel Foucault explained that we needed *a new economy of power relations*.[29] The author here refers to philosophical issues concerning his preferred topics – madness, alienation, crime, sexuality – which, *a priori*, are not directly linked to the context of organisations. However, Foucault himself said that his concepts, his books should be used as *small toolboxes*,[30] and that methodology is more important for dismantling, deconstructing and understanding problems than the themes themselves. In other words, while the subjects which interested Foucault seem to be far removed from the concerns of organisations, the methodology he applies can nonetheless be quite relevant.

The issue at hand here is just as much power as it is resistance to power, more precisely, the forms of resistance to power, or to powers, which innovation will bring about. In order to identify these forms of resistance, we must first understand what exactly is meant by power. With the help of Foucault, we can define power not so much as a relationship but as a mode of action of some individuals on others. In the collective imagination, "power" means hierarchy, domination, structures of power, leadership, order and submission. While all of these are true, such a vision of power is simplistic, because there can also be hierarchy without domination or power. For example, in situations where the hierarchy does not have the capacity or means to exercise it. Therefore, it is the exercise of power, power in action which should be examined.

In "The Subject and power", Foucault skilfully explains that one of the roles of philosophy since the Enlightenment has been to monitor the excessive powers of political rationality. He goes on to explain that the relationship between rationalisation and excesses of power is obvious, so it is not a question of banally analysing the power relationship and how it is exercised – the dominant-dominated mode – but rather of proposing a new mode of investigation for understanding power through the observation of forms of resistance to power: *Rather than analysing power from*

---

[29]Michel Foucault, "Le sujet et le pouvoir", in *Dits et écrits II*, Gallimard, "Quarto", 2001, p. 1041. Michel Foucault, "The Subject and Power" in *Critical Inquiry*, Vol. 8, No. 4, The University of Chicago Press (Summer, 1982, pp. 777–795).

[30]Michel Foucault, "Des supplices aux cellules", in *Dits et écrits I*, Gallimard, "Quarto", 2001, p. 1588. *Essential Works of Foucault, 1954–1984*, New Press, 2001.

the point of view of its internal rationality, it consists of analysing power relations through the antagonism of strategies.[31] Foucault looks at power in a traditional way: power of men over women, of parents over their children, of psychiatry over the mentally ill, of medicine over the population; but power can be examined far beyond these institutional systems.

Financial institutions exert great power over individuals in a particularly ruthless way. The banking system is fundamental for carrying out all the possible steps of everyday life: paying for something, receiving payments, paying a deposit for a house, getting a loan, etc. However, despite its critical role in society, its accessibility remains challenging. A traditional analysis highlights that there is a very clear exercise of power in the bank-user relationship, and the only reason this is changing is thanks to the strategies of resistance which have emerged. While the emergence of online banking in the early 2000s desacralised the banking system, it is above all the networks of resistance, the networks of power, which have helped reshape the bank-client relationship. This is very true with what is commonly known as "crowdfunding", a method for financing projects without calling on the traditional actors, i.e. banks. Disintermediation, i.e. the emergence of a direct relationship between the project owner and the investor, is the descendant of traditional underwriting, and has developed particularly thanks to the Internet and social media. Financing therefore no longer needs to go through banks, because the only thing which matters is the relationship between investors and recipients. The intermediary has a very limited role, sometimes even non-existent.

What holds true for the banking system holds equally true for many of the services we have already mentioned. And in each case, the value map, which was previously hijacked by a very small number of players who ultimately held power, is redrawn entirely. This is the case with multinationals or with conglomerates in the tourism sector, which saw resistance to the power they held emerge through Airbnb, and it is also the case with taxis, in France, where the concentration of a very small number of players granted these dominant players sufficient power to define prices, to establish the offer they wanted, where they wanted and when they wanted.

---

[31] Michel Foucault, "Le sujet et le pouvoir", in *Dits et écrits II, Op. cit. Michel Foucault, "Le sujet et le pouvoir", in Dits et écrits II, Op. cit.*, p. 1041. Michel Foucault, "The Subject and Power", *Op. cit.*, pp. 777–795.

Michel Foucault denounced the power of institutions, of power apparatuses such as schools and prisons, but also the power held over our bodies in the context of medical care. The power exerted by physicians over patients is determined by the knowledge they possess, by the attitude they take and by the context, whereby the individual requiring care is led into a position of inferiority. It is indeed power networks which undermine established, hierarchical and structured power. Therefore, it is not surprising that in the medical sector, a power of resistance developed denouncing patients' living conditions and the quality of care. Many Internet platforms now give patients the opportunity to evaluate their stay in a hospital or clinic, and even though patients do not dare express their discontent in front of doctors, nurses and administrative staff, they have no qualms about venting their views on chat rooms, where they can give their own account of the care and explanations they received, but also the general atmosphere, how pleasant the staff was, the meals, how they were treated, etc. Many medical centres have understood this and make sure that they circumvent resistance by integrating comments, advice and feedback into their value proposition. This is the case of the famous Shouldice Hospital in Toronto, the Alexandra Health Care in Singapore or the Narayana Hospital in Bangalore, to name just a few. They even try to stifle resistance by encouraging their clients to share, easily and on a regular basis, their patient-client experience.

The question of knowledge ownership has always been an issue of power control, as is the case in the medical field, but as is also the case with schools, of course. Here too, the pockets of resistance were never completely silenced. Take for example the popular universities in the 19th century or the University of Vincennes at the turn of May 68. In recent years, traditional education has nevertheless been challenged by a large number of pockets of resistance, as illustrated in our previous examples of the Khan Academy or the école42 in France. All these emerging models reject education based on a dominant-dominated model and advocate a more horizontal transmission of knowledge, where everyone contributes to the construction of knowledge as they learn. The example of a course on innovation is indicative of this paradigm. How can a course on innovation be delivered in a traditional learner-teacher system, when dozens of innovations emerge every week on the market, all over the world, all the time, across all industries? At a time when our classrooms are increasingly international, increasingly connected, a vast majority of students are aware of the innovations which are taking place. How can the teacher individually be aware of all of them? In other words, how can a Professor in Innovation be constantly aware of all current innovations, which students will definitely ask about? The only possible way forward is the co-construction of courses. The system needs to change so as to enable students to think about innovation, beyond the confines of the classroom, and think about learning, think about sharing with their classmates as well as with their teachers. And instead of simply questioning the teacher about an innovation they have heard about, why not give students the opportunity to bring these experiences into the lesson, to describe the innovation in question, to share it, and help others understand it. The role of the Professor, then, would be to help students analyse it, to help them understand what is at stake above and beyond methodology, experience and academic knowledge. This would no longer be a "top-down", teacher-student approach, but rather a process of joint construction. These new forms of learning also include peer-to-peer assessment, where students assess each other's work. A student who understands a lesson will have no difficulty in explaining it to a classmate, using different vocabulary than the teacher, and referring to other sources of shared knowledge. These new modes of learning are developing. In addition to the examples mentioned above, this paradigmatic shift is being adopted by more and more innovative institutions around the world. Once again, it is the resistance associated with recent technological innovations which makes these approaches possible, it is the opposition to established systems which fosters the development of these networks, these alternative strategies.

Resistance never attacks power or institutions directly, what it attacks are in fact the effects of power. It is not about attacking a university, but about challenging the ways in which knowledge is disseminated. Foucault made this very clear when he explained that *what defines a power relationship is a mode of action, which does not act directly and immediately on others, but which acts on their own action. An action on the action.*[32] In the examples presented above, none of these forces of resistance wanted to seize power for themselves, it is simply not something they are fighting for, what they denounce are the actions and consequences of power. These resistant proposals articulate alternatives which established historical actors condemn because they wish to safeguard the effects of power they have always possessed and which afford them monopolistic advantages. The networks of resistance *do not look for the "chief enemy"*

---

[32] *Ibid.*

but for the immediate enemy,[33] what they seek is to remove the hierarchical pretensions of the dominant players.

When resistance emerged in the field of mobility through a proposal to put people in contact with each other for travelling, the established power structures condemned the substance of the proposal, the new player, the application, the organisation which initiated the proposal, in other words "the immediate enemy". Looking at the bigger picture, however, we can see that the "chief enemy", was in fact new technologies, deregulation, evolution in user behaviours. In other words, the evolution of the environment which brought about innovation. Only by understanding, accepting and/or collaborating with this chief enemy can traditional players thwart the resistance, simply because the resistance will then no longer exist. When a car rental company condemns, criticises and calls for the disappearance of a car-pooling platform, such as BlaBlaCar, it is attacking the immediate enemy, but not the "chief enemy". The immediate enemy is only the consequence of the chief enemy. Consequently, action should be geared towards the environment. This can be through legislation, for example, which could evolve so as to ensure traditional rental companies can offer a similar service. Maybe what they need to do is adapt to or integrate a new technological paradigm, or to adapt the offering to the changes in customer needs.

Here again, as with crowdfunding, care services, education, Foucault shows us that what is at play here is the struggle of individuals in their status, struggles which *assert the right to be different, and they underline everything which makes individuals truly individual.*[34] Resistant proposals assert the right to propose a new way of being, a new way of doing. Resistant proposals assert individuality, personality, not to say personalisation, which traditional players failed to develop. Power structures are not interested in individuals, they want subjects, they want to impose a truth which must be slavishly acknowledged. In essence, they are the antithesis of resistant proposals. And that is precisely why forces of resistance are not interested in power, in seizing that power for themselves: what they fight for is a proposal which is radically different. *The main objective of these struggles is to attack not so much "such or such" an*

---

[33] *Idem.*
[34] *Idem.*

institution of power, or group, or elite, or class but rather a technique, a form of power.[35]

Struggles and resistance

For Foucault, struggles and resistances are divided into three axes: those which oppose forms of domination, those which denounce forms of exploitation and those who fight everything which restricts the individual. The domination of major organisations, the forms of exploitation they practice, by more or less taking the individual hostage, have regularly given rise to resistance. Computer operating systems are an example of this. Linux is a form of resistance to the quasi-total domination of American giant Microsoft. The same is true for knowledge. Up until a few decades ago, knowledge was found in certain books, dictionaries and encyclopaedias. The advent of collaborative tools for knowledge creation and transmission such as Wikipedia have drastically called into question the power of traditional books, which, in a way, represented a form of domination. Now, the "power of knowledge" goes through debates – by all and for all – through agreements, through tangible evidence. This spells the end of the traditional tools of domination of age-old powers, a new norm for the acquisition of knowledge is emerging.

An example of Foucault's second form of struggle can be found in the illegal file sharing platforms which emerged around the 2000s, such as eMule or Napster. These platforms were not so much developed to avoid paying for a music album or a film, but rather to make a statement, bordering on anarchism, questioning distribution costs and the margins of intermediaries in general. It is a resistance to the forms of exploitation represented by the world's major music and film distributors. It is also a resistance to the goliaths of the music industry who are less interested in launching and developing talent than in increasing profits.

As for the last struggle, against that which restricts or subjugates the individual, the subjugation which everyone can experience can be found in particular in schools, where the standardisation of teaching tends to force each pupil into a particular way of being, way of thinking; and the resistance is to be found in the alternative methods which have been developed, such as Montessori or Martenot, which give pupils more room

---

[35] *Idem.*

to to express themselves, which ensure that they learn at a pace which matches the speed at which they understand, the way they learn and their capacity to assimilate knowledge. Resistant proposals fighting against subjugation are also emerging, and are just as valid, in the political sphere. Movements such as Occupy Wall Street, Podemos, or Nuit Debout have taken a significant share of the political chessboard. These movements, which have very clearly benefited from the Internet for establishing networks of like-minded people, for recruiting, for communicating, for sharing the information they wish to disseminate nationally and more widely for some, have ultimately created new networks of powers. These are non-hierarchical networks of horizontal powers, which stand up to a political system which they no longer accept, who resist against methods they no longer accept, mainly because these methods confiscate power, subjugate individuals. The citizens who set up these networks of resistant power reject the established system in which election ballots only serve to confiscate power from individuals, and instead seek to show that politics can be a place which elevates citizens, a space for collaboration, without however annihilating the individual.

These forms of struggles reshape power relations, but more generally, reshape relations according to a triad of security-confidence-transparency. Blockchain technology, which was launched in 2008, along with the digital currency called bitcoin, is highly symptomatic of this. Blockchain is a storage technology which enables the transmission of information from one individual to another in a transparent and secure manner, directly peer-to-peer without any control or centralising body. It acts as a ledger of sorts, containing the entire history of interactions between its users. All interactions are secure, visible by all users without any intermediary, which means anybody can verify the validity of the chain. It first grew popular in the context of monetary transactions and asset transfers. However, the development and applications of blockchain technology are limitless, whether for establishing a contract with many stakeholders or as a registry. We could perfectly imagine using it to create legislation. All citizens could contribute to drafting the legal text by adding their own contributions. These would not be hosted by an Internet giant, but by all participating citizens. All proposals would be transparent to all, contributors, readers, and of course citizens, who are those most affected by any laws. In this context, blockchain could tear down the walls of power. There would be no representatives of the people, because the people would represent themselves; no hierarchy confiscating power with an assembly which decides on and passes laws, but multiple stakeholders who take democracy and their destiny into their own hands.

The three forms of resistance, or struggles, which Foucault highlights are extremely relevant and enlightening today, in contexts and spaces which the French philosopher probably never even imagined, because most of the phenomena creating the paradigm emerged as a result of technological innovations. The peer-to-peer culture (sharing files, data, methods between users without a central server) necessarily entails cultural and societal shifts, struggles and resistance. This has significant consequences on the notions of hierarchy and human networks.[36]

Michel Foucault had thoroughly analysed the issue of power in a number of fields, and from different angles: philosophy, sociology, the State, institutions, religions and pastoral power in particular.

However, power and power relations are also rooted in the economic sphere, and maybe even more so – particularly now, the beginning of the 21st century – than in institutional apparatuses, which have been almost completely discredited, and religions, which have largely lost their standing as devices of power. Power between individuals within organisations and between organisations is predominant and plays out at all levels, with employees as well as with customers and partners of the organisation. While the author of *Discipline and Punish* offers a seminal, enlightening analysis of power and its mechanisms in terms of method, he somewhat staggeringly plays down the power of companies and organisations, and this is revealed when he somewhat naively states that *sometimes the power was exercised by private ventures.*[37] However, it would appear that, at least in recent decades, this is precisely the space in which power relations have been unfolding.

In other words, the question of power and who holds it, of the effects of power and who transmits and who receives it, and of power strategies and their corresponding tools and networks, does not necessarily lie where we expect it to. It has been entirely reshaped over the last two, maybe three decades. Resistance can be found in the streets, but not only; resistance speaks through a few proponents of change, but not only; resistance denounces, but not only; resistance also proposes solutions, alternative methods, ways to ensure that resistance is not just resistance for the sake

---

[36]Pekka Himanen, *The Hacker Ethic and the Spirit of the Information Age*, Random House, New York, 2001.

[37]Michel Foucault, "The Subject and Power" in *Critical Inquiry, Op. cit.*, pp. 777–795.

of it, and brings forth proposals which are intelligent, complete and lasting.

A redistribution of value

The shattering of power structures as they may have existed in the past and still exist today – sometimes overwhelmingly – entails a number of consequences. Firstly, power is no longer concentrated in the hands of and controlled by a limited number of players who hold exclusive rights on the offer; secondly, increased participation by beneficiaries, users and customers; and thirdly, a redistribution or sharing of value. In the hotel industry, in mobility, health care or the delivery industry, many oligopolies have formed and have in fact confiscated the financial value of the market, which is only distributed among a limited few. Whether talking about ACCOR, G7 Taxis or Taxis Bleus (both belong to the same company), or pharmacies, they hold the keys to what is on offer, the pricing conditions, and of course, the profits. The arrival of competitors, as we have pointed out with examples such as Uber, Airbnb and others, also entails an overhaul of the redistribution of value. First of all, value at the level of the offer, by providing different services as well as a new variety of proposals; and value at the level of the players, by multiplying the possible players to propose the offer; lastly, a redistributed financial value. To give a simple example, foreign tourists travelling to Paris will not spend less during their stay because they are staying at an Airbnb. Overall, they will spend just as much during their visit, it is simply that they will not have to spend most of their money on accommodation. This means they can spend more on outings, visits, buying products – purchases they might not have made had it not been for the competition of the hotel business, whose rates are prohibitive in the French capital. According to the Paris Tourist Office, in the past, tourists used to dedicate 70% of their budget to accommodation in traditional hotels; now they spend only 40% on accommodation, but spend the same overall amount during their stay, thereby benefiting a larger number of players.[38] This is a new distribution of value, made possible by the recent emergence of innovative services. Remember, however, that we must be careful – at least at this stage – not to qualify or pass

---

[38]Étude Asterès, Airbnb, study on the contribution of Airbnb users to the Paris economy, 2013.

judgment on these innovations, or say whether they are "good" or "bad". Because innovation always precedes the legal framework which governs it, many of these services emerge without a clear legal status or with inadequate legislation. As a result, tensions have arisen between the traditional players, who have seen their sources of income disappear, and the new entrants. New entrants, on their part, have considered these markets significant and interesting enough to take over some of these market shares.

Organisations such as Compte-Nickel,[39] KissKissBankBank, Boursorama[40] were all developed on the fringes of the banking system. Their proposal uses the codes of the traditional banking system, offers services from the banking system, without however possessing all the characteristics of traditional investment, private or retail banks. These services capture some of the value which was once reserved for traditional establishments. Their development and growth bear no comparison with that of historical organisations. What causes traditional players to denounce these new entrants is seeing their clients defect and their profits dwindle.

Are these developments, which affect all sectors, from education to driving schools, from banking to hotels, an extreme development of the liberal and capitalist system, or are they in some way its explosion? Is their existence the sign that it has reached its breaking point? Is not the arrival of micro-organisations, of competition, the harbinger of the end of a past capitalist system made up of large corporations which control, with very few players, our way of consuming, of moving around, of financing ourselves? Have citizens not regained some of their freedoms through the destruction of traditional walls? Does this not develop new forms of economies, whether they are called collaborative or transformative economies? When citizens, in their free time, can become a delivery service – Amazon Flex – when any individual who owns a car can become a driver – UberPop – when a fan writes articles on Wikipedia thereby contributing to the world's largest encyclopaedia, do these not constitute challenges to the bastions of power built by and hitherto controlled by major, financially significant companies? It is not simply that Larousse, FedEx, Taxi Parisien are being challenged. They are gradually being replaced by common men who propose an alternative offer in a

---

[39] A French alternative banking system established in 2014.
[40] A French online banking platform.

structured way. This is once again a reversal of power relations, or rather, to be more precise, a networking of powers, which is taking place, and whose chief resource is no longer "the firm" with its dictatorial power, but a network of individuals whose freedom is preserved. It is important to stress here that it is not that one firm replaces another. Airbnb does not replace ACCOR, whether in terms of shareholders, employees or customer relations, almost everything opposes these two companies. When a great number of Uber drivers in Paris decided to set up their own driving company, there was nothing to prevent them from doing so. They already had the required status to work on behalf of UBER, and preferred to set up a different community model, rather than the one proposed by the American structure, which they were able to set up within a few weeks.

What enabled this is the banishment of authority over the masses. This is what triggered the collaborative economy, which has grown not only by way of the multiplication of players, but also of the involvement of all citizens. Without contributors, YouTube could not exist, nor would Wikipedia. The same can be said about Airbnb and its hosts, or UberPop and its car owners, and so on and so forth. The contribution of a certain number of people is what makes it possible to design a collaborative offer. Of course, not everyone has to become a contributor, these can even represent only a minority of the population as a whole. The vast majority of people who visit YouTube or Wikipedia are viewers or readers, respectively. In the same way, only a tiny fraction of people use their vehicles to offer driving services, but everyone has the opportunity and the freedom to if they so choose, for the benefit of all, which is the very essence of the collaborative economy.

From the end of hierarchy to the development of circularity: The advent of a flat world

Concomitantly, this dimension of the collaborative economy has brought about a circular economy. There is no hierarchical structure any more, with one single structure holding all the power. Instead, there is circularity, where anyone can become a player, a supplier, provide a service, or produce an offer. It is also what can be called a form of "flat"[41]

---

[41] Thomas Friedman, *The World Is Flat: A Brief History of the Twenty-first Century*, Farrar, Straus and Giroux, 2005.

organisational innovation, i.e. an organisation where layers and interme-diaries disappear. Everything is done on the surface, in a linear fashion. The organisational skeleton is deconstructed so that it is flatter, more hori-zontal. This does not mean that there is no body which implements and structures supply and demand, but what it does mean is that this interme-diary is entirely dependent on the players of this offer, who are at the same time customers and/or suppliers. This means this "body" has no hold on them – or only a very weak one – this forces it to systematically operate within a new balance of power in which it is not exactly identical to other players, but is infinitely more so than in a traditional hierarchical struc-ture. This innovative construction of new, "flat" organisations can be found in many other circumstances. This is the case of workplaces where open spaces show a willingness to break down hierarchical structures, known to promote communication and discussion, breaking down possi-ble physical as well as psychological barriers.

This concerns not only organisational innovation. The development of iPod and its iTunes service are also part of this "flat innovation" approach, both in terms of the actual devices and the service. When it was launched, the iPod was very small, very thin, with no buttons whatsoever, was touch sensitive, and flat. Alongside this, the iTunes platform destroyed hierarchical structures: it put artists, record labels, retailers and buyers on the same level by making access to music as quick and easy as possible. All consumers needed was an Internet connection and a connec-tion to their computer to purchase and listen to music. Apple's offer not only nullified the role of record stores, but also removed their hierarchy, the power these had to select one artist over another, one music genre over another, thereby enabling consumers to buy music depending on the organisation *they* wanted. The expertise and advice of the record store became irrelevant, as did the point of sale itself. Apple flattened these roles and functions, and gave back to consumers the choice to buy what they wanted, when they wanted. And so, in the early 2000s, the Californian company had understood the trend of the flattening of the world. However, it failed to recognise this again 10 years later, and organisations such as Deezer or Spotify understood that the last remain-ing structure – iTunes – had to be flattened too. The drawbacks of iTunes – users had to download the platform, they had to purchase the service, and the dependence on the Cupertino-based company – pushed the development of a different type of online music platform for stream-ing music. Earlier, platforms such as Myspace had already understood this, and in particular the value of the direct relationship between the composer or performer and the listener.

This is also true for the written word, with the development of online magazines and newspapers, there is no need for newsstands or bookshops to sell books. This affected publishing also. Nowadays, anyone can publish a book. What used to be called self-publishing now boils down to digital printing at virtually no cost. Publishing has always been in a relationship of power and hierarchy, with a publisher at the top, a reading committee which subjectively chooses to publish such and such a work. Then the diffuser and the bookseller, who arbitrarily or on commercial terms, decide to promote a particular work. The same goes for book promotion, which was, as it often still is, based on connections, networks or interests which are not necessarily objective. Today, writers have at their disposal dozens of offers for publishing a text in book form, and interactions have been flattened. Anyone can turn their text into a book. Of course, it will not be backed by the support of a well-known brand, will not be a "book" in the traditional and noble sense, but this text can nevertheless be printed and put into book form, can be marketed and distributed. The author takes on a very participative role in such a project, and also contributes to the marketing of the text, its communication and distribution, usually via social media.

Deconstructing ancient worlds to build our own: The case of education

There has certainly never been such a big gap between the way the world is advancing and the way we teach. Irrespective of the level of education, the teacher-learner principle has not been called into question for many, many decades. Classes are taught in classrooms, the teacher at the board addresses the novices who sit quietly, homework is still commonplace, and obviously assessments, electivity and correction are still the common attributes of education today. School is indeed a device of power as denounced by Foucault, and it is all the more complex to challenge when elitism allies with corporatism.

Over the last century, the world has evolved very rapidly, brutally and drastically, but the way of teaching has remained unchanged. The teacher stands at the front, the learners sit at their desks, they write down what they are required to learn, look at the board and that is it. Clothing aside, we are still using methods from another century, another age.

Yet the education sector too is affected by the organisational flattening brought about by innovation. Less than 20 years ago, students walked into the classroom with a defined perimeter of knowledge acquired in previous years, whether in the same course, in a previous education level, or in even in another school structure altogether. Today, professors have no way of knowing whether or not the student entering the classroom has already taken the same course, maybe a similar level course at a competing university which publishes its courses online or on a knowledge dissemination platform. How do you deal with a student who sits in the classroom and who, a week or a month prior, decided to take this course in another institution? Is this situation not bound to happen more and more often? Should we condemn a student who is passionate about a subject simply because their knowledge or interest could jeopardize the pedagogical approach prepared by the teacher? Education has always depended on the quality of teachers and students, who, together, founded brands which stand for prestige and excellence, and renown. The globalisation of education only accentuated this phenomenon in the recruitment of both the best teachers and the best students. The inertia of the sector has reinforced this dynamic, which is why the higher educations at the top of rankings are also those which have a very prestigious brand. In fact, education operates within a very strong hierarchical structure with a form of dominant–dominated relationship, with at the top the prestigious brand of the school, the excellence of the teachers who form disciples whom they consider worthy. The phenomenon of flattening seen in many sectors should also challenge the education sector, as well as the credibility rightfully given to knowledge platforms. Moreover, the development of online courses from different universities means that the students of today and of tomorrow will be tapping into different structures in order to develop their knowledge. Is the best innovation course still Harvard or ESSEC? Or maybe HEC or Stanford? Tsinghua or the National University of Singapore? It is probably safe to say that the quality of innovation courses in these academically high-ranking universities is similar. However, we could legitimately say, for example, that the course on technological innovation is the best at Stanford given its long experience in this field, that the course on responsible innovation is the most relevant at ESSEC given its pioneering spirit in this field, that the financial innovation course is maybe not the best at HEC despite their significant investments in this area, that the innovation course in Asia might not be particularly relevant at Tsinghua given its central geographical location, or that the entrepreneurial innovation in Singapore course is superior to others considering the number of start-ups developed in the city-state. What prevents a student based in Mumbai from taking all these courses so that they can learn from the best on the different facets of innovation? Once again, there is a flattening movement, whereby all courses are aligned and available so that individuals can learn as much as possible on a theme or topic. The education of tomorrow will consist of a set of small structures offering an ultra-personalised meta-structure according to what one is interested in. Will the education of tomorrow be built like a box of Lego, where everyone can pick "bricks" to build themselves up according to their individual goal? Universities and higher education institutions need to understand this evolution of education. Turning inward and considering themselves the best is what will lead the system to its demise. The structures dispensing education as well as the organisation of education and the courses themselves all have to be designed anew.

It is obvious that in such a context, technologies play a major role, in whatever form: tablets, computers, the Internet, and especially artificial intelligence. It is not a question of being for or against artificial intelligence, but of knowing how it should be integrated into education. If bots are capable of offering restaurant recommendations between users based on their location, they are no less capable of connecting students around the world working on the same theme. And self-improving software would enable learners to progress, by pointing out common mistakes and, for example, how best to succeed at a given subject. At the end of the day, it is essentially the personalisation of education, which every teacher would dream of achieving but is de facto not possible in the current system. Conversely, artificial intelligence could help teachers to rethink the way they teach, as many software programs can detect recurring weaknesses in students' work and highlight what elements maybe not adequately addressed in the syllabus or the pedagogical approach.

Artificial intelligence, like other innovations, is redesigning education and gives people the opportunity to learn outside the walls of a brick-and-mortar school, so they can personalise content, improve teaching, evaluate with greater relevance, etc.

Technology, the flattening structures and collaboration are the future of education. Let us go back to the example of teaching innovation. Teaching this discipline in today's context is fraught with challenges. It is a very exhilarating discipline to teach: you work constantly on what is new, what offers a different perspective, what makes life simpler or more rewarding. However, exciting as it may be, this discipline is not simple to teach because of one of its qualities: its omnipresence. Innovation is everywhere. If you have ears, eyes, a nose or a mouth you are the target of a recent innovation. It is omnipresent. It overflows, spreads, invades our everyday life, you cannot turn around without seeing a new innovation which has appeared in the last weeks, days or hours, whether it is in Silicon Valley, Silicon Sentier or Silicon Shenzen. The globalisation of information precipitates the existence of a new object, or a new service which ends up on screens all over the world at the same time. Obviously, those who are most receptive to this context are the ultra-connected: teenagers, young adults, students, whose everyday life is largely rhythmed by a compulsive need to check their communication devices. Knowledge pertaining to new innovations is no longer limited to over-achieving nerds. It is accessible and of interest to everyone. Whoever is interested in a particular sport, art, or any hobby or topic for that matter, knows what innovation are being developed in this field, anywhere in the world. What is problematic for teaching innovation is not so much the proliferation of innovations, but rather the exponential coverage they get, and interest they garner.

While teaching innovation is about understanding how the world was so as to understand how the world is, and to make assumptions about what it will be, the greatest challenge, however, is to understand the present world, in order to identify possible avenues for considering its future. One solution would be to rely on those who have steeped themselves in information on these topics and can offer relevant insight to the classroom. Indeed, students are not only the most receptive to this issue, they are also the ones who will make up the world of tomorrow. In other words, such a system would enable the emergence of assumptions about the world to come. Consequently, it is paramount to ensure that the classroom is a space to monitor, explore and develop innovations. Insofar as possible, all innovations should find their way to the classroom in order to build up the educational landscape. In practical terms, this can be achieved through the Facebook or Twitter account of the course or through its shared wiki or blog. Innovation should be the lifeblood of the course, each session acting as fab'lab.

While students are in the best position to be receptive to, share and highlight innovations, this does not necessarily mean that they comprehend them. That is where the teacher–decoder comes in. Young students and experienced teachers alike are always blinded by the lights of the present, and methodological analysis, academic rigour and perspective are the only things which can help us understand the innovations which flood our everyday lives, so that, ultimately, we are not overpowered by them.

We can no longer teach the same way as we did when social networks did not exist, when those who today collect and gather knowledge – Google, Amazon, iTunes, etc. – were in their infancy. How could we ignore several billion people connected to social media, which for many are the first – and sometimes the only – media they watch. Social media should, in fact, become one of the first channels for education. Our goal here is not to glorify the giants of the digital economy, but by educating these uber-connected populations, by helping them achieve a Deleuzian deconstruction of these platforms, we will enable them not to be crushed by these giants, but rather to use them so as to reconstruct the knowledge which is still needed.

The role of the teacher is undergoing a transformation. The teacher is no longer the mere bearer of hierarchical knowledge; the teacher is also an organiser, a decoding expert, a manager, a knowledge "scout" or of a form of raw knowledge which is brought to the heart of the education model. The sacrosanct teacher-learner dynamic has run its course, class-rooms are no longer airtight. Maybe we should tear them down before students do.

We are already living in the world of flat innovation, and this concerns music, publishing, workspaces or even planet Earth, which has never been this "flat" with the considerable development of air transport, covering increasingly long flight distances with an ever-decreasing number of stopovers.

Innovation takes on many forms, crosses many sectors and spans many regions. No one is spared from the power of the Innovator, their strength, will and desire. Innovation advances inexorably, unethically, unapologetically and without compassion, in a cold and dehumanised manner. Relentless and indiscriminate, innovation and the innovator care about little other than the act of creating and doing, or generating value in whatever form and regardless of collateral damage. Can innovation be thwarted? Is it at all possible, in a Utopian way, to give a soul to innovation?

Chapter 3

The Need for Responsible Innovation

One has to look out for engineers, they begin with sewing machines and end up with the atomic bomb.

Marcel Pagnol
Critique des critiques

How Far Should We Take Innovation?

As a result of innovation, animal populations and species are disappearing. The massive development of technologies, products, consumer and non-consumer goods has had and continues to have a direct consequence on the depletion of natural resources. It is undisputable that the atmosphere, soil and oceans are deteriorating due to anthropogenic activity and our constant quest for economic growth. Increasing urbanisation is profoundly and lastingly changing the balance of the biosphere. These challenges are global: acid rain and radioactive pollution know no borders, and the "7th continent" made of plastic is adrift in the Pacific beyond national waters. These are the direct consequence of the unpredictability of the innovations introduced onto a market. When chlorofluorocarbons (CFCs) were launched in the 1950s, there was no way of knowing that in the 1970s and 1980s we would discover that they were dangerous greenhouse gases and were causing stratospheric ozone depletion.

In the 16th century, French philosopher François Rabelais said *Knowledge without conscience is but the ruin of the soul*,[1] proving himself to be particularly visionary. This observation does not apply only to the environmental impact of science: electronics have invaded our everyday lives with communicating objects; the "digitalisation of the world" is becoming a global challenge; nanotechnologies are ubiquitous in food, clothing, furniture, cars, etc. And this is certainly only the beginning, considering the advances still to come in the exploitation of the human body and its avatars with the trivialisation of automation.

At the same time, emerging digital technologies, alongside new means of communication which derive from them, have been instrumental in democratic upheavals, enabling populations to raise international awareness about complex political situations and in circumventing limitations to freedom of expression in order to rally public opinion to their cause. Medical advances, supported by technology, are praised by their beneficiaries. In light of this, the concept of innovation, like that of science, should be put into perspective with the Greek term *deinon*, which expresses both what is terrific and terrifying, concepts which merge together to express the power of opposites. Sophocles illustrated this idea in *Antigone* with the example of the man *Skilful beyond hope is the contrivance of his art and he advances sometimes to evil at other times to good*.[2] Indeed, it is the man, the individual who proposes an innovation, who – whether consciously or unconsciously – can make an innovation tend towards evil or towards good. There was a period when religion weighed so heavily on the collective consciousness and institutions that it inhibited certain possibilities for progress, for example in reproductive choices. Today, this constraint has completely disappeared, at least from lab benches. Moreover, scientists have not always had the means to fulfil their ambitions. In the last few decades, however, there has been a clear technical and technological acceleration with the increase in genetic knowledge, our growing understanding of DNA structures and the advent of cloning, etc. Today, the problem is no longer an issue of moral

---

[1] François Rabelais, *Gargantua and Pantagruel, Complete. Five Books of The Lives, Heroic Deeds And Sayings Of Gargantua And His Son Pantagruel.* Translated into English by Sir Thomas Urquhart of Cromarty and Peter Antony Motteux. Retrieved from https://www.gutenberg.org/files/1200/1200-h/1200-h.htm.

[2] Sophocle, *Antigone*, trad. P. Mazon, Les Belles Lettres, 1955, p. 86. Sophocle, *Antigone*, Loeb Classical Library. Translated to English by Hugh Lloyd-Jones.

acceptance or scientific capability. It is an issue of duty to do or not to do in the name of ethics and responsibility.[3]

Progress can be seen as a meta-model for change, dealing with the general perspective of evolution, that of knowledge, with hope for the future of mankind. Innovation, on the other hand, refers to more precise, technically, scientifically and socially targeted developments, often considered in relation to the market. In a way, then, innovation is the child of progress, constantly seeking to adapt to the needs of individuals. Innovation enabled the emergence of products and services which less than a century ago were pure science fiction. This is the case of transhumanism, whose self-professed aim is to improve the human condition through life-enhancing techniques, such as eliminating ageing and increasing intellectual, physical or psychological capacities.[4]

The Case of Transhumanism

Responsible innovation emerges in a very particular context with the massive deployment of the Internet and the disruptions it has brought with it, whether it be in the management of databases, social networks, education, or the redefinition of entire sectors in both industry and services. Around the same time, in the mid-1990s, another, considerable disruption was introduced: transhumanism. This is particularly relevant because it demonstrates that innovation is not necessarily linked to commercial entities, that it can emerge in the medical and paramedical field, that it can affect an extremely broad ecosystem and raise philosophical, technological, sociological, legal and even anthropological questions.

---

[3]The birth of the first "saviour sibling" in France 2012 is one of many examples. The parents of a little girl with a genetic disease decided to have a second child in order to save their first born. The parents of this "saviour sibling" benefited from a double preimplantation genetic diagnosis. The embryos carrying the disease were discarded, and the medical team selected from among the healthy embryos the one most compatible with the genetic makeup of the first born, and implanted it in the mother's womb. This is a formidable technical prowess, but one cannot help but wonder about the development of such a success which borders on eugenics.

[4]www.transhumanism.org.

The emergence of transhumanism

Of things some are in our power, and others are not.[5] Thus begins the famous *The Handbook of Epictetus*, a lapidary work for the practice of Stoic discernment. This maxim, also known as a spiritual exercise,[6] invites us not to try to control or alter events over which we have no control. While so many complain about their fate, the Stoics learn wisdom by practicing not to want things to be other than they are. In doing so, you will never experience misfortune because you will preserve the inner balance of your passions, but also align your being with the order of the world. The world, as our fate, as our environment, conditions us endlessly. However, Western culture, in its most recent historical manifestations, has granted humanity the possibility of extricating itself from this condition, or at least of expanding its condition, or at the very least, of pushing back its boundaries and blurring its finiteness. Transhumanism, an extension of the Promethean faculty of mankind to ward off the blows of fate by repairing the accidents of its existence, now aims at increasing humanity's longevity, motor capacities, as well as intellectual, muscular, etc. Through technology, increasing our own power is within our reach. Does this new control we have over nature – and particularly over *our* nature – also grant us some form of control over our destiny and our environment which are no longer impervious to our will? As we grow better and stronger thanks to transhumanism, are not the vicissitudes of destiny and these "things" which happen to us and which escape our control (genetic inheritance, hunger, disease) destined to sink into oblivion? Is not transhumanism shifting the limit which Epictetus drew in his time, reducing infinitesimally all the things which are not in our "power"? Descartes, in his "provisory code of morals" in *Discourse of the Method*, urged to *change the order of my desires rather than the order of the world.*[7] Will we not soon be able to change the order of the world rather than the order of our desires?

---

[5]Épictète, *Manuel*, trans. J. Pépin *in Les Stoïciens*, Bibliothèque de la Pléiade, Gallimard, 1952, p. 1111. Epictetus, *A Selection from the Discourses of Epictetus With the Encheiridion*, Translated to English by George Long. Retrieved from http://pioneer.chula. ac.th/~pukrit/bba/Epictetus.pdf.

[6]Pierre Hadot, *What is Ancient Philosophy?* trad. M. Chase, The Belknap Press of Harvard University Press, 2004.

[7]Descartes, *Discours de la méthode*, in *Œuvres*, Bibliothèque de la Pléiade, Gallimard, 1953, p. 142. René Descartes, *A Discourse on Method*. Translated to English by John Veitch. Retrieved from https://www.gutenberg.org/files/59/59-h/59-h.htm.

French surgeon Laurent Alexandre, also CEO of a DNA sequencing company, once stated at a conference that many of the people who were in the audience that day would live a 1,000 years. This practitioner, now recognised as one of the world's leading specialists in the field of transhumanism, explained that in doing so, *the man of the future would be like a website, forever a "beta version" of himself, a prototype organisation dedicated to continuous improvement.*[8] This surprising analogy is rooted in the fact that one of the world's largest companies, Google, is now at the forefront of the technical advances which will, according to the motto of Calico, a biotech company established by the Internet giant, enable mankind to fight aging and ultimately "kill death". It is common knowledge today that Google has become the main sponsor of the transhumanist movement. Constantly "updating" humanity like a website means augmenting it through technology, thanks to the convergence of four types of technologies grouped under the acronym Nanotechnology, Biotechnology, Information technology and Cognitive (NBIC) science, and the consequences of which continue to unfold in our economy and our lifestyles. This new transhumanist desire to turn humans into ever-evolving digital beings is reflected in a recent fundamental restructuring of Google, leading to the establishment of a new parent entity called Alphabet, thereby relegating the famous search engine to the rank of one single letter among 26 possibilities. It is as if Google was trying to become a dictionary of the future of the digital age, whose pages would be just as many services aimed at defining the human species of the future.

Transhumanism is a major phenomenon of our time, which, as it develops, raises profound questions which we must address. What is transhumanism? How did it originate? To what exactly does this term refer?

Understanding transhumanism and post-humanism

The term "transhumanism" was first coined in 1927 by biologist Julian Huxley, brother of Aldous Huxley, the famous author of *Brave New World*. In *Religion without revelation* the evolutionary biologist stated: *The human species can, if it wishes, transcend itself – not just sporadically, an individual here in one way, an individual there in another way, but in its entirety, as humanity. We need a name for this new belief.*

---

[8]Laurent Alexandre, *La mort de la mort*, JCLattès, 2011, p. 25. Our translation.

Perhaps transhumanism will serve: man remaining man, but transcending himself, by realizing new possibilities of and for his human nature.

"I believe in transhumanism": once there are enough people who can truly say that the human species will be on the threshold of a new kind of existence, as different from ours as our is from that of Peking Man. It will at last be consciously fulfilling its real destiny.[9] However, transhumanism was effectively born as a movement in and of itself in the 1980s under the impetus of American futurists from the American cyberculture. Nick Bostrom defines it as *intellectual and cultural movement that affirms the possibility and desirability of fundamentally improving the human condition through new applied reason.*[10] The self-professed goal of transhumanism is to advance the human condition through life-enhancing techniques, such as eliminating ageing and increasing intellectual, physical or psychological capacities.[11]

Through its purpose of supporting bodily improvements, transhumanism is a multifaceted concept which can be divided into two categories. First, mechanical transhumanism, which is characterised by adding prostheses or orthoses made of inert matter to a living organism. Most often, these enhancements are specifically designed to make up for a physical impairment, a missing sense or a missing limb, and are often highly publicised. For example, the carbon prostheses of South African athlete Oscar Pistorius, designed to enable him to compete at the highest level in the discipline of running, or the first total artificial heart produced by Carmat and implanted in a patient with heart failure on 18 December 2013, a world first. Sometimes, these enhancements are the work of one single person. This is the case of Nicolas Huchet, who in 2002, made a bionic hand using a 3D printer to replace the limb he lost in a work accident. Following this, he set up a project to offer affordable Bionic hand prostheses, in order to promote the democratisation of bionic technology. The second category of enhancements is organic transhumanism, which is characterised by the direct manipulation of organic matter through genetics or grafting. It concerns genetic engineering, an area with a high potential for development in the coming decades. Thanks to gene therapy we

---

[9]Julian Huxley, "Transhumanism", *Ethics in Progress*. 6(1), 2015, 12–16; doi: 10.14746/eip.2015.1.2y, ISSN 2084-9257.

[10]Nick Bostrom, "Transhumanism FAQ: A General Introduction, version 2.1". Retrieved from http://humanityplus.org/philosophy/transhumanist-faq/, 2003.

[11]www.transhumanism.org.

are already able to insert genetic mutations into the cells of individuals who have a medical condition, whatever it may be. This type of therapy targets mainly diseases such as different forms of cancer. As far as transplants are concerned, a distinction is often made between allografting and autografting: allografting, as its etymologically indicates, requires another living individual to donate an organ to be transplanted into the patient's body (this may be a kidney transplant, for example). Autograft involves using the patient's own organic substance, as is the case with a bone marrow transplant, for example.

Considering transhumanism from the dual angle of mechanical transhumanism and organic transhumanism raises the question of when this typology emerged, and also how this axiological classification was established. The most commonly accepted vision assumes that transhumanism would initially be more organic, enabling the human species to increasingly augment its life expectancy and cognitive capacities. Then, this form would ultimately give way to a mechanical model, carried by an artificial intelligence which would make our carnal envelope obsolete. This superior civilisation would therefore be exclusively made up of highly sophisticated robots, death-proof and endowed with creative thinking.

Considering that today, both types of transhumanism are only in their infancy (whether in terms of robotics or genetic engineering), there is not strictly speaking one type which would supplant the other. Therefore, the question of the historicity of the transhumanist typology has yet to be answered.

In this perspective of modifying the human body through techniques, a new distinction is to be made between two types of transhumanism. First, the transhumanism which repairs, i.e. *the Repaired Man*. This form of transhumanism concerns itself with repairing the human being when the body presents a deficiency or a malformation, using orthoses, prostheses, or artificial organs. This kind of transhumanism is already a reality. Next, the transhumanism which enhances, i.e. *the Augmented Man*. This is a more futuristic transhumanism which offers an improvement to biological functions, or enhances human potentialities. While this second modus operandi of transhumanism is still in its infancy, many consider the transition from Repaired Man to Augmented Man as a continuum. Would the two modalities therefore also correspond to two moments in the long process of achieving transhumanism? In the field of genetic engineering, for example, in France today, 29 out of 30 embryos detected with trisomy 21 are aborted. French scientist Laurent Alexandre states that *the next step will be to select genetic variants which promote high IQ, which the Chinese are in the process of identifying as part of their gifted sequencing program. Tomorrow, they will produce several embryos and choose the one with the best expectation of high IQ.*[12]

This perspective plunges us into a "wicked problem", which shows us the positive side of transhumanism, of this innovation which offers a cure to a large number of diseases, the possibility for people with certain conditions to regain freedom, and overall a positive advance for the Repaired Man. But at the same time, it raises a great many ethical considerations for the Repaired Man – and, by corollary, also for the Augmented Man. Of course, this raises the question of cost and the inequality this can generate between the populations who can afford it and those which cannot and who will, therefore, ultimately remain inferior, prisoners of their condition. It also raises psychological issues, because the Repaired Man is made whole on a physical level through transhumanism, but what of his psychological state? His physical impediment may have psychological repercussions, and how are these addressed? Among many other issues, we must also reflect on the status given to the Repaired Man? If a mechanical or biological "repair" makes him better than he previously was, might this not push individuals to also want this or that prosthesis? This is all the more true in the case of the Augmented Man, who seeks performance at all costs. Whether it is on an intellectual, biological or physical level, through sports for example, the Enhanced Man is on a quest to transcend the limitations and the boundaries of the human condition.

Even though the promoters of transhumanism themselves warn of the risks which may emerge from these new techniques, they remain convinced that the benefits outweigh any potential negatives in order to fight against evils such as poverty, disease, disability, malnutrition, dictatorial states, etc. These theorists claim that their ultimate goal is the quality of life of individuals. Progress is only valued in light of this final objective. Consequently, the concept of "nature" is something nebulous, which is an obstacle to progress.[13]

---

[12]Laurent Alexandre, "Après l'homme réparé, l'homme augmenté?" in "Les Échos" on April 17, 2015. Our translation.

[13]Nick Bostrom and Anders Sanders, "The Wisdom of Nature, An Evolutionary Heuristic for Human Enhancement", in *Human Enhancement*, J. Savulescu and N. Bostrom (eds.), Oxford University Press, 2008, pp. 375–416.

That said, the human species has always sought, in one way or another, to achieve progress, to modify itself, whether knowingly or not. In *On the Origin of Species*, Darwin even emphasised that the human species as we know it has certainly not reached its definitive form, that it is in fact in its initial stage, and will continue to evolve.[14] Raymond Kurzweil, one of the theorists of transhumanism, echoes Darwin and stresses that the pace of technological change is accelerating crucially and that the next few decades will see radical technological advances, but also a technological singularity which will profoundly and definitively change the nature of humankind.[15]

This is why we also talk about post-humanism: simply put, transhumanism is the condition for the advent of the post-humanism. Post-humanism is linked to a certain theory of evolution, since it sees itself as the next stage of human becoming. French entrepreneur Jean-Michel Besnier reminds us that it was the German philosopher Peter Sloterdijk who first coined this term in the context of a colloquium on Heidegger and the end of humanism.[16] According to Sloterdijk, humanity was to create a new value system adapted to the emergence of new beings, resulting from the convergence of the new NBIC technologies in the human body. He argues that transhumanism is still poorly defined, but should be characterised as a bridging vector towards the future stage of post-humanism.

That being said, the concept of "post-human" has not yet received an unambiguous definition from transhumanists. As Besnier says in his article "Posthuman": *Between Nicolas Bostrom (founder of the World Association of Transhumanism), Max More (to whom we owe extropians) and Ray Kurzweil (director of the Institute of Singularity), there is a near-total lack of consensus: the first states he wants to achieve the well-being and perpetuation of humanity, the second to eliminate the entropy which is dooming us to extinction, and the third to prepare for the coming of a Singularity which will make our species obsolete.*[17]

---

[14]Charles Darwin, *On the Origin of Species, Op. cit.*

[15]Raymond Kurzweil, *The Age of Spiritual Machines*, Viking Adult, 1999.

[16]Jean-Michel Besnier, *Demain les posthumains : Le futur a-t-il encore besoin de nous ?* Fayard 2010. Our translation.

[17]Jean-Michel Besnier dans l'article « Post-humain » *in Encyclopédie du trans/posthumanisme: L'humain et ses préfixes*, sous la direction de : Gilbert Hottois, Jean-Noël Missa et Laurence Perbal, Vrin 2015. Our translation.

"Post-human" as a concept emerged within a technophile countercul-
ture of the 1960s, which hoped that humanity would expand so as to
include cyborgs, androids, robots and other intelligent objects. It is a zeit-
geist, a fantasy, but not a recent one. It draws its legitimacy from the tide
of opinion which rejected humanity for what it had shown itself to be in
recent and current history, capable of all monstrosities. The posthuman,
then, emerges as a successor to the human, more dignified, less fallible: a
sort of anxiolytic, which makes up for our inadequacies and conjures the
Promethean shame[18] of being human. The German philosopher Günther
Anders described this feeling as what mankind felt when faced with its
own creations, which are the result of a rationalised technical process
which can be mastered from start to finish. A striking example is the position of the writer Jean-Michel Truong,[19] a member of the transhumanist
movement, who hopes for the advent of the post-human, in order to ward
off a humanity guilty of having brought upon itself the most appalling
attacks (Hiroshima, Auschwitz, etc.).

The Innovator and transhumanism

Elon Musk founded Neuralink[20] with the aim of developing a brain-
machine interface, the epitome of mankind's desire for absolute control.
Mankind strives to do everything possible to ensure that the brain can be
fully under control, with the underlying assumption that it needs to
be repaired. This is also the stated ambition of Kernel.[21] These proposals
are grounded on the idea that the brain needs to be improved, increased
and made more efficient. The fusion between human intelligence on the

---

[18]Günther Anders, *The Obsolescence of Man*, Volume II: On the Destruction of Life in the
Epoch of the Third Industrial Revolution.

[19]Jean-Michel Truong, *Totalement inhumaine*, Les empêcheurs de penser en rond, 2003.

[20]*"Neuralink is developing ultra-high bandwidth brain-machine interfaces to connect
humans and computers"*. https://www.neuralink.com/.

[21]"Machines of all kinds can help us along the way, but our vision is one in which we
humans maintain and expand our authorial power. The advanced intelligence of tomorrow
is a collaboration between the natural and the artificial. United, unheard of possibilities
abound. We're building off two decades of breakthrough research, working closely with
private partners and scientists to get usable solutions in the hands of people everywhere.
We're starting with potential applications for patients with cognitive disorders". http://
kernel.co/.

one side – with the brain – and artificial intelligence on the other – with computers – means that we are able to develop a new type of brain, more powerful than that of humans, sharper than that of machines. The organisation developed by Musk heralds the end in the coming decades of mankind's dependence on the "natural" brain, with the limitations we are given at birth. This dimension can only be made possible through the initiative of an innovator who has the means to bring together multiple skills: engineers, neurologists, doctors, programmers, who, together, will contribute to the success of innovation. Such an expression of transhumanism or posthumanism could be seen to signal the end of the human brain as we have known it for thousands of years, and perfectly underlines, as with other illustrations of transhumanism, that the Innovator operates transversally, across all professions, all functions, all disciplines.

The Innovator can be a doctor, a philosopher, an entrepreneur, an artist, a sportsman, etc. The Innovator can exist in any and all strata of society, and that is precisely why it is all the more important to raise understanding amongst society as a whole of the definition and responsibility of Innovators. Many innovators do not necessarily recognise themselves as such, and therefore do not necessarily act with the responsibility that is incumbent upon them in their quality as innovators, driven only by the desire to ensure the success of their idea. This is very apparent with transhumanism, which is, in fact, the expression of an age-old human desire. Mythology is replete with examples of mankind's desire to live longer, such as in The Epic of Gilgamesh, in which the Fountain of Youth had the particularity of giving eternal youth to anyone who drank or bathed in its water. In Roman mythology, the goddess Juno bathed in this fountain to regain her virginity. In Irish folklore, there are tales of a fountain which was said to heal the wounded. Humanity has been obsessed with immortality for at least 3,000 years. The first "scientists" long sought the Elixir of Life, a legendary potion which was believed to have the virtue of prolonging life indefinitely or preserving youth. What's more, humanity is not just interested in staying young or prolonging life, it is obsessed with exploiting science to its fullest potential. One example is Daedalus, an Athenian character from Greek mythology, whose name in Greek means "crafted", "to work cunningly". He is an inventor, a sculptor and a great architect, combining aesthetic genius and technical ingenuity, known in particular for designing the labyrinth to trap the Minotaur for ever, and from which Ariadne escapes thanks to the famous thread, on the advice of Daedalus.

Daedalus also invented flying, as portrayed in the myth of Icarus. Daedalus, the "ancestor" of the Innovator embodies the *techné* – technique – the path to attaining control over the world, and affording the opportunity for those who so request, like Minos, to abandon themselves to their *hubris*, the excess, to achieve their crazy schemes... Daedalus embodies a form of science without conscience: if science and technology can achieve it, then it should be done. Things are no longer accepted the way they are. And this mastery sought after by mankind in myths can also be found in the Bible. In Genesis, we can read: *Be fruitful and multiply and fill the earth and subdue it, and have dominion over the fish of the sea and over the birds of the heavens and over every living thing that moves on the earth.*[22]

Historically science is a branch of philosophy, and many philosophers are also scientists. This is the case of Descartes who wrote *A Discourse on Method* in 1637. This marked the beginning of the Modern period, filled with just as much ambitions as that of mythology. He says: *But as soon as I had acquired some general notions respecting physics, and beginning to make trial of them in various particular difficulties, had observed how far they can carry us, and how much they differ from the principles that have been employed up to the present time, I believed that I could not keep them concealed without sinning grievously against the law by which we are bound to promote, as far as in us lies, the general good of mankind. For by them I perceived it to be possible to arrive at knowledge highly useful in life; and in room of the speculative philosophy usually taught in the schools, to discover a practical, by means of which, knowing the force and action of fire, water, air the stars, the heavens, and all the other bodies that surround us, as distinctly as we know the various crafts of our artisans, we might also apply them in the same way to all the uses to which they are adapted, and thus render ourselves the lords and possessors of nature.*[23] Therein lies the challenge Descartes set himself: to make us masters and possessors of Nature. This stance, which was legitimate in the 16th century – all the more so as it concerned itself with the preservation

---

[22] Genesis 1:28 [NRSV].
[23] Descartes, *Discours de la Méthode*. Gallimard, Bibliothèque de la Pléiade. (édité et remanié en 1953), p. 168. René Descartes, *A Discourse on Method*, Translated to English by John Veitch. Retrieved from https://www.gutenberg.org/files/59/59-h/59-h.htm.

of human health[24] – was rarely questioned, and the race for progress and innovation, which feeds economic development, has continued to accelerate.[25]

A century later, Condorcet in his *Outlines of An Historical View of the Progress of the Human Mind*, takes Descartes' thinking one step further. He says: *We feel that the progress of preventive medicine as a preservative, made more effective by the progress of reason and social order will eventually banish communicable or contagious illnesses and those diseases in general that originate in climate, food and the nature of work. It would not be difficult to prove that this hope should extend to almost all other diseases, whose remote causes will eventually be recognized. Would it be absurd now to suppose that the improvement of the human race should be regarded as capable of unlimited progress? That a time will come when death would result only from extraordinary accidents or the more and more gradual wearing out of vitality, and that, finally, the duration of the average interval between birth and wearing out has itself no specific limit whatsoever? No doubt man will not become immortal, but cannot the span constantly increase between the moment he begins to live and the time when naturally, without illness or accident, he finds life a burden?*[26] Prolonging life, eradicating diseases: such were the challenges of the 18th century.

Following in the footsteps of Descartes and Condorcet, La Mettrie crossed the line which Descartes had not dared to. In *Man a Machine*, he argues that the human body as a whole is a machine. So, he says: *Let us now go into some detail concerning these springs of the human machine. All the vital, animal, natural, and automatic motions are carried on by their action. Is it not in a purely mechanical way that the body shrinks back when it is struck with terror at the sight of an unforeseen precipice,*

---

[24]Emmanuel Faye shows that the end sought is not first of all the "conveniences" which are to be found on earth, but "the preservation of health" in order to make men "wiser". This implies having knowledge of the "causes" of our problems and of "all the cures that nature has provided us with". Cf. E. Faye *Heidegger, l'introduction du nazisme dans la philosophie: autour des séminaires inédits de 1933–1935*, Albin Michel, "Idées", 2005.

[25]The first critics were noted in the early 1960s, notably through Rachel Carson, *Silent Spring*, Mariner Book Edition, 2002.

[26]Condorcet, *Esquisse d'un tableau historique des progrès de l'esprit humain*, édition dite Prior-Belaval, Vrin 1970, p. 236. Condorcet, *Outlines of An Historical View of the Progress of the Human Mind*.

that the eyelids are lowered at the menace of a blow, as some have remarked, and that the pupil contracts in broad daylight to save the retina, and dilates to see objects in darkness? Is it not by mechanical means that the pores of the skin close in winter so that the cold cannot penetrate to the interior of the blood vessels, and that the stomach vomits when it is irritated by poison, by a certain quantity of opium and by all emetics, etc.? that the heart, the arteries and the muscles contract in sleep as well as in waking hours [...]?[27] He argues that the human mind ought to be considered as a continuation of the sophisticated organisation of matter in the human brain: the human species is but a superior animal. The philosopher seeks to remove all mystery from life and compares the human body to a machine in order to better understand it. Benjamin Franklin, for his part, discussed the idea of being able to stop and start the course of life at will.[28]

When we combine both the ambitions of men and the physiological evolutions which Darwin identified, it is only natural, then, that the notions of Overman and the "will to power" emerged. In the 19th century, Nietzsche evoked this *will to power*[29] which we have already discussed and refers to "becoming more". For the German philosopher, particularly in *Thus Spoke Zarathustra*, there is always a tendency for power which manifests everywhere by taking different forms and functions with regard to individuals or organs.

From Descartes to Nietzsche, philosophy follows in the footsteps of mythology and science in its pursuit of human development. Science fiction is not far behind. Authors such as Arthur C. Clarke, author of *2001: A Space Odyssey,* or Isaac Asimov who invented the term robotics, a word now part of our everyday vocabulary. Science fiction anticipates what will become reality. In 1985, in *Blood music*, Greg Bear shows the possible separation of humanity into several branches: natural humans; mechanised humans; and biologically modified humans. How is this different

---

[27] Julien Offray La Mettrie, *L'Homme-machine*, édition présentée et établie par Paul-Laurent Assoun, Paris, Denoël, 1981, p. 192sq. Julien Jean Offray de La Mettrie, *Man a Machine*. Translated to English by Gertrude Carman Bussey. Retrieved from http://www.gutenberg.org/files/52090/52090-h/52090-h.htm.

[28] Nick Bostrom, "A history of transhumanist thought", *Journal of Evolution and Technology*, 14(1), 2005.

[29] Friedrich Nietzsche, *Fragments posthumes sur l'éternel retour*, *Op. cit.* Friedrich Nietzsche, *On the Geneaology of Morals, Op. cit.*

from what we are witnessing 30 years later with repaired humans, augmented humans and now genetically modified embryos?

Currently, not a day goes by without revealing the evolution of the human individual in their existential, physical and intellectual entrenchments. And what is very noticeable is the integration of these human enhancements into society. This is particularly true for sports, for example with Bob Radocy, who uses different prostheses for different sports. Or Jeremy Campbell, who wanted to be the first leg amputee athlete to launch a discus over 60 metres. He managed to launch it 62 metres (the world record is now 74 metres). The most significant case, however, is Pistorius, the first athlete to participate in both the Olympic and Paralympic Games in London in 2012.

A further milestone was achieved, with Neil Harbisson, an Irishman known for his ability to hear colours. In 2004, he became the first person in the world to wear an *eyeborg*. The fact that his "eyeborg" is included in his passport photograph is interpreted by some as official recognition of Harbisson's condition as a cyborg. In the same spirit, Rob Spence wants to be implanted with a camera to replace his damaged eye. This last example underlines the fact that the boundaries between having a prosthesis to make up for a disability and having a prosthesis to "perform" better are becoming more and more blurred. Indeed, Rob Spence's camera eye enables him to see better, to record, to zoom in, just like a camera. Once more we are faced with the duality between Repaired Man and Augmented Man.

We are at a critical point, not so much in that these developments and aspirations are new, because they have long been imagined and desired by mankind, but rather because they are becoming reality. This moment in time, this transition from one period to another, from desire to reality, is more or less what we call Singularity. The founder of the Singularity Movement, Ray Kurzweil, is an academic and is also the strategic director of Alphabet. He explains that the Singularity is a future period in time which he estimates will take place around 2045 at which point technological change will be so rapid and its impact so great, that human life will be forever and irreversibly transformed. Neither utopian nor dystopian, this era will transform the concepts we rely on to give meaning to our lives from market models to the human life cycle, even death.

According to its founder, understanding the Singularity will *alter our perspective on the significance of our past and the ramifications for our future. To truly understand it inherently changes ones view of life in general and one's own particular life. [...] The Singularity will represent the culmination of the merger of our biological thinking and existence with our technology.*[30] Elon Musk's Neuralink project, this merging of the brain and the computer, demonstrates that the Singularity is already in the making. While this innovation is presented primarily as a solution to cure diseases such as Parkinson's, it is also shown as a way to improve memory, to benefit from the discoveries of artificial intelligence, in short, to surpass the limitations of the human body.

The only difference between myths and our contemporary society is that now we know that we are capable of actually making these things happen. It is precisely in this gap between the will to do and the actual doing that responsibility must carve out a place for itself. The desire to go beyond our simple human condition, of being immortal, the best, the most beautiful, the strongest, the most intelligent, dates back to the time when man was man. And it is perhaps this which has enabled the human species to be one of the most evolved beings in nature. That being said, how far do we have to go? Must we innovate at all costs? How much responsibility lies in the hands of the Innovator? Or with the player who puts all these devices on the market?

The Emergence of Responsible Innovation

Being accountable for one's actions

To a certain extent, the term "responsible" is polysemic, maybe even trivialised. What does responsibility mean today? For whom? To what extent? Within what limits? What does it mean to be responsible in an unprecedented context of increasing technology and its escalating impacts, at a time when globalisation is accelerating? From here onwards, the human being is forced to assume responsibility *for* the world and *in* the world. More particularly, the Innovator is concerned with the responsibility of the world they design through the new products and services they launch on the market.

The responsibility of the Innovator is all the more important as they find themselves in a new context which articulates both the modern period

---

[30]Raymond Kurzweil, *Humanité 2.0 : la bible du changement,* M21 éditions, 2007, p. 31. Raymond Kurzweil, *The Singularity Is Near: When Humans Transcend Biology,* Penguin books.

in which we live and the search for sustainable and responsible development with a view to preserving mankind and its environment. Thanks to advances in science and technology, we now have an understanding of the world in all its complexities and in how we exploit it. These developments offer a plethora of possible actions, but at the same time raise ethical, social and civic questions, given the new risks entailed by these developments, and that it is impossible to determine these ahead of time, whether in terms of success or unforeseen applications. French author François Ost explains that in this context, responsibility needs to be redistributed for we *now appear responsible, or at least co-responsible, for a collective action whose developments and effects are largely unknown to us, and so, the circle of proximity which made me accountable only towards those close to me and my neighbours is broken, and so, the bond of simultaneity which made me accountable for the immediate, or at least proximate, effects of the actions I take today is distorted.*[31] The frameworks of responsibility and caution are evolving because so too is the breadth of our ability to act, even compared to 30 years ago. Responsibility remains individual, but extends globally, it is attributable to a subject, but not only.

Moreover, whereas responsibility was linked to proximity, to a clear spatio-temporal delimitation, it has now become timeless, spatially boundless and with unlimited multi-reciprocity. In other words, responsibility needs to be reconsidered because the back and forth between individual and global responsibility is as confusing as it is intense. Jean-Louis Genard explains that: *More than clearly identifiable actions, we are faced with a multiplicity of decisions which, together, can have far-reaching effects. In short, responsibility is both everywhere and nowhere. Actions have been taken, decisions have been made, sometimes with dramatic consequences. But responsibilities are not identifiable at all, unless they relate to the organisation or the network, which does not correspond to our spontaneous understanding of the idea of responsibility. The latter remains attached to individualised identification.*[32] To this we might add that this has the effect of diluting responsibility.

Although the very concept of responsibility can be difficult to grasp spontaneously (as it is often associated with ethical, moral, respect and

---

[31] François Ost, La *Nature hors la loi*, La Découverte, p. 267. Our translation.
[32] Jean-Louis Genard, "Le temps de la responsabilité", in Gérard Philippe, Ost François and Van de Kerchove Michel (eds.), *L'Accélération du temps juridique*, Brussels, Publications des Facultés universitaires, Saint-Louis, 2000, pp. 105–125. Our translation.

awareness issues), it has a very precise definition, on which its Latin etymology sheds light: *respondere,* i.e. to answer for one's actions. This makes sense with liability as defined in the Civil Code: *Any act whatever of man, which causes damage to another, obliges the one by whose fault it occurred, to compensate it.*[33] To answer for one's actions is to take responsibility for them, to recognise oneself as the perpetrator. Responsibility also has a moral dimension. To answer ("respond") for one's actions is to take responsibility for them, to recognise oneself as the perpetrator. Responsibility also has a moral dimension. It refers to the moral obligation to right a wrong, to fulfil a duty, to assume the consequences of one's acts.

There is a link between responsibility and freedom. To be free is to take responsibility for one's actions. To be responsible is to be able to answer for them, precisely because of this freedom. Consequently, a prudent man who wants to be absolutely free will take on as few responsibilities as possible, simply because it will be difficult for him to assume them. If we can be free, independent in society, what about when we are at work? Can we, as managers, preserve the freedom we cherish as citizens? The hierarchical structures, the administrative and operational organisation of companies are difficult to reconcile with freedom. However, individuals can only be held accountable for their own actions if they are completely free. In an economic context, where the labour market is in a constant state of tension between supply and demand, employees do not feel totally free to accept or refuse certain demands from their management.

The versatile nature of the concept of "responsibility" is reflected in language. In English, there are three different words to define the notion of responsibility: *responsibility, liability* and *accountability.*[34] The latter term very directly implies the notion of being accountable to others: to a board of directors, to the general public, to customers. Innovation must be thought out in the light of these new constraints and the multiplicity of responsibilities which are emerging. Since responsibility has different connotations and meanings, it cannot be understood in the same way by

---

[33]Article 1240 of the French Civil Code (version of 2016). Translated to English by John Cartwright, Bénédicte Fauvarque-Cosson and Simon Whittaker.

[34]Responsibility concerns the responsibilities incumbent upon a person, the things they are in charge of, liability essentially concerns legal issues, while accountability refers to questions of transparency, towards the population, for example.

all players in a globalised economy. This necessarily leads to misunderstandings about what to do from one country to another, from one culture to another.

Without even questioning the problems of language, the notion of responsibility is, by nature, complex, not only because it involves others, but also because it expresses several dimensions within the same individual. We are at the same time manager, innovator, citizen, parent, husband, wife. This raises the very clear issue of the interaction between the private and professional spheres, and the interdependence between managers and citizens, between innovators and the recipients of the innovation as a whole. Is the action I am taking as a manager one I would wish for as a citizen? As Marc Neuberg sums up, the responsibility of innovation lies in the consideration of situation within a value system shared by all the actors impacted by that process.[35]

Principle of responsibility – Principle of responsible innovation

We cannot date the emergence of the concept of responsible innovation. It is the result of a set of catalysts, a chronological process integral to the issue of corporate social responsibility, which originally came about as a way of examining the involvement of the business world in in society. Howard Bowen, considered the founding father of corporate social responsibility, is one such example. He defines the social responsibility of managers as *the obligations of businessmen to pursue those policies, to make those decisions, or to follow those lines of action that are desirable in terms of the objectives and values of our society.*[36] However, the issues of corporate social responsibility have little practical relevance to innovation.

More recently, Gro Harlem Brundtland, in her 1987 report on the concept of sustainable development,[37] shows how important it is to take

---

[35] *La Responsabilité : questions philosophiques* de Marc Neuberg. Presses universitaires de France, 1997.
[36] Howard Bowen, *Social Responsibilities of the Businessman*, Harper & Brothers, 1953, p. 236.
[37] Gro Harlem Brundtland, *Our Common Future* – Report of the World Commission on Environment and Development, New York, United Nations General Assembly, 1987.

future generations into account in our actions within organisations. More precisely, to succeed in defining viable schemes which reconcile the three ecological, social and economic aspects of human activities: the "three pillars" to be taken into account by communities, businesses and individuals.

As for responsible innovation itself, it can be traced back to philosopher Hans Jonas. In *The Imperative of Responsibility* Jonah questions whether humanity should continue to exist.[38] If the answer is yes, then humanity must adopt a new behaviour of care and concern for the world. This duty of care is incumbent upon the Innovator, since they are the pillar of responsibility towards civil society. This is both worrying and encouraging because it implies that if the Innovator does indeed have such a hold on society by deploying new ideas, new products and innovations, then, by corollary, they can also change the world by integrating the dimension of responsibility into their projects. This is the principle of responsible innovation. In 1979, in *The Imperative of Responsibility,* Jonas had already developed the idea that human knowledge surpasses predictive knowledge, without employing the actual label of responsible innovation. It is therefore fundamental, in his view, to develop an ethical approach so as to close this gap. Without rejecting science and technology, Jonas exposes the need to deploy a humane form of responsibility so as to face up to the risks inherently brought on by technology and which imperil humanity.

Responsible innovation and social innovation

The concept of responsible innovation is fully in line with the philosophy of responsibility as proposed by Hans Jonas. In this respect, it is important to differentiate responsible innovation from social responsibility. Social responsibility, or inclusive innovation, concerns itself with innovating so as to understand better the issues faced by the most disadvantaged populations.[39]

---

[38] Hans Jonas, *The Imperative of Responsibility: In Search of an Ethics for the Technological Age,* University of Chicago Press, 1985.

[39] Formally, social innovation is defined by the Bureau of European Policy Advisers (BEPA) as meeting social needs while also creating new social relationships. BEPA's main vocation is to act as a bridge between the European Commission's policy makers and

This can mean developing very low-cost battery-powered refrigerators to avoid temperature changes in countries where electricity is not stable, or battery-powered electrocardiographs developed in India for farmers in remote areas. All such innovations are crucial for these populations. Social and societal innovation is enjoying very strong growth, thanks to the development of technological possibilities.

Responsible innovation, however, is something else. It does not propose responsibility as an end in itself. On the contrary, it considers that responsibility should not be the preserve of social innovation alone, but rather should be present above and beyond these issues. While the customer potential for low-cost battery refrigerators or tablets computers is considerable, it is still below standard demand. However, it is in the main standard markets, the largest ones, that responsibility must be applied, both in terms of purposes and processes. A social innovation is not necessarily a responsible innovation. For example a low-cost car accessible to all can be made with polluting materials.

The inaccurate understanding of responsible innovation and its trivialised use are not without consequences. Responsible innovation must be taken into account in all innovation strategies, all processes, all developments and for all targets – young and old, well-off and less well-off, urban and rural, Europeans, Asians, Americans, However, by being associated with solely social aspects, it runs the risk of being relegated to issues, albeit important, but which do not constitute the everyday life of the economic, competitive and globalised world in which we live. In other words, responsible innovation does not aim to take on social issues, or even to say how to be innovative in the face of such issues. Its aim is to become involved in the innovation processes of all organisations, so as to assess the question of responsibility, in industry as well as in services, in advanced technologies as well as in basic manufacturing.

The objective of responsible innovation, then, is to integrate – throughout the innovation process, from design to market launch – measures which promote environmental sustainability, the use of non-polluting materials, waste sorting, recycling, protection of workers, customers,

---

stakeholders from the civil society. Inclusive innovation, on the other hand, aims to deliver high-performance products, processes and services at very low cost to poor people, from housing to transportation and medicines to computer technologies. Above all, these innovations must be extremely affordable. See the Statement by Dr. R.A. Mashelkar during the World Bank S&T Global Forum, December 2009.

employees, etc. The role of responsible innovation is also to take into account those who will be impacted by the innovation, whether directly or indirectly. Responsible innovation here is not the quest *per se* for improving the environment, human health and working conditions, but rather the act of integrating all these dimensions, whatever the innovation. While there is a strong need for innovations with a responsible and social purpose, integrating responsibility into innovation processes is much more crucial. This is because responsible innovation encompasses all existing and future structures, whatever their size, sector or location. If an organisation implements a program to recycle its technology products within structures which hire people with disabilities, then it can be said to have a social component. The same applies to a banking institution which develops microcredit for the poorest populations. These are two examples of innovations with a social purpose. Responsible innovation, however, lies above all in the fact that the technology company does not use Chinese or Brazilian rare earths for its production, nor toxic products which could harm employees, workers or users. For a financial institution, responsible innovation lies not so much in the purpose as in the method: what is the source of the funds, what is the risk of over-indebtedness for the contractors, etc.? Even though integrating people with disabilities into social life, or ensuring poor populations can access credit is positive, this must not be done at all costs. Above all, what is important is to know how to focus responsibility efforts on what has the greatest impact on society, something which is crucial throughout the innovation process as a whole.[40]

In the same way, it is important to dissociate responsible innovation from the concept of Responsible Research and Innovation (known as RRI), which is defined as: *transparent, interactive process by which societal actors and innovators become mutually responsive to each other with a view to the (ethical) acceptability, sustainability and societal desirability of the innovation process and its marketable products in order to allow a proper embedding of scientific and technological advances in our society.*[41] However, responsibility cannot have the same scope in research

---

[40]Other forms of innovation such as *jugaad* or cradle-to-cradle are also useful and enable innovation to be rethought in a socially benevolent way. However, these innovations, important as they may be, remain marginal compared to "traditional" innovations and do not necessarily raise questions about the innovator as an individual.

[41]René Von Schomberg, *Prospects for Technology Assessment in a framework of responsible research and innovation*, in: Technikfolgen abschaetzen lehren: Bildungspotenziale transdisziplinaerer Methode, Wiesbaden, Springer VS, 2011, pp. 39–61.

as it does in innovation. Even if these two concepts are intimately linked, they are far from being identical and are not subject to the same objectives and constraints in their fields of application. Where research has an epistemological scope; innovation has an objective of performance in a competitive context with the ultimate goal of materialising and marketing a product. Based on this fundamental difference in purpose, responsible innovation is applied in an operational manner, where RRI remains a theoretical concept which is not very well suited to organisations looking for concrete tools to help the innovators in their day-to-day work.

Reducing the Uncertainty of Innovation

The other issue which responsible innovation tries to solve is reducing the uncertainty of innovation. In other words, when considering the launch of a new product or service, the role of responsible innovation is to ensure that the time of greatest uncertainty in the life cycle is taken into account. The more the life cycle is under control, the more responsibility will be under control, since it is also a question of anticipating the end of the product's life, its destruction, its elimination. This means that while a sound understanding of the life cycle of a product or service is primarily intended for forecasting sales, communication or follow-up operations, it is also a valuable tool for responsible innovation.

The crucial element in this cycle is Moore's chasm,[42] because this is what makes innovation uncertain. This is due in particular to two factors which particularly influence the dissemination of innovation: mass media and opinion leaders. Social networks are a typical example of an unpredictable "gap". Facebook, for example, had never anticipated the billions of people which would sign up to the database. The platform's leaders were overtaken by their innovation and found themselves at the head of a gigantic database which now imposes a responsibility they had not initially anticipated or even wanted. The diagram of the life cycle of a product or service shows this chasm, this gap, between early adopters and others. The main challenge for a responsible company is to anticipate this chasm by developing a comprehensive vision of this life cycle. In this way, a company can put a product on the market having developed it already anticipating the entire responsible process: traceability, reflection on consumption, use and possible social, economic and environmental

---

[42] Geoffrey Moore, *Crossing the Chasm, Op. cit.*

impacts. However, the unpredictability of innovation strongly undermines the validity of this approach. If success exceeds expectations, will the supplier still have the capacity to supply demand responsibly, given its carbon expenditure for example? Will the recycling processes always be the same? Will employees be able to absorb the additional workload? If it fails, what to do with the unsold goods? Innovation, therefore, is imbued with uncertainty. It is not a matter of abandoning innovation due to this uncertainty. It is simply a matter of anticipating future possibilities, successes and failures, and different uses. This involves developing exhaustive hypotheses for the innovation process as a whole, always keeping in mind the product cycle once this innovation is on the market. Although not all hypotheses can be imagined, most of them can certainly be anticipated.

The thrusts of responsible innovation

Extensive research has been carried out in order to define responsible innovation, under the initial impetus of Bernadette Bensaude-Vincent.[43] More specifically, three interacting determinants have been developed for understanding the challenges of responsible innovation. These determinants can interact, but must also be considered separately from one other.

Questioning the answers to be given to the needs of individuals

This first pillar of responsible innovation is decisive: must we always respond to the needs of individuals? We have already addressed the issue of needs and more specifically that we do not create needs but rather respond to conscious or unconscious latent needs. That being said, is it because a need exists that we must necessarily meet it?

Responsible innovation questions the obsession of organisations of having to systematically respond to the needs of individuals by

---

[43] See the editorial by Bernadette Bensaude-Vincent, at the *Colloque innovation responsable* of April 29, 2009, Collège de France. *Responsible Innovation: Managing the Responsible Emergence of Science and Innovation in Society*, edited by Richard Owen, John Bessant, Maggy Heintz Wiley 2013. *Introduction to Responsible Innovation Criteria. A Guide to Entrepreneurs and Innovation*, Interreg IV B-207G – KARIM Project is co-financed by the European Union. Xavier Pavie, Victor Scholten and Daphne Carthy, *Responsible Innovation, from Concept to Practice*, World Scientific 2014.

challenging the relevance of the systematic provision of a response to every single need detected. Should a company systematically launch the innovation which meets an identified need? In other words, just because there is a need does not necessarily mean that there has to be an answer. Should innovation strategies systematically have the reflex of setting innovation in motion as soon as a need is detected? Is it because high school students do not want to do their homework that we need to launch an online service where others do their homework for them?[44] Is it because a fraction of the population has certain sexual desires that we need to organise holidays which meet this demand?[45]

If consumers want to listen to music while on the go, outside of their car and their living room, while commuting, on a walk or running, and with great practicality thanks to dematerialisation, is it, however, necessary and justified to have twenty different generations of iPods in less than 10 years, when we know that the construction of each device requires the extraction of rare earth elements, a process known to be particularly polluting? Is it because individuals want to become homeowners that we should necessarily develop services at all costs to enable them to purchase their dream house for which they do not really have the debt capacity?

Measuring the direct consequences of innovations

This dimension is linked to two elements: on the one hand, the uncertainty of implementing any innovation and, on the other hand, the inability to anticipate the impacts of products or services on the health of current users and their lifestyles, as well as on future customers.

This inability to predict is all the more acute because, at the same time, there is an innovation race which leads to rapid, sometimes even hasty decisions. The competitive environment, the atomisation of markets, compels competitors to launch their latest innovation as quickly as possible, without really considering the consequences. As an example, we might mention the tragic and infamous case of the Ford Pinto, a car which was left on the market even when it was known that there was a risk of

---

[44]*Libération*, March 7, 2009, "Faismesdevoirs.com ferme déjà ses pages".
[45]Examples of websites include: pleasuretours.com; alternativephuket.com; globalfantasies. com; temptation.originalresorts.com; affordable-adult-vacations.com; wildwomenvacations. com; pornweek.com.

the petrol tank exploding at the slightest shock.[46] In this example, this was due to the blatant dishonesty of the company's leader; other times, however, business leaders might do the right thing to avoid any risk. For example, the exact impact of radiation from mobile phones on the heart or other organs remains unclear – the scientific studies carried out on the subject are still far from conclusive and are often divergent. This is a direct consequence of the innovation, and the Innovator must understand that they bear responsibility for what they are potentially doing to the recipient of the innovation. In the case of subprime mortgages, the direct impact was obvious, and the innovator ought to have put in place a system for protecting those who were going to benefit from this scheme (or maybe even turn them down when this was relevant). We can also consider the example of consumer credit. On a regular basis, commercial courts recall the catastrophic situations of families facing over-indebtedness. The spiral in which these households find themselves is very often the result of revolving loans, taken out through major retailers, but also through the websites of specialised credit institutions when they make a purchase or when they have an exceptional need. The direct impact of this proposal is the delicate situation in which the borrower will find himself in order to repay the credit with interest rates which can be more than excessive. Let's not forget the massive appearance of robots in industry and in everyday life, which could destroy up to 70% of jobs in the coming years.[47] This is a direct consequence of innovation, and it does not necessarily mean that this innovation has to be eliminated, but simply that the consequences must be considered and the question must be asked as to whether it is possible to accompany this inevitable change for the most-affected categories of workers.

Considering the indirect impacts of innovations

The third and last axis concerns the need to consider that an innovation has consequences beyond the framework from which it emerged. In order

---

[46] Jonathan Raymond, "La Ford Pinto : le contre-exemple américain", *Le Polyscope Le journal de l'École polytechnique de Montréal* 36, 2003.

[47] Melanie Arntz, Terry Gregory and Ulrich Zierahn (2016), "The Risk of Automation for Jobs in OECD Countries: A Comparative Analysis", OECD Social, Employment and Migration Working Papers, No. 189, OECD Publishing, Paris. Retrieved from http://dx.doi.org/10.1787/5jlz9h56dvq7-en.

to achieve this, we must fully accept the idea that we all interact with each other consciously or unconsciously and within an ecosystem. Whereas the previous axis concerned the impacts of innovation on its users, here it is a question of considering that the launch of an innovation will certainly have an impact on its customers, but that non-customers might also be impacted. A certain maturity is required to achieve this degree of responsibility, since we are talking about being accountable to someone who exists outside of the scope of our actions. The innovation brought about by a scientist or a product manager can induce sectorial permeability which had not initially been foreseen. For example, this could be the launch of a new, faster, more powerful aircraft, but which presents the downside of emitting higher noise levels. The Innovator needs to assess the consequences of the innovation in terms of flight crew, ground staff and customers, but also in terms of the impact on local residents, whether human or animal. It is the entire ecosystem around airports which is affected, as highlighted by the Grenelle de l'environnement summit in France, which outlined measures to be taken.[48] The same is true when selling an air-conditioned vehicle which will consume on average 15% more fuel than a car which does not use this option.[49] The CO_2 emissions will not only impact the driver of the vehicle, but also passers-by and cyclists with whom the car will share the road.

The construction of dwellings near a road has a direct consequence on the development of the lungs of those who live there, even if they themselves never use these roads. The nanomaterials in Japanese socks offer great comfort and mean socks remain odourless. However, when socks are washed, the nanomaterials end straight up in the wastewater which can be discharged into rivers, the sea, eaten by fish, come into contact with plants, etc. These are the indirect impacts causing the entire ecosystem to be disrupted. The subprime crisis did not only affect customers and lenders, but also those who were totally unrelated to this proposal but who, through the financial game of securitisation, were negatively impacted by this innovation. When we put our savings in a savings account or a life

---

[48] https://www.vie-publique.fr/eclairage/268585-le-grenelle-de-lenvironnement-quels-engagements. It should also be noted that measures to reduce noise pollution for the well-being of local residents also increase aircraft kerosene consumption at the same time.
[49] Laurent Gagnepain, "La climatisation automobile, Impacts, consommation et pollution" in *Repères* published by the French Environment and Energy Management Agency – Transport Technologies Department, 2006.

insurance policy, for example, what is this money used for? Do banks invest these funds in companies which may indirectly harm citizens?

These three questions are fundamental to initiating a responsible innovation process. Faced with the impossibility of controlling the uncertainty of innovation, these considerations are intended to help the players of innovation to at least measure it.

The process of responsible innovation

These three axes of responsible innovation can be found in the innovation process described above,[50] which consists of five steps.[51] This ensures that responsibility is not limited to the development of new products and services and that it permeates and is integrated into all the levels of the company. The key to responsible innovation strategy lies, first and foremost, in a commitment by the organisation as a whole to integrate responsibility at all levels of the company and ultimately, to control the achievement of its objectives. This strategy consists of five steps[52]:

Step 1: Complying with the law

The first step in the process concerns the company's compliance with existing laws and regulations. This may seem obvious, but the legal conflicts between Samsung and Apple, for example, are proof that it is still possible, in some cases, to neglect a thorough examination of existing patents held by a competitor. This step provides a solid foundation for moving on to the second step of the process.

Step 2: Anticipating future legal constraints

The second step is to anticipate future legislations without waiting to be forced to do so. The challenge here resides in turning compliance with

---

[50] See the section describing the innovation process on page xx of this book.

[51] Ram Nidumolu, Coimbatore Krishnao Prahalad, and M Madhavan Rangaswami, "Why Sustainability is Now the Key Driver of Innovation", *Harvard Business Review*, 2009, pp. 57–64.

[52] Xavier Pavie, *L'innovation responsable, levier stratégique pour les organisations*, Eyrolles, 2012.

standards into an opportunity for innovation, through the early implementation of impending or future regulatory obligations which will require the company to change its approach in the near future. By anticipating new or future legislation, the company stands out from its competitors, because it was the first to move, to innovate on an aspect which will ultimately concern all market players. This requires a certain ability to anticipate and shape regulation as well as an ability to work with other companies, including competitors, so as to facilitate the implementation and enrich the emergence of innovative solutions. The opportunities for innovation in this stage lie in using compliance as an incentive for the company and its partners to experiment with sustainable technologies, materials and processes.

For example, in the 1990s, Hewlett Packard was aware that copper used in electronic components was particularly toxic. Anticipating a possible regulation on this use, the R&D department worked for about 10 years on a substitute mixing silver, tin and copper. A European directive to this effect was issued on 1 July 2006 and HP was clearly able to get ahead of its competitors.

Step 3: Thinking of the value chain as an ecosystem

This step is about becoming a driving force for an entire ecosystem and in particular, suppliers. The central challenge is to increase the efficiency of the value chain, by building it in such a way that all actors and organisations are dedicated to responsibility. This requires the organisation to develop expertise in techniques such as carbon management and life cycle assessment. It also requires the ability to redesign operations, use less energy and water, produce fewer emissions and waste, and ensure that suppliers and retailers carry out their green operations efficiently. The opportunities for innovation in this stage lie in the development of sustainable sources of raw materials and components.

In 2008, Walmart required its Chinese suppliers to reduce their CO_2 emissions by 5% by 2013 and increase the efficiency of their energy production by 25% in 3 years. In order to guarantee this is effectively carried out, Walmart developed a three-phase process: the initial assess its suppliers' behaviour and actions; verify the commitments made; and finally, encourage suppliers to develop their commitments through other factories.

Step 4: Developing responsible products and services

This stage is about creating the idea, product or service within the organisation. This consists in integrating into the five traditional phases of innovation (ideation; feasibility; capability; launch; and post-launch)[53] both the axes specified above, as well as the hypotheses of the possible evolutions of the product given its uncertain nature once on the market. In this step, at each phase of the process of developing responsible products and services, the risks and direct or indirect consequences of the project on various social, economic and environmental factors are either assessed or at least taken into account in order to be measured more accurately once the product or service is launched. In order to ensure that the risks of the project are effectively taken into account once it has been launched, there is a need to formulate a series of assumptions related to the potential benefits which will have to be measured after the launch. This stage is intended not only for creating, designing and marketing products or services which promote responsible behaviour, but also for developing these offers by ensuring that their impacts – during their development and once they are on the market and acquired by consumers – are monitored so that the necessary measures can be taken should they prove to be particularly negative.

Step 5: Drive change

The final step in this process consists in bringing about lasting changes not only at the level of the organisation but also at the level of the industry in which it operates. This is achieved in three ways:

(1) Developing responsible business models

This phase involves finding new ways of delivering and acquiring value, which will change the basis of competition. The skills required for the business to reach this stage are the ability to understand what consumers want and to find different ways to meet those requirements, as well as the ability to understand how partners can increase the value of the offering. This stage offers opportunities for innovation, in the development of new technologies which will significantly change the value chain.

---

[53] See the section describing the innovation process on page 29 of this book.

(2) **Promoting responsibility and raising awareness**

Innovation is a strategic lever for increasing responsibility in production methods and market consumption patterns. The responsible company has a duty to communicate with consumers and to raise awareness about responsibility among the public. This therefore requires the development of an effective means of dissemination to inform the public about the company's responsibility and its offers.

(3) **Creating the next practice platform**

The aim here is to question the dominant logic behind today's business model through the prism of responsibility, with a view to creating new responsible offers. In order to achieve this, the organisation needs to know how renewable and non-renewable resources affect business and industrial ecosystems. It must also be able to syncretise business models, technologies and regulations in the different sectors. The opportunities for innovation in this stage are found in the creation of platforms and ecosystems which will enable customers and suppliers to share resources, so that these to benefit everyone.

The entire process is designed to help innovators, using a traditional method, to question, anticipate and develop responsible innovation, not only for the innovators and their employees, but for all stakeholders, so that they understand what their role is in innovating responsibly.

The limits of responsible innovation

In the 10 or so years since the emergence of the idea of responsible innovation, a number of organisations have begun to take a close interest in this concept, whether in the energy, communication[54] or automotive sectors. Following the crisis in 2007, banks and insurance companies had no choice but to rethink their innovation process.[55] This was fruitful, as many ideas emerged through these processes, and some banking organisations

---

[54] As an example, the Engie group and La Poste in the Lorraine region developed a number of relatively structured think tank on responsible innovation, particularly between 2010 and 2015.

[55] In France, the "Club Innovation Finance" has been running a project called DRiM for almost 2 years to help its members develop a responsible innovation process based on Design Thinking techniques. See Xavier Pavie, Corinne Jouanny, Daphné Carthy and François Verez, *Le design thinking au service de l'innovation responsable*, Maxima, 2014.

have even sought to develop new offerings which integrate end-to-end responsibility for employees, investors, customers and the rest of the ecosystem. This has led to the setting up of financial investments which respect socio-environmental issues, and bank accounts with reasonable and balanced interest rates.

However, while the responsibility of innovators in these organisations brought about a very concrete reflection on possible actions for innovating responsibly, only a small part of the organisations in each of the sectors has really taken on the task of conducting a responsible innovation policy. This has an impact on competitiveness which, in the short term, is detrimental to companies which are working towards deploying such an initiative.[56] To be more precise, studies show that a structure which conducts a policy of responsibility does benefit from a large number of advantages: strong employee loyalty compared to the market in which it operates; better customer loyalty; employee engagement resulting in improved productivity; and a high level of trust from its entire environment, whether speaking of suppliers or institutions with which it deals, etc. However, all of these benefits only become apparent over a relatively long period of time. Effective employee loyalty can only be measured after several years, and the same applies to employee engagement as well as the trust the company has built up within its ecosystem. Innovating responsibly is a long-term commitment, and in an increasingly competitive context the temptation is great to overlook these areas in favour of a less responsible but more profitable approach in the short term. Disembodied shareholding as it has developed over the last few decades does nothing to help. When investors entrust their money to an organisation to make it grow – pension funds, investment organisations – and do not even know where it is invested, the only thing they are concerned about is how long it will take to get their money back and at what rate. As a result, the intermediary's only concern will be to generate margin and profit for the company in which they invest, and as quickly as possible. This pushes the question of responsibility to the background, and investors will think twice before investing in trust, commitment or loyalty.

---

[56] It should also be noted that the term "responsible- innovation" is often understood as a barrier to innovation. The term "innovation" is characterised by development, growth, headway and progress. The term "responsible" is understood as a hindrance, a form of inertia, patience.

In the end, this situation does not encourage organisations to undertake this type of initiative because the lack of collective responsibility penalises them in the short term. In other words, if a company decides to apply a responsible innovation process and its competitor does not, in the short term, the former will likely be facing financial hardship due to higher costs, because the return on investment will only be tangible after a long period, with fewer investors because most seek immediate profit. In fact, responsible innovation is doomed to failure. One way forward might be cooperation with competitors, which is neither rare nor impossible. This is often done for establishing norms and standards, or, more illegally, to collude on rates. In the case of a project between banks and insurance companies, the establishment of a "coopetition"[57] structure enabled the project to move forward between competitors, but here again, not all operators in the sector agreed to come to the table and there was nothing to prevent competitors from adopting their own approach, thereby undermining the ambition pursued among responsible players.

Perhaps the fundamental problem is that initiatives such as responsible innovation are about addressing processes rather than behaviours. Responsible innovation is, in fact, a deconstruction of modes and methods of innovation in which each phase, each stage is called into question. It is about challenging the status quo and establishing evaluation criteria throughout the process so as to gauge whether the innovation will respect the environment, employees, customers and the ecosystem in the short, medium and long term. The fact remains that none of these actions are binding on the one hand, and on the other hand, they are constantly underpinned by subjectivity and interpretation. In addition, given the uncertainty of innovation, there is always a margin of error, a lack of knowledge which the entrepreneurs will always view to their own advantage, thereby failing to take into account the risk incurred for others.

Moreover, there is something deleterious about this process because it can be perceived carrying the responsibility in and of itself, thereby diluting the responsibility of the Innovator. In other words, to use the process of responsible innovation without questioning ourselves would be akin to the manager of a marshalling yard in Nazi Germany, working without

---

[57]Xavier Pavie, Corinne Jouanny, Daphné Carthy et François Verez, *Le design thinking au service de l'innovation responsable, Op. cit.* Xavier Pavie, Corinne Jouanny, Daphné Carthy and François Verez, *Le design thinking au service de l'innovation responsable, Op. cit.*

questioning the orders he was carrying out. Hiding behind the method without demonstrating critical thinking or discernment is detrimental precisely because the key resides in applying critical thinking and using the process of responsible innovation only as a tool, a means, but not as an end in itself.

In 1961 the first version of the book *Winnie the Pooh* by A.A. Milne was published, and these are its opening lines: *Here is Edward Bear, coming downstairs now, bump, bump, bump, on the back of his head, behind Christopher Robin. It is, as far as he knows, the only way of coming downstairs, but sometimes he feels that there really is another way, if only he could stop bumping for a moment and think of it. And then he feels that perhaps there isn't. Anyhow, here he is at the bottom, and ready to be introduced to you.*[58] This quote is very relevant for understanding metaphorically both responsible innovation and, above all, the fundamental role of the Innovator. In order to survive, Christopher must eat breakfast every morning, he must feed himself or else he will end up withering and disappearing. However, if every morning he bangs his bear's head against the stairs, the bear will also end up perishing, falling apart and disappearing. There are many ways for Christopher to go downstairs for breakfast and take care of his bear. He could carry the bear in his arms, put it on his shoulders, put it in a bag, etc. But he prefers to go down the stairs and let the bear's head hit each step, for only one reason which is in the quote: he does not stop to think about it.

Similarly, an organisation needs to be nurtured, to grow, to acquire value. That is what keeps it alive, and what enables it to survive when it is sometimes surrounded by vigorous competitors. Nevertheless, should we never stop to think, letting innovators unconsciously damage individuals and the environment as Christopher does with this little bear? Can we, in one way or another, help them think, and if so how?

The Path to Innovation-Care

Critique of responsibility

This notion of "responsible innovation" therefore seems fraught with limitations, which ultimately hamper its understandability by the public

---

[58]Alan Milne, *Winnie the Pooh*. London: Methuen & Co/Ltd, 1926.

and even its implementation within the structures of innovative organisations. Not to mention the fact that it remains a process rather than a behaviour which should be adopted. The concept of "responsibility" itself raises a number of challenges, as pointed out previously, in particular the risk of dilution of responsibility.[59] However, the dilution of responsibility in general, and of responsibility as it pertains innovation in particular, has resulted in a failure to take account of its consequences. We feel less concerned by the impact of an innovation when it has been diluted in a managerial chain.[60] Accountability is only possible when we can control all aspects of something, however small it may be.

The concept of "responsibility" is also problematic in terms of the destination of this responsibility: for what and for whom would an innovation be responsible? We could also imagine a responsible innovation solely aimed at safeguarding the interests of shareholders. Consequently, what does it matter what actions are taken? So, we must ask ourselves what is the object of responsibility? Is it the preservation of generations to come? Or of the current generation? Is responsibility toward groups, communities or individuals? These are questions which need to be asked, all the more so if we refer back to the meaning of the term "responsibility" in the 18th century, time at which it encompassed a notion of solidarity. This particular influence harks back to the restructuring of schemes of civil responsibility, including the idea of risk prevention. It is from this point forward, with the emergence of insurance and compensation, for example, that responsibility was disconnected from the notion of fault. Responsibility has become a tool for allocating risk rather than a principle for regulating behaviour. This came with a paradoxical consequence: the deresponsibilisation of action.[61] Laurence Engel explains that: *responsibility without fault tends to lead to the weakening of responsibility. Upstream, before a decision is taken, and because it results in the attribution of responsibility left and right without consideration for the behaviour of those involved, it acts as an anaesthetic and numbs action, thereby producing a feeling which is completely opposite to that of responsibility.*

---

[59]Walter Baber, *Organizing the Future: Matrix Models for the Postindustrial Policy*, Alabama, The University of Alabama Press, 1983.

[60]*Idem.*

[61]François Ewald, *Histoire de l'Etat-Providence*, Folio, 1996, p. 86. Melinda Cooper (ed.), *The Birth of Solidarity, The History of the French Welfare State.*, Translated to English by Timothy Scott Johnson, Duke University Press.

Downstream, because it fails to identify the mistakes which may have been committed and therefore essentially 'destroys' the feeling of responsibility as the person who pays compensation for the fault may publicly say that it is not their fault.[62]

Therefore, through this judicialization of responsibility, the substance of the subject's responsibility and relationship both to oneself and to others lost its essence.[63] The notion of responsibility had genuine meaning insofar as it was an action voluntarily chosen by individuals, for individuals, but was impoverished as soon as it became "confiscated" by prescriptive bodies.[64] Thus, underlines François Ewald, *being responsible, in a situation where a person is the guarantor for others, means deciding; means the very act of making a decision. This is a dimension which is completely foreign to law insofar as, responsibility in law is defined in terms of a norm and as a breach of a norm. However, strictly speaking, there can be no responsibility when a person is subject to a norm. The experience of responsibility begins precisely when a person makes a decision without being able to refer to a norm.*[65] This is the dimension to which Pedersen refers when he underlines the distance in responsibility between "do not harm" and "do good".[66] This once more raises the issue of abiding by a norm, which is different from doing good. To "do good" is going beyond the norm in a positive and deliberate fashion.

One last critical aspect regarding the notion of "responsibility" is that it has become devoid of meaning. Since the financial crisis, everything has become "responsible", as if by magic. From consumer credit to the latest mobile phone devices, everything is now labelled "responsible". After the *greenwashing* which some organisations had no qualms in using so as to give themselves a "greener" image, today we are witnessing

---

[62] Laurence Engel, "Réguler les comportements", in T. Ferenczi (dir.), De quoi sommes-nous responsables?, Éditions Le Monde, 1997, pp. 80–89. Our translation.

[63] See Guido Gorgoni's very comprehensive article, "La responsabilité comme projet", in Christophe Eberhard, *Traduire nos responsabilités planétaires. Recomposer nos paysages juridiques*, Bruxelles, Bruylant, 2006, pp. 131–146.

[64] François Ewald, *Histoire de l'Etat-Providence, Op. cit.*, p. 86. Our translation.

[65] François Ewald, "L'expérience de la responsabilité", in *De quoi sommes-nous responsables*, *Op. cit.*, pp. 11–36. Our translation.

[66] Esben Rahbek Pedersen, "Modelling CSR: How Managers Understand the Responsibilities on Business Toward Society", *Journal of Business Ethics* 91, 2010, 155–166. Table II: Key groups of societal responsibilities.

responsibility-washing. Many companies convey a certain image of responsible behaviour without it being a reality.

While there is an evident need for responsible innovation, the term itself is clearly no longer appropriate. It is outdated, not sufficiently clear or too trivialised. It is tainted with a passive, defensive connotation, but most importantly, it fails to determine its purpose with sufficient precision and therefore seems unsuitable.

Herbert Hart proposed the notion of "role-responsibility"[67] to characterise the situation of a person who has the responsibility (role) of managing the interests of others. Role-responsibility refers to a meaning of responsibility which brings into play a network of transversal responsibilities at the crossroads between ethics and law. Although this concept does indeed seem of interest for the issue under review here, it does not seem sufficiently adapted because, just as for the term "responsibility", "managing the interests of others" could strictly speaking only concern the preservation of shareholders' interests, regardless of the means used.

Paul Ricoeur also highlights that the term *respondere* is often misunderstood. Instead, the author argues, we should use *imputare*, i.e. imputation. According to the author, the notion of responsibility should be broadened so as to include the notion of imputation, in order to enhance the dimension of the relationship to others. His arguments are very close to the questions raised for responsible innovation. He says: *the new meaning ascribed to responsibility in the technological age calls for an orientation openly directed towards a distant future which goes far beyond the time foreseeable consequences*.[68] However, the term "imputation" is too close to legal considerations because imputation seeks the "fault", it characterises it for the subject, which is useful, but in no way sufficient. If the effect sought is to instil fear among innovators with the idea of imputation, the direct risk is that this will lead to a contraction, or even the abandonment, of innovation. Moreover, imputation looks to the past, whereas what we are trying to achieve is a forward-looking, prospective view, for future innovations.

There is a clear need for a new term, a new dimension, a new understanding which can make up for the shortcomings we have just listed, the overall lack of substance. This new concept should provide us with a

---

[67] Herbert Hart, *Punishment and responsibility*, Oxford University Press, 1968, p. 213.
[68] Paul Ricoeur, "Le concept de responsabilité. Essai d'analyse sémantique", in *Le Juste 1*, Paris, Seuil 1995. pp. 281–282. Our translation.

better understanding of what is at stake in the relationship of the individual both with himself and with others. In other words, it is about thinking about innovation as a means whose goal would result in an "improvement" for individuals. In that sense, then, innovation would take care of them. This would cast light upon an aspect which responsible innovation does not emphasise, or at least not enough. Introducing the notion of "care" would naturally lead innovation towards more desirable outcomes, for individuals and society alike. When coupled with the notion of innovation, it could usher in a paradigmatic shift in the role of the Innovator, and help us to set up a more accurate approach of what responsible innovation should be. This paradigm could be placed under the aegis of Plato who said, in *The Republic* that the State ought not be established so that *any one class in the State happy above the rest; the happiness was to be in the whole State.*[69] To paraphrase the Athenian, to innovate-care is to innovate for the State while seeking not only the exceptional happiness of a single group, but rather happiness for as many individuals as possible, that is to say civil society as a whole.

What is care?

Care can be understood as solicitude, taking care of someone or benevolence.[70] It reflects the universal[71] expression of human concerns about the world in which we live. It is used by many academics and practitioners in different disciplines. Although this term has been adopted by sociologists, social workers, psychologists, lawyers, politicians, philosophers, geographers, anthropologists and engineers, it is important that today we

---

[69] Platon, *République*, trad. Léon Robin, *in* Platon, *Œuvres complètes I*, Gallimard, « Bibliothèque de la Pléiade », 1950, IV, 420b, p. 980. Plato, *The Republic*, Translated into English by B. Jowett. Retrieved from http://www.gutenberg.org/files/1497/1497-h/1497-h.htm.

[70] Sandra Laugier et Patrcia Paperman, "La voix différente et les éthiques du *care*" in Carol Gilligan, *Une voix différente, pour une éthique du* care (1982), French translation by Annick Kwiatek, reviewed by Vanessa Nurock, Champ-Flammarion, 2008, p. XXIX. Carol Gilligan, *In a Different Voice: Psychological Theory and Women's Development*, Harvard University Press, 1982.

[71] Carol Gilligan, *Une voie différente. Pour une éthique du care*, Paris, Flammarion, 2008, pp. 50–59; as quoted by 9. Molinier, S. Laugier and 9. Paperman, *Qu'est-ce que le* care? Petite Bibliothèque Payot, 2009, p. 7. Carol Gilligan, *In a Different Voice: Psychological Theory and Women's Development*, Harvard University Press, 1982.

question its position within the managerial sphere, particularly with regard to innovation.[72] Moreover, considering that the notion of care is intimately linked to the interrelationship between individuals, Joan Tronto, one of the most influential scholars on the concept of care, stresses the need for institutions, cities and States[73] to question the concept of care. This makes sense because, for the proponents of the ethics of care, morality stems from experiences related to everyday life and to the moral problems faced by real people in their ordinary lives.[74]

Originally, Tronto and Berenice Fisher defined care as *On the most general level, we suggest that caring be viewed as a species activity that includes everything that we do to maintain, continue, and repair our "world" so that we can live in it as well as possible. That world includes our bodies, our selves, and our environment, all of which we seek to interweave in a complex, life-sustaining web.*[75] When care is associated with innovation, it deviates slightly from this definition, because not all technological, scientific, economic, or other innovations are intended to "repair" the world or our bodies – even if this may have been the ambition of progress. However, based on this definition, innovation-care can already in part be defined as deliberately avoiding what care seeks to implement. In other words, innovation should not run the risk of destroying the world, the environment or individuals.

Another way in which the notion of innovation-care deviates from this is that care focuses on the present whereas innovation care focuses on the future. While care aims to take care of those who need it now, innovation-care seeks to meet people's future needs while still taking care of

---

[72] Joan Tronto, "*Care* démocratique et démocraties du *care*", French translation by. B. Ambroise, in P. Molinier, S. Laugier, P. Paperman, *Qu'est-ce que le* care?, *Op. cit.*, p. 35. Joan Tronto, *Caring Democracy: Markets, Equality, and Justice*, New York University Press, New York, 2013; Pascale Molinier, S. Laugier and P. Paperman, *Qu'est-ce que le* care? *Op. cit.*, p. 8.

[73] Joan Tronto, "*Care* démocratique et démocraties du *care*", *Op. cit.*, pp. 36 and 54. Joan Tronto, *Caring Democracy: Markets, Equality, and Justice*, New York University Press, New York, 2013.

[74] Sandra Laugier et Patricia Paperman, "La voix différente et les éthiques du *care*" in Carol Gilligan, *Une voix différente, pour une éthique du* care, *Op. cit.*, p. V.

[75] Berenice Fisher and Joan Tronto, 1990, as quoted in J. Tronto, *Moral Boundaries. A Political Argument for an Ethic of Care*, Routledge, New York, 1993. Quoted in "*Care* démocratique et démocraties du *care*", *Op. cit.*, p. 37. Our translation.

them. This again raises ethical issues about what we should and should not do to "take care" of society. More specifically, when these issues are considered insofar as how they relate to innovation, the question which arises is: "How should we live?" For Bernard Williams, this question is the foundation of ethics, which he attributes to Socrates.[76] The question "how should we live?" in fact expresses a want, a need for ethics, which is precisely what a philosophical approach endeavours to provide. It does this by asking the more fundamental ethical question – which also happens to be Socratic: what is the kind of knowledge I need if I am to live a good way of life? This means that innovation-care is based on two pillars. On the one hand, "taking care of oneself" or, as the Greeks called it, *epimeleia heautou*,[77] and on the other hand, ethics, which here is related to Socrates, but which, as we will see, can also take a Kantian approach.

These details are important for our topic because, from the origins of "care", as pushed by Carol Gilligan, care has been understood as a form of ethics, more particularly a feminine ethic, because where it first emerges is within the family setting – we take care of those around us and who love us unconditionally – and is transmitted from one generation to the next from mother to daughter. However, numerous analyses have since shown that we are not born with an inherent sense of care, it is a quality we acquire, we *become* caring.[78] This transmission, then, is not genetic, it takes place through education, and gender barriers are gradually disappearing. Therefore, if care is able to transcend genders, as has cultures and borders, it follows that it is quite capable also of transcending social spheres to also take hold in the spheres of economics and management.

Characterising innovation-care

There are two ways of linking innovation with care: care-innovation and innovation-care. In order to understand this, we must first go back to the

---

[76] Bernard Williams, L'Éthique et les Limites de la philosophie, trad. M.-A. Lescourret, Gallimard, 1990, p. 7, after *The Republic*, I, 352d.

[77] Michel Foucault, *L'Herméneutique du sujet*, Cours au Collège de France. 1981–1982, "Hautes études", Gallimard-Seuil, 2001, pp. 6–13.

Michel Foucault, The Hermeneutics of the Subject, Lectures at the Collège de France, 1981–1982, edited by F. Gros, General Editors: F. Ewald and A. Translated to English by Graham Burchell. Retrieved from http://www.rebels-library.org/files/foucault_hermeneutics.pdf.

[78] Pascale Molinier, Sandra Laugier, Patricia Paperman, *Qu'est-ce que le* care?, *Op. cit.*, p. 15.

work of Tronto and Fisher, who explain that care consists of four phases: caring for someone or something (care-about); caring for someone (care-for); giving care to someone (care-giving); and being the object of care (care-receiving).[79]

Innovation associated with care can be found in at least three of the above-mentioned categories. An innovation can indeed be oriented towards "care-giving", a scientific innovation in the medical field for example. Innovation can also be aimed at "taking care of someone" (care-for). Companies providing childcare or cleaning services, tutoring, etc. are very much in line with this aspect of care. In these first two categories, therefore, services and products can be developed where care lies at the core of the economic proposition.

Lastly, innovation can also be linked to the notion of "care-about". This is not about a new product or service to be offered, it is about developing innovations, irrespective of the sector, market, product or service, with concern for the individuals which make up society. It is driven by a form of care about others. This does not take the form of a response in and of itself, but rather as a response to the consequences of innovation on the individual. In other words, when you launch a new banking service, are you sure that it "takes care" of the person who will use it? It is about questioning whether this service will penalise those who sign up for it, or take them "hostage".

It is important to differentiate innovation-care and care-innovation. The latter focuses more particularly on innovations in relation to care needs (childminders, baby-sitters, cleaning, etc.). Innovation-care, however, means taking others into account when assessing the impact of innovation. As such, it can apply to innovation in itself, be it technological, scientific or economic. It is within these different areas that the question of care, that is, the fact of taking care of others, arises.

Modes of expression of care

The challenge of innovation-care is above all to bringing back innovation into society, to the individuals which comprise it. As stated earlier, innovation is trapped in the managerial strata and only listens to the market, to

---

[79] Joan Tronto "*Care* démocratique et démocraties du *care*", *Op. cit.*, p. 37. Joan Tronto, *Caring Democracy: Markets, Equality, and Justice*, New York University Press, New York, 2013.

detect commercial potential. Innovation-care, however, takes account of the society within which the product or service is to be launched, so that, in turn, the innovation can take individuals into account. This could be interpreted as adopting a Cartesian approach, in as much as Descartes' defence of the idea of the human beings as "masters and possessors of nature" was – as already discussed – intimately linked to the idea of progress in favour of the preservation of the individual and the conservation of health.

For Tronto, care can only exist through collective consciousness, because all of us benefit from it. This means that it is the attention we pay to the caring for others which enables collective care to emerge. However, this raises the question of know-how: what do we know about caring for others? What do we know about what is done for us? Or of the gestures, the intentions of others towards us which weave the maintenance, the coherence and even the aesthetics of our lives.[80] How can managers know what it means to take care of others? These questions are all the more acute when it comes to innovation: what do we want in and for our lives? How should we respond to these desires? With what intentions and coherence?

The innovation-care approach asks these questions about all forms of innovation in order to build them up according to profound individual needs. This requires questioning each decision to place an innovation on the market when the purpose of the innovation in question is in contradiction with, or at least very far removed from, declared universal principles. Business strategists have long understood the economic aspects of innovation. The question here therefore is to think beyond the market share which this or that innovation will provide. The vulnerability of a company lies not so much in its balance sheet as in the consequences for individuals – whether employees, customers or citizens – who work for or benefit from it. To paraphrase Kant, the desired goal here is to innovate for others as we would for ourselves.

Tronto highlights that the notion of "care" is dyadic, establishing a relationship between two kinds of individuals: the care-giver and the care

---

[80]Bérénice Fisher and Joan Tronto, « Toward a feminist theory of caring », in Emily K. Able, Margaret. Nelson (dir.), *Circles of care. Work and Identity in Women's life*, Albany, State University of New York Press, 1990, quoted in Joan Tronto, *Moral Boundaries... Op. cit.*, French translation *Un monde vulnérable. Pour une éthique du* care, La Découverte 2009, p. 143. Repris dans Pascale Molinier, Sandra Laugier, Patricia Paperman, *Qu'est-ce que le* care ?, *Op. cit.*, p. 19.

recipient – a relationship where the balance of power is in favour of the former.[81] Analogously, this superiority of the giver over the receiver is also to be found in the concept of innovation-care, albeit in a different form. The innovative company or the innovator exerts power over clients – the beneficiaries of the innovation, whom they know, whom they have studied extensively, whose needs they have clearly identified, etc. – and whom the firm or the innovator will be able to help. This balance of power, which the innovator may be tempted to abuse, is a fundamental element of innovation-care, which would then be formulated in these terms: to what extent can I exploit the vulnerability of the person who needs me? To take a more extreme – but very real – example, to what extent does a weapons manufacturer who innovates by developing a better performing device really take into account the person who is going to buy it? Of course, without going so far as weapons, this also applies to food and new technologies. For example, it is not yet clear whether extra-high voltage lines have a health impact.[82]

Spheres of the individual

This is the context in which the dichotomy between the private versus the professional sphere plays out with regard to innovation in general, and for the Innovator in particular. For some years now, Western companies – and governments for that matter – have been promoting the need for a clear separation between our professional and personal life: the famous work/life balance. By the same token, however, this results in a potential lack of awareness or even disregard for the effects of one on the other. By expecting a manager to be a citizen like any other when they walk out the office, by corollary, means that a manager is expected to leave aside their role as a citizen when they walk back in to the office. To what extent does the manager, when they have before them an innovation which has high

---

[81] Joan Tronto, "*Care* démocratique et démocraties du *care*", *Op. cit.*, p. 36. Joan Tronto, *Caring Democracy: Markets, Equality, and Justice*, New York University Press, New York, 2013.

[82] See the report by French senator Daniel Raoul on the effects on health and the environment of electromagnetic fields produced by high and very high voltage lines ("Les effets sur la santé et l'environnement des champs électromagnétiques produits par les lignes à haute et très haute tension") submitted to the French Parliamentary Office for the Evaluation of Scientific and Technological Options, May 2010.

potential for their company and which could earn them bonuses and pro-
motions, question whether the company should give up on the innovation
given the hypothetical risks it may present for their fellow citizens?

Therefore, there is a disparity between power and care, and this disparity is the source of possible conflicts for managers. How can managers
answer this question? Based on their judgement or values? Their morals?
The catch, however, is that both morals and values are very difficult to
determine universally.[83] A morally-valid decision in Asia might not be
considered so in Africa. Breaking this down even more, moral sensitivity
varies from one person to the next, and also between men and women.[84]
Today's most significant innovations transcend borders and continents.
This manager/citizen dichotomy needs to be explored anew. Should we
continue to support the manager/citizen separation or, on the contrary,
should this dichotomy be better articulated in order to strike a more desirable balance?

There is a need for redefining responsibility within innovation, taking into consideration all players, regardless of their role and function,
that is to say a responsibility which reflects on the individuals likely to
be impacted by the innovation – be they customers, citizens, potential
customers, etc. Not only must the Innovator understand that they are
also and at the same time a citizen, but also that the professional sphere
exists only to take care of the private sphere. This is what Empedocles
tried to teach us, reformulated by Jean-François Balaudé: *There can be
no just and harmonious human community unless its members also think
and behave as members of the larger community of the living.*[85] In other
words, the Innovator must in all circumstances remain a citizen, an individual working for civil society, for the community to which they
belong.

The interaction between the private and professional spheres translates in an interdependence between manager and citizen, between the
Innovator and all the many recipients of the innovation. Ultimately, the
private and public spheres merge and become one.

---

[83] Mark S. Schwartz, "Universal Moral Values for Corporate Codes of Ethics", *Journal of
Business Ethics* 59, 2005, 27–44.
[84] Sandra Laugier and Patricia Paperman, "La voix différente et les éthiques du *care*",
Op. cit., pp. III and XXIV.
[85] Jean-François Balaudé, *Le Savoir-vivre philosophique*, Grasset, 2010, p. 117.

Competitiveness, interdependence and short-term vision

What the innovation-care model highlights is that self-sufficiency is not an option, and both the Innovator and the end consumer must accept this immutable dimension. This situation of interdependence between innovators and the direct or indirect recipients of the innovation can easily be understood. Nevertheless, it is seldom or insufficiently integrated, because of factors exogenous and endogenous to the firm.

Exogenous conditions

The exogenous conditions which limit the understanding of this interdependence, and therefore of innovation-care, are intrinsically linked to the economic pressure in which firms operate, and even more so to strong and global competitiveness, which, in turn, puts pressure on innovation processes. Firms must at all costs be competitive and productive and, if they do not want to be crushed by the intense competitive context, they must also constantly renew themselves. A form of economic Darwinism seems to operate, which entails a fight for economic survival which results in the elimination of the weakest.

In order to understand this, we need to look at a survey conducted between September 2009 and January 2010, in which 1,541 CEOs and senior managers in the public and private sectors representing organisations and companies of all sizes in 60 countries over 33 sectors were interviewed.[86] The results show that there is a typology of companies which are described as being "financial standouts", particularly in terms of innovation. The economic differences between "standouts" and other organisations are based on their short- and long-term performance. This is based on annual operating margin growth over 4 years from 2003 to 2008 to measure long-term performance. The same analysis was performed over 1 year from 2008 to 2009 so as to measure short-term performance. From this, they were able to identify these "standout" organisations: those which succeeded in improving their operating margin both in the long and short term. It should also be noted that these "standouts" were able to survive better during crises, thanks to their robustness, which they built and constantly reinforced in this highly-competitive environment.

---

[86]IBM Institute for Business Value, *Capitalizing on Complexity*, IBM Corporation 2010.

Two particularities of these "standouts" are worthy of note. Firstly, these organisations take on the responsibility of making decisions in the face of uncertainty: 16% of them are more likely than others to implement iterative strategic planning processes rather than formal annual planning processes.[87] Secondly, they demonstrate an ability to make decisions much faster than others: 54% declared they were in favour of quick decisions.[88] Yet it is precisely these two factors which undermine responsibility in innovation as they fail to foster reflection on the possible negative consequences of an innovation. By definition, making decisions in uncertainty is conducive to risks. Being able to make a decision quickly is just as risky as not having any control over the many factors and consequences at play. Of course, we should guard against concluding too hastily that being a "standout" necessarily means undermining the responsibility associated with innovation. This calls for a detailed analysis of the innovations and processes brought out by these "standouts". Moreover, it would be necessary to analyse a set of companies with so-called "responsible" innovations and compare their performance with both the market averages in their sector and those of that of these "standouts".

Endogenous conditions

Endogenous conditions are intimately linked to the first. Both deal with two major axes. First of all, the length of time a CEO stays in their position is constantly decreasing. Over the last 10 years, the average term of a CEO has decreased by 25%.[89] When asked about this situation, CEOs claim that between the moment they take on their position and leave it, they barely have enough time to establish a strategy. It is expected that sole focus – and obsession – be the next financial report, regardless of when they joined as CEO. However, such reports cannot be published without also announcing a strategy, future innovations and projects, even if they are only in very early stages. They denounce the "hype" syndrome which they have no choice but to play into in order to reassure the markets and/or shareholders and/or employees. This leaves no room for doubt, questions, even if it the very essence of innovation is that it exists in a

---

[87] *Idem.*

[88] *Idem.*

[89] Ken Favaro, Per-Ola Karlsson, and Gary L. Neilson, "CEO Succession 2000–2009: A Decade of Convergence and Compression" for Booz&Co, *Strategy Business*, 59, 2010.

state of uncertainty. In order to retain their position, these leaders have to maintain the PR buzz surrounding their announcement and to guarantee the success of the innovation. As a result, competitors jump on the innovation train, leading to media hype. It is no longer a question of aiming for the innovation of the year award, but rather the announcement of the year, which can be measured directly by the evolution of the company's share price on the stock market. This mechanism is very short, and therefore the time CEOs stay in position is more and more short-lived. The pressure of the markets and shareholders on short-term profitability takes a toll on CEO's lifespan and they complain that they do not have the time to implement a real strategy or to implement a series of successful innovations.

We must also highlight another factor which is endogenous to the company whose responsibility is once again put on the shoulders of CEOs. The CEOs have a particularly close link with innovations, and are often considered as their fathers. In a survey of 1,130 business leaders from all sectors and all continents, surveyed CEOs clearly stated that they bore the ultimate responsibility for innovation. A total of 50% stated that "I am the innovator" or that the innovation belonged to "all employees"[90], which implies that CEOs retain ownership, since they are at the apex of the hierarchy. This relationship presents a number of challenges for the development of a possible innovation-care, in particular, it raises a primarily egological question. If an innovation fails, is it the leader who takes responsibility for its failure? If so, how and to what extent? Is there not an obsession for innovation whenever pride and ambition come into play?[91]

Understanding interdependence as a means of balancing exogenous and endogenous conditions

The innovation-care approach works on both the exogenous and endogenous conditions of the company through an awareness of interdependence. Interdependence arises in the internationalisation of goods and services; between individuals, whether they are managers or employees; within individuals, when these are both manager and citizen. Whether we like it

---

[90] IBM, "Global CEO Study", 2008.
[91] For example, the behaviour of Lee Iacocca, the CEO of Ford regarding the Pinto model. Jonathan Raymond, "The Ford Pinto: The American Counter-Example", *Op. cit.*

or not, there is always interdependence. A care-driven approach means accepting this interdependence by taking care of oneself as well as others. This awareness of interdependence means recognising that acts of violence against others always penalises us, just as we benefit from the care of others.[92] This is why theories of care always stress the importance for human life of showing that all of us depend on the services provided by others in order to satisfy even the most basic needs.[93] From the perspective of care, the self and others are not represented as separate, distinct entities: the relationship constitutes the central object from which the moral subject perceives needs and responds to this perception. Each of these perspectives captures the relationships between the self and others.[94]

Interdependence is everywhere, from medicine to driving on a road, from education to information, from management to collaborating within a project-group. Integrating this aspect requires leaving the egological sphere, which is the most difficult thing for businesses and their leaders find to do in general, and particularly within the context of innovation. The aim of innovation-care is two-fold: it is to show that innovation is not a solitary endeavour and that failure is not a sign of weakness but rather the result of distinctly human characteristics. As an example, a study of aircraft accidents has shown that if crew members rely solely on the pilot's understanding of the situation at face value, they are unable to correct an error. Therefore, if pilots and the rest of the crew learn to recognise their mistakes and accept their weaknesses, together, they can solve problems more effectively.[95]

Innovation-care and self-control

Innovation-care is the awareness of the interdependence which exists between individuals, firms, nations, citizens, managers, clients, users, etc. Innovation-care means being aware of the porosity between these players, of the interactions which take place at the crossroads of the private and

---

[92] Carol Gilligan, *Une voix différente, pour une éthique du* care, *Op. cit.*, p. 123.

[93] Sandra Laugier and Patricia Paperman, "La voix différente et les éthiques du *care*", *Op. cit.*, p. IX.

[94] *Ibid.*, p. XXXIII.

[95] Joan Tronto, "*Care* démocratique et démocraties du *care*", *Op. cit.*, p. 5. Joan Tronto, *Caring Democracy: Markets, Equality, and Justice*, New York University Press, New York, 2013.

public spheres. Once the Innovator becomes aware of living within a process in which they themselves benefits from the care of others, and that they themselves are impacted by innovations, then they can understand the notion of care as it applies to their practice. Only then will they be able to be "caring".

Once these intertwined processes are understood, innovation will no longer claim to be acting on behalf of others to bring them happiness. It is a natural temptation of innovation, but it is also a temptation which can be detrimental to care. Tronto differentiates between "good" and "bad" care, by giving the example of colonisers who, in past centuries, were convinced they were not exploiting the colonised peoples they wanted to rule.[96] The same question may be raised about innovation.

The "standout" companies from the report mentioned earlier seem to take this path of listening to others, and seem more particularly concerned with listening to their customers, placing them at the forefront of their proposals. Putting customers at the heart of their strategy becomes almost an obsession. In fact, for 95% of these firms, i.e. 14% more than the other types of firms, "getting closer to the customer" was their absolute priority.[97] However, there is more to innovation-care than this. While the Innovator may believe something is "good" for themselves, or even their customers, it may not be so for the rest of society. This is why an innovation-care approach requires listening to the opinions of others. This does not refer to the opinion of existing or potential customers, but rather to all of those who may well become impacted by the innovation to come. This ties in with one of the axes of responsible innovation.

This is a particularly sensitive issue because, from the perspective of the customer, the worthwhile innovations are those which happen incrementally. However, the major issues about the impact of innovations arise when disruptive innovations occur. Incremental innovations are, by definition, more predictable because they are already, at least partially, on the market. Disruptive innovations actually require much more attention because the impacts they will have are, by definition, unprecedented. This is compounded by the fact that the very concepts of disruptive or incremental are not understood in the same way across the world.[98]

---

[96] *Ibid.*, p. 39.
[97] IBM Institute for Business Value, *Capitalizing on Complexity*, IBM Corporation, 2010.
[98] Norma Harisson, *Disruptive innovation in China*. Lecture given at CEIBS (China Europe International Business School) Shanghai, June 30, 2010. During this conference,

Therefore, innovation-care requires a holistic approach, whereby it is not only a matter of acting according to what is good for oneself or for the company, but also according to what is good for society as a whole and how the innovations being brought about will impact it. A cigarette manufacturer must take non-smokers into account; a household detergent manufacturer must take into account the disposal of its products in water as well as the children who will come into contact with these products; a car dealer must take into account pedestrians and cyclists with whom cars share a road.

In the end, the paradigm shift brought about by the innovation-care model is a resurgence of Kantian principles, in particular his different formulations of the categorical imperative. The first of these is particularly relevant: *Act as if the maxim of thy action were to become by thy will a universal law of nature.*[99] It highlights interdependence: the obligation to look at the global impact and the fact that others may, at the same time, have the same concerns as yourself, instead of adopting a personal, individual outlook. This principle could be the foundation of innovation-care: acting with care means bringing our actions into line with a universal outlook on the impact of the actions we are about to take.

The second principle is: *So act as to treat humanity, whether in thine own person or in that of any other, in every case as an end withal, never as means only.*[100] Here, innovation-care is analysed from the point of view of the preservation of humanity, which should be considered as an end in itself. Like the previous principle, this one seeks to place the individual as a necessary prerequisite for action. Kant was obviously not discussing innovation when he wrote these principles. However, he was a great observer of the Enlightenment and therefore of the many problems arising from progress and science, as Rousseau condemned in his *Discourse on the Arts and Sciences.*[101]

Norma Harisson returned to the issue of incremental *vs* disruptive innovation, pointing out that what is incremental for the American market can be disruptive for the Chinese market. This explains why, globally, innovation in China is incremental from Western innovations, especially in terms of the *business model.*

[99] Emmanuel Kant, *Fondation de la métaphysique des mœurs* in *Métaphysique des mœurs*, I, *Fondation, Introduction*, trad. Alain Renault, p. 97. Emmanuel Kant, *Foundation for Metaphysics of Morals in Metaphysics of Morals*, Translated to English by Thomas Kingsmill Abbott. Retrieved from http://www.gutenberg.org/files/5682/5682-h/5682-h.htm.

[100] *Ibid.*, p. 108.

[101] Jean-Jacques Rousseau, *Discours sur les sciences et les arts*, Garnier-Flammarion, 1992, pp. 29–56. Discourse on the sciences and the Arts, translated by Ian Johnston, Richer Resources Publications, 2014.

From innovator to innovator-carer?

The principles of Kant, and more generally innovation-care, call for a completely new behaviour on the part of mankind, a new way of being with others and oneself. When Hans Jonas introduced the "responsibility principle" he even questioned whether humanity had a right to exist.[102] If the answer to this question is yes, then it is fundamental that human beings evolve towards a new behaviour, one that is caring for the world. This is a new stance which individuals at large must know how to take. Confronted with the rise and the power of technology, faced with ever-increasing globalisation, human beings find themselves obliged to assume responsibility for what happens *in* and *to* the world.

This is the responsibility of the Innovator, and raises the question of the profile of the Innovator, the stance they should adopt. The Innovator should carry in themselves a caring behaviour. However, usual studies about innovation, whether in management, economics or sociology, focus much more on innovation as a process and therefore concern themselves what the Innovator does rather than who they are.[103] Even when this aspect is addressed, the question of the responsibility of the Innovator remains side-lined. Schumpeter saw the Innovator as an athlete with a strong taste for conquest, a "wild spirit" which yearned for success.[104] Recent literature on entrepreneurship questions the personal characteristics of the Innovator-entrepreneur, but neither Robert[105] nor Sahlman[106] deal with the issue of responsibility. None of the types of innovators Norbert Alter defined in his typology (central; specialised; relay; follower) bear this characteristic.[107] The only elements which emerge from

---

[102]Hans Jonas, *Le Principe responsabilité. Une éthique pour la civilisation technologique*, (Trad. J. Greisch, 1998) Paris, Flammarion, 1979, pp. 95–106. Hans Jonas, *The Imperative of Responsibility: In Search of an Ethics for the Technological Age*, University of Chicago Press, 1985.

[103]Renelle Guichard and Laurence Servel, « Qui sont les innovateurs ? Une lecture socio-économique des acteurs de l'innovation », *Sociétal*, 52, 2006, 26–31.

[104]Joseph A. Schumpeter, *Théorie de l'évolution économique*, trad. Jean-Jacques Askett, Dalloz, 1999. François Perroux (1935), *La Pensée économique de Joseph Schumpeter*, Presse de Savoie, 1965, p. 83.

[105]Edward Robert, *Entrepreneurship in High Technology: Lessons from MIT Beyond*, OUP, New York, 1991.

[106]William Sahlman, "How to write a great business plan", *Harvard Business Review* 4(75), 1997.

[107]Norbert Alter, "Entreprise: les innovateurs au quotidien", *Futuribles*, January 2002.

existing research on the profile of the Innovator is that innovators are often seen as iconoclasts, eccentrics, out of the norm, marginals or even deviants *because they display behaviours which are in opposition with established norms*.[108] This element, which is significant, echoes Foucault, who regularly used the term "innovation" to evoke behaviours, particularly sexual behaviours, which went beyond established norms.[109]

Less traditional or academic works more frequently explore the question of the profiles of innovators, they too fail to address the issue of the responsibility the Innovator should bear. For example, Tom Kelley's latest best-selling book, *The Ten Faces of Innovation*, does not address the issue of the innovator's responsibility at all. The author defines three categories of behaviours in the face of innovation ("learners", "organisers" and "builders"[110]) and delineates their specificities, but none of these are ever described as possessing (or as being the one who should possess) responsible qualities.

Stigmatisation and self-control

Integrating responsible behaviour into innovation through behaviours and policies does not involve additional constraints or elements likely to curb innovation. Obviously, it is not a question of stigmatising innovation, or agreeing with Rousseau who saw progress as the symbol of the degradation of mankind, or even of trying to demonstrate that our natural state would be more profitable.[111]

---

[108]Norbert Alter, *L'Innovation ordinaire*, PUF, 2003, p. 18. Our translation.

[109]Michel Foucault, *Le Courage de la vérité, Le gouvernement de soi et des autres II*, Cours au Collège de France. 1984, éditions Hautes Études, Gallimard-Seuil, 2009, p. 228. Cf. Michel Foucault, « Le triomphe social du plaisir sexuel : une conversation avec Michel Foucault », *in Dits et Écrits II*, 1976–1988, Gallimard, « Quarto », 2001, pp. 1127–1133. Cf. également, Richard Shusterman, *Vivre la philosophie – Pragmatisme et art de vivre*, trad. Christian Fournier et Jean-Pierre Cometti, Klincksieck, 2001, p. 45. Richard Shusterman, *Practicing Philosophy: Pragmatism and the Philosophical Life*, New York: Routledge,1997.

[110]Thomas Kelley, *The Ten Faces of Innovation: IDEO's Strategies for Defeating the Devil's Advocate and Driving Creativity Throughout Your Organisation*, Broadway Business, 2005. No more elements in Jean-Philippe Deschamps, *Innovation Leaders*, Jossey-Bass, 2008.

[111]Jean-Jacques Rousseau, *Discours sur l'origine et les fondements de l'inégalité parmi les hommes*, Flammarion, 1989. *Discourse on the Origin of Inequality*, Dover Publication, 2004.

Two qualities seem necessary. First of all, as mentioned earlier, the ability to question the impact of a responsible innovation and, in this respect, to come to grips with the three aspects Bensaude–Vincent underlined. Secondly, the ability to slow down the pace of innovation so as to attempt to bring it into line with the economic, social and societal sphere in which it will be implemented. This latter point can easily evolve toward self-control as the Stoics understood it, that is, closely linked to the notion of freedom.[112] Being able to control oneself is being free from one's passions, from external elements or events which may occur, and so on. Being able to control oneself for the Innovator-carer means to be able to free oneself from the market, from economic pressure, from situations where an innovation would be launched without having duly assessed its possible consequences. This is not to say that we should be blind to the context in which innovation unfolds, but neither should we be dependent on it. In fact, if the product or service launched is truly innovative, then these issues are secondary.

For the Innovator-carer; being a master of oneself also means being able to determine one's own motivations in acting and launching an innovation. Why is this innovation good in itself, for oneself and for others? This is how one can become the master of the innovation process, right down to its deepest consequences. For the Innovator-carer, however, self-control also means giving up on their passions, just as the Stoic masters gave up on their passions. Even if these passions are attractive and pleasurable, the Stoics endeavoured to control them so as not to yield to them.[113] The Innovator-carer, therefore, must achieve a certain wisdom which no one else can match: they must be sensitive to the needs of others, but must only act on what they know, because others rely on them.[114] They must be able to foresee the actions which could result in suffering,[115] because they more than anyone else are responsible for everyone's well-being.[116] In so doing, it is the ethics of care as a whole, based on the

---

[112]See the preface in Pierre-Maxime Schuhl and the Introduction by Émile Bréhier in *Les Stoïciens*, translated into French by É. Bréhier, Gallimard, "Bibliothèque de la Pléiade", 1962. An important element found in Epictetus' *interviews*.

[113]*Idem.*

[114]Carol Gilligan, *Une voix différente, pour une éthique du* care, *Op. cit.*, p. 93. Carol Gilligan, *In a Different Voice: Psychological Theory and Women's Development*, Harvard University Press, 1982.

[115]*Ibid.*, p. 215.

[116]*Ibid.*, p. 235.

precept of non-violence and of doing no harm,[117] which will prevail in the field of innovation.

Therefore, even if an innovation can significantly increase turnover, contribute to achieving objectives and generate a significant benefit, the Innovator-carer should be able to give up on it if it jeopardises in any way the act of caring for others, for society. The Innovator-carer therefore acts as a form of conscience. Not only for the Innovator themselves, but also for their company, organisation or society. The Innovator-carer is to act in the name of the common good, not only their own. Responsible-innovation involves the assessment of the consequences of an innovation on the community, innovation-care involves caring for the community. As such, innovation-care potentially has a positive and benevolent role to play in the community and in civil society, and the Innovator-carer is the first student of the ethical Kantian principle: "What ought I do?"[118] This leads to the understanding that responsible innovation has a predetermined role to play in terms of its impact, whereas innovation-care takes care of others as a prerequisite.

Care and performance

Kindness and care for others are key-notions for innovation-care, and contribute to the evolution of the very notion of care, because, as we have said, care here refers to the act of caring for others. For Janet Finch and Dulcie Groves, care is even a *feelings of affection and responsibility combined with actions that provide responsively for an individual's personal needs or well-being, in a face-to-face relationship*.[119] From motherhood, to cleaning or childminding, there are professions and professional arrangements which are linked to care. While the initial approach to care was very feminist, it would be relevant to look at innovation-care from a female perspective, because women are very receptive and adapt more

---

[117]*Ibid.*, p. 277.

[118]Emmanuel Kant, *Logique*, Vrin, 1965, p. 25. Emmanuel Kant, *Kant's Introduction to Logic, and His Essay on the Mistaken Subtilty of the Four Figures*, Forgotten Books, April 5, 2018. Translated to English by Thomas Kingsmill Abbott.

[119]Francesca Cancian and Oliker Stacey, *Caring and Gender*, Thousand Oaks, Pine Forge Press, 2000; cited in Joan Tronto, "*Care* démocratique et démocraties du *care*", *Op. cit.*, p. 36. Joan Tronto, *Caring Democracy: Markets, Equality, and Justice*, New York University Press, New York, 2013.

easily to innovations,[120] and women's lives, compared to men's, are more dependent on social interaction and personal relationships.[121]

Managers and innovators should become part of the official "deliverers" of care, perhaps even more so than its "traditional operators", because they are in charge of individuals who may become directly or indirectly impacted by their innovations.

It should be stressed that the expression "innovation-care" is characterised by a hierarchy, in which "care" is subordinate to the idea of innovation. Although we have proposed that Innovator-carer should know when to give up on innovations, there is no denying that their first attribute is to aim for economic performance. Care is not responsibility; it is not corporate social responsibility; and it is not sustainable development either. Last but not least, care is not a framework or a constraint for innovation. It is a device which can be articulated alongside it, but in no way is it positioned as a goal in and of itself. For innovation, as a known instrument for performance, growth, sustainability and the improvement of people's lives in the broadest sense of the word, is what must take precedence. This primacy should be absolute and unambiguous: because innovation comes first ontologically, it is necessarily towards care that organisations, leaders and innovators must look. Moreover, striving for the well-being of all, for a caring behaviour from the very inception of the innovative movement do not entail sacrifice.[122]

This means that performance is at the core of innovation-care, that there is no possible amphibology in this new integration, and this is capital. Any other interpretation would be a misunderstanding of the meaning

---

[120]Ellen Garbarinoa, Michal Strahilevitzb, "Gender differences in the perceived risk of buying online and the effects of receiving a site recommendation", *Journal of Business Research*, 57, 2004; S. Güzin Mazman, Yasemin Koçak Usluel and Vildan Çevik "Social Influence in the Adoption Process and Usage of Innovation: Gender Differences", *World Academy of Science, Engineering and Technology*, No. 49, 2009. And also Carol Gilligan, *Une voix différente, pour une éthique du care, Op. cit.*, p. 25. Joan Tronto, *Caring democracy: markets, equality, and justice*. New York: New York University Press, 2013.

[121]Carol Gilligan, *Une voix différente, pour une éthique du care, Op. cit.*, p. 23. Joan Tronto, *Caring Democracy: Markets, Equality, and Justice*, New York University Press, New York, 2013.

[122]Carol Gilligan, *Une voix différente, pour une éthique du care, Op. cit.*, p. 92. Joan Tronto, *Caring Democracy: Markets, Equality, and Justice*. New York University Press, New York, 2013.

of care in general, and of innovation-care in particular. Innovation-care does not mean providing a basic service of an inferior quality, under the pretext that what is important is the care for others.

The sense of "care" is something which develops alongside something else. "Care" in and of itself, means nothing. At best it would be a new form of compassion. Developing care is, in fact, all the opposite: it should deal with concrete events, with reality, following the approach of the pragmatist current as developed on the American continent. Without the focus on innovation, innovation-care would remain a given-without a gift. Some existing tools can accommodate innovation-care, such as Moore's Chasm[123] or Martin's Virtue Matrix,[124] for example. Furthermore, its concrete approach means it can also be implemented within existing corporate strategies assessment methods, such as the *Dow Jones Sustainable Index*,[125] for example. Innovation-care can just as easily be based on quantitative axes which include composite indicators to evaluate one's ability to innovate-care.

Classical philosophy saw "commitment" as the fundamental paradigm for implementing a truly philosophical life-style. Such a commitment would be reflected in both the mind and actions and summarised in the famous *theōria/praxis* articulation. It is also the Greek *elenchos* – commitment – which is to *think well to act well*.[126]

The innovation-care model is still in its infancy, and the way in which it will be integrated into business models has yet to be defined. Nevertheless, just as the classic Greek philosophers did for philosophy, it is important to think of innovation-care as a commitment. That is to say, along two approaches: intellectual productions, theories and speeches; and actions. Like other sciences, management and business need to take into account these two aspects in innovation-care, both for their own development and for the development of individuals and for society.

---

[123] Geoffrey Moore, *Crossing the Chasm, Op. cit.*
[124] The Virtue Matrix: Calculating the Return on Corporate Responsibility (HBR OnPoint Enhanced Edition) by Roger Martin, *Harvard Business Review*, December 1, 2002.
[125] https://www.spglobal.com/esg/performance/indices/djsi-index-family.
[126] Jean-François Balaudé, *Le Savoir-vivre philosophique, Op. cit.*, p. 188. Our translation.

Chapter 4

The Innovative Individual at the Heart of Our Questioning

What I call spiritual exercises, that is, practices designed to transform the self and enable it to reach a higher level and gain a universal perspective, in particular through physics, through an awareness of one's relationship with the world, or through an awareness of one's relationship with humanity as a whole.[...] Is any of this meaningful currently? I think there is a continuity of these practices coupled with a discontinuity. Over the centuries, these spiritual exercises continuously resurface.

Pierre Hadot
What is ethics?

The Qualities of the Innovator

Innovation questions our past, our progress and our present, all with a view to informing our future. It is a shifting theme, which relies on the notion of change so as to ensure our continued existence. This in no way diminishes the existence of creative destruction. This movement – whether endured, chosen, triggered, or on a macro– or micro–economic scale –, never ceases to apply, to nations as well as to organisations. The most recent of such waves is the current challenge of oligopolies through collective, collaborative proposals. This emerged as a result of a movement questioning and challenging the power which the people no longer recognise nor accept: the capitalism of the 1970s, for both its confiscation of offers, power and money, and its inability to propose alternative offers to citizens. On many occasions we have tried to characterise the person behind these provocations, these changes, these innovations: the Innovator. To what extent do they bear responsibility for what they develop? To what extent, after all, should not all the questions we ask be addressed to them and them alone?

Hitherto, innovation has never emerged spontaneously from outside a human being, and innovation is always the product of the Innovator. For the Innovator is the entrepreneur, of course, the "person in charge" of innovation, but they are just as much a biologist, a scientist, a mathematician, an agricultural engineer, an astrophysicist, etc. It is a mistake to conceive of the Innovator only as the person who is in charge of developing profit on behalf of a private organisation by offering a new product or service. Pasteur, Lumière, Curie, Edison, Watt, Ampere, Bell, etc. None of these innovators developed their innovations in the pursuit of profit. Nonetheless, they fathered innovations which have indisputably had a lasting impact on society.

Therefore, what we are to examine is not so much innovation *per se*, but rather the Innovator. All questions arising from the consequences of innovations, their roles, their developments ultimately boil down to examining a *fait accompli*. Therefore, in the face of novel developments, the crucial question might be to ask whether the innovator of yesterday and of today can be the Innovator of tomorrow, a time fraught with increasing challenges and burdens? In light of this new reality, ought we not redefine the qualities and the characteristics to be had by the Innovator?

It is increasingly essential for the Innovator to be enlightened, capable of questioning the short-, medium- and long-term stakes, capable of assessing opportunities as well as risks. In other words, someone capable of acting responsibly. It is perhaps in these terms that the Innovator of tomorrow ought to be shaped: a responsible being capable not only of formulating the right questions for ensuring the sustainability of their organisation – which is a prerequisite – but also of demonstrating benevolence towards others, no matter how far-removed they are from their activities.

It goes without saying that examining the role of the Innovator, their qualities and characteristics in these terms is an innovation in and of itself. Traditionally, we expect the Innovator to be a leader, a unifying force, a creative person, a winner. However, these properties do not align with those we need to find in the Innovator of tomorrow.

If we consider that it is the matrix of the Innovator which needs to be redefined, how, then, can this be achieved? Is it in the education of innovators? There is, in fact, no such thing as specific training for innovators. All that is offered today are courses *about* innovation for individuals from a wide range of backgrounds, such as engineering, management or even medicine and law among many others, since, as discussed, innovation appears in many places. Some may ask what *disciplines* should be used so as to help the Innovator develop the required qualities. However, when we ask the Innovator to question the innovations they generate responsibly, it is the *behaviour* of the Innovator we should look at. The Innovator cannot merely be a technician in a given field, rigorously applying methods which foster the emergence of an innovation. The Innovator must demonstrate extra-ordinary attitudes, habits, behaviours because the Innovator is in direct contact with the world, often without realising it. What needs to be done, then, is to rethink the very *essence* of the figure of the Innovator, the person who changes the world, anew, with a fresh perspective.

Innovators and Philosophers: Mode of Being and Similarities

There are several reasons why philosophy seems the strongest avenue to help redefine the Innovator and their role, or, to be more precise, for the Innovator to rethink their role. First of all, it should be noted that philosophy and innovation have much in common.

The act of questioning

Philosophy is essentially a discipline of questioning. Philosophers are intrigued by the world, questions its inner-workings, questions what seems to be taken for granted, and seeks to understand. Aristotle expresses this clearly: "*It is through wonder that men now begin and originally began to philosophize; wondering in the first place at obvious perplexities, and then by gradual progression raising questions about the greater matters too, e.g. about the changes of the moon and of the sun, about the stars and about the origin of the universe. Now he who wonders and is perplexed feels that he is ignorant (thus the myth–lover is in a sense a philosopher, since myths are composed of wonders); therefore if it was to escape ignorance that men studied philosophy, it is obvious that they pursued science for the sake of knowledge, and not for any practical utility*".[1] Philosophers pursue knowledge, and the speculations they formulate are hypotheses for understanding the world they see before them. The quest for understanding natural phenomena, understanding the origin of the world stems from wonder, but also from refusal. Philosophers and scientists alike refuse to take for granted the answers which may have been given to them through myths and religions. It is through research, the establishment of hypotheses, the formulation of structured, organised, analysed, rigorous answers that knowledge, insight and thought have advanced.

In the same way, what characterises the Innovator is their refusal to take existing situations for granted. Whether talking about the invention of electricity, of the car, of the steam engine or of the Internet, in each case, the Innovator's opposition to existing situations is what allowed for these initiatives to emerge. Like philosophers, the Innovator questions the inner-workings of the world, how it operates, who is involved: what is the context? What are the forces at play? The Innovator then works to improve this world. In the examples mentioned above, it may seem the innovators brought them about towards a utilitarian end. This would reduce the Innovator to a mere entrepreneur. The Innovator, like philosophers, exists in all fields, lands and peoples. As an example, we need only look at the field of philosophy itself, which is filled with inventors and innovators. As we have demonstrated with art or with sport, innovation is by no means exclusive to world of finance or business. Philosophy has been the stage for many innovations, in many contexts and in many forms. When philosophy, an oral discipline *par excellence*, shifted to writing, this constituted a major innovation. Thanks to the written word, philosophy spread more widely and more rigorously. This constituted a strong innovation, which generated an undeniable creation of value, even if this was not measured in profits. When philosophy extended to aesthetics – in Antiquity of course, but mainly with the considerable contributions of Baumgarten or Burke – this, too, was a form of innovation. When Brillat-Savarin wrote *The Physiology of Taste*, philosophy opened up to the culinary and gastronomic field. Innovation in philosophy, then,

---

[1]Aristotle, *Metaphysics*, 982 b 13 Aristotle. Met. 1.982b Aristotle *Aristotle in 23 Volumes*, Vols. 17 and 18, Harvard University Press, Cambridge, MA; William Heinemann Ltd., London, 1933, 1989, Translated to English by Hugh Tredennick. Retrieved from http://www.perseus.tufts.edu/hopper/text?doc=Perseus%3Atext%3A1999.01.0052%3Abook%3D1%3Asection%3D982b.

emerged in the form of new themes which had not yet been addressed. As such, this could be referred to as incremental philosophical innovation. However, innovation also came in the form of new methods. Socrates innovated with the maieutic method, i.e. with a new method of questioning; as did Aristotle with his novel approach to logic. With *A Discourse on Method*, Descartes clearly innovated by marking a departure from the scholastic tradition and by seeking to build a thought founded on solid, rigorous, scientific and technical foundations. More recently, Pierre Hadot can also be seen as an innovative philosopher, in his invitation to approach Greek philosophy as a way of life. The same can be said of Michel Foucault, who explores the political space, sexuality or the "marginalised", and at the same time builds "little toolboxes" so as to give us the means to decipher other types of issues, paradigms and knowledge. Contemporary philosopher François Laruelle also offers an interesting example. Since the 1980s, he has developed the idea of non-philosophy, and openly declares that it is possible to invent in philosophy: *Philosophy is to be created, and that is good news. It is not set in its history, its institutions, its texts, its unconscious: it is always other than its past. It must be invented when new knowledge, such as technology and science, haunts the encyclopedia.*[2] For Laruelle, not only does philosophy invent, but it has no choice but to innovate at the risk of otherwise disappearing, devoured by other "competing" disciplines. The new objects which haunt everyday life, the evolution of science and technology, force philosophy to renounce its conservatism, to change itself.

The quest for progress

There is another similarity between philosophy and innovation: the quest for progress. From the Latin *progressus*, which translates as to advance, "progress" is to march forward, the evolutionary process oriented towards an ideal term, it is that which advances and develops over time. The roots of innovation can be found in those of progress, and first and foremost the progress of knowledge, the evolution of knowledge. There is an inextricable link in philosophy between understanding and progress. Understanding can only be achieved through progress, and progress can only be achieved by understanding. The "wonder" which characterises the

---

[2]François Laruelle, *En tant qu'un*, Aubier, 1991. p. 2. Our translation.

origin of philosophy led philosophers to question the phenomena which surrounded them, they began to understand and therefore to progress in the knowledge of what caused them wonder. Always, and still today, philosophers have sought to understand, or to advance their understanding, and therefore knowledge. This explains why the first scientists, physicists or chemists were philosophers. From Leucippus and atomism to Democritus and Epicurus, or the alchemists of the Middle Ages or of the 16th century such as Paracelsus,[3] or, more recently, chemists like Berthelot, all these great thinkers operated just as much in the field of science as that of philosophy. They were intellectuals of progress, they advanced science as well as knowledge, by articulating both discovery and thought. Philosophy is the child of progress and evolution, whether this progress is "natural", scientific or intellectual.

Similarly, the very *raison d'être* of the Innovator lies in progress, which is the essence of their being, which they use and brings into existence. Whether it is in terms of new products or services for the business world, or in the development of new techniques for the sportsman or musician, the Innovator seeks to bring about progress, to enable their discipline, their field, their industry or the organisation in which they are involved to advance towards the ideal version of itself. Political innovator Lee Kuan Yew is perhaps the leader who has most focused on the notion of progress for his society. This was a life-long obsession, and he successfully took Singapore from a third world country to one of the richest in the world within the span of one generation.[4] After inheriting a jungle in 1965, in 50 years, he managed to develop a garden city with one of the lowest infant mortality rates in the world, one of the highest life expectancies, almost no unemployment, a stable government, a universal health care system and an education system considered the best in the world. In the business world, the quest for progress took on different shapes and the automotive sector is regularly held up as an example. When Ferdinand Porsche launched his first Volkswagen in 1937, he was committed to progress for all, convinced that he could build the "people's car", a vehicle accessible to all. This is not very different from Carl Miele who, also in Germany and a few years earlier, set up a factory to manufacture milk

---

[3] Already in the 15th century, Paracelsus tried to experiment with the "chemical" reproduction of life. See Bernadette Bensaude-Vincent, *Histoire de la chimie*, La Découverte, 2001, p. 35.

[4] Lee Kuan Yew, *From Third World to First*, Harper, 2000.

centrifuges and then the famous washing machines, seeking, through innovation, to bring about progress for all.

Creativity

Perhaps somewhat surprisingly, the philosopher can be seen as a creative person. *Creare* in Latin is to create, and a creative person is he who masters the art of creating. The act of creation, often associated with artistic productions, is the action of inventing, founding, producing something hitherto unknown. This can be a literary genre, a methodology, a play and of course a book. The philosopher is a creative person because they never stop producing something, most often original, both in substance and form. As presented earlier, through progress, the Philosopher brings about a new method, a new philosophy, so to speak, in order to advance thinking. In that sense, then, the philosopher is creative. This creativity is expressed when the philosopher proposes a form of originality or a new way of sharing or conveying his message. The Garden of Epicurus, for example, a creative place where a number of very different individuals were brought together as a community outside the city, was a novel proposal for doing philosophy differently. Aristotle created the Lyceum, Plato invented the Academy, both in order to develop a place to do philosophy in a different way. When Descartes decided to use the "I" in *A Discourse on Method*, he marked a creative break as well. We should also mention Montaigne, who turned a travel diary into a philosophical essay whose aim was to "make" as he "makes" his book: *I Myself Am the Matter of My Book*[5] he clearly states. Far from the image of the soporific, boring philosopher filling pages and pages of writing without concerning himself with contributing anything imaginative either in substance or in form, Montaigne developed new writing proposals, carving out a new space for ideas.

Of course, there can be no innovation without creativity, and the Innovator constantly feeds on creativity. While creativity brings new things to a market, as the notion of progress reminds us, the Innovator can also create new spaces for developing their idea. This is what George

---

[5] Montaigne, *Essais*, mis en français moderne et présentés par Claude Pinganaud, Arléa, 2002, p. 13. Montaigne *The Essays of Montaigne, Complete*, Translated to English by Charles Cotton.

Lucas imagined with the Pixar studio, bringing together artists, production managers, engineers and designers. The Innovator imagine new ways of understanding their customers, this is precisely the proposal of *design thinking* as developed by Rolf Faste in the 1980s. Creativity can also lie in the method, and that is what Steve Jobs conveyed when he stated that his job was to connect the seemingly unconnected dots of creativity which were in the United States, Asia or Europe. If the Innovator do not possess this quality of being creative, then they must immerse themselves in sources of creativity which may lie among their customers, potential customers, suppliers, competitors or the researchers around them. There are many techniques for detecting creativity, even the faintest signs, whether conscious or unconscious, in all these partners who surround them. Without creativity the source of innovation eventually dries up, leading to the continuous reproduction of pale, unoriginal copies, mere improvements, but nothing more. It is the same for thought; if philosophers do not become more creative in how they think and in the dissemination of knowledge, then philosophy would fail to advance and would eventually run dry. For both philosophers and innovators, creativity is the key to survival.

Commitment

Creativity cannot materialise out of sheer will, it cannot materialise through will power in an instant. Whether for a Philosopher or an Innovator, creativity is a state of mind, a heightened state of alertness which means they are able to detect when potential ideas present themselves. The Philosopher is constantly analysing the world. This is a necessity for Seneca, who reminds us that we must continuously "unroll" our mind so that we can attend to all that it holds, so that this wealth may be readily accessible whenever the need requires.[6] Plotinus expresses the same idea when he urges us to do with our soul as a sculptor would stone, cutting away, smoothing, polishing it, making it pure.[7] And this is not

---

[6]Sénèque, Lettre 72 à Lucilius: « il faut sans cesse étudier la philosophie », in *Les Stoïciens, Op. cit.* Seneca, Ad Lucilium Epistulae Morales, London, William Heinemann, New York; G. P. Putnam's Sons. Translated to English by Richard M. Gummere, https://en.wikisource.org/wiki/Moral_letters_to_Lucilius.

[7]Plotin, *Ennéades*, I, VI (1), 9, 13, trad. Émile Bréhier. Plotinus *The Six Enneads*, Translated to English by Stephen Mackenna and B. S. Retrieved from http://www.documentacatholicaomnia.eu/03d/0204-0270,_Plotinus,_The_Six_Enneads,_EN.pdf.

specific to Ancient philosophy. The contemporary space is replete with philosophers who consider the practice of philosophy ought to be carried out continuously, day and night. Therein lies the distinction for Thoreau between a philosopher and a professor of philosophy.[8] This does not mean that one cannot be one and both at the same time, and there are many philosophers who are professors of philosophy, from the Pre-Socratics to Michel Foucault among others; just as there are philosophers who are not professors of philosophy. Cleanthes was known as a water-carrier, Marcus Aurelius was emperor, Spinoza cut optical glasses. This did not prevent any of them from being fully philosophical and thinking about their own ideas all the time, imagining concepts, analysing their favourite themes. Because the philosopher is in direct contact with the world they are trying to come to grips with and to advance through thought, science and reflection, his entire body and soul are constantly at work at the philosophical level, whatever else they may be doing. The philosopher toils tirelessly, endlessly, working himself into the ground with philosophical tasks. From Diogenes, who, as legend has it, died meditating wrapped in his cloak, to Wittgenstein, who worked on his deathbed,[9] philosophers are reputed for being obsessed by their work, driving themselves sick or insane, like Nietzsche. Unlike the novelist or the essayist, the Philosopher pours their life and soul into their work, be it written or oral. Descartes died of pneumonia following the morning lessons he was giving in the middle of the Swedish winter, and Merleau–Ponty died at his desk, resting his head on a book by the author of the *Metaphysical Meditations*. Schopenhauer, who was inhabited by his thoughts, convinced of his intuitions and for whom nothing came before his work, was also found dead sitting on his chair. For philosophers, their own health is secondary, as is the health of those around them. They die for their work and ideas.

This is reminiscent of the founder of Apple who, despite suffering from a chronic condition, was consulted daily by his team of developers, and who insisted on going on stage, even at the end of his life, to present

---

[8] Henry David Thoreau, *Walden ou La vie dans les bois*, French translation by L. Fabulet, Gallimard, 2007, p. 18. Henry David Thoreau, A Week on the Concordand Merrimack Rivers; Walden, or, Life in the Woods; The MaineWoods; Cape Cod, by Henry David Thoreau, Edited by Robert F.Sayre. Retrieved from https://azeitao.files.wordpress.com/2007/05/walden.pdf.

[9] Ray Monk, *Wittgenstein, le devoir de génie*, trad. Abel Gerschenfeld, Flammarion, 2009, p. 564. Ray Monk, *Ludwig Wittgenstein: The Duty of Genius*, Penguin Books, 1991.

his firm's latest product. His life was devoted to the innovations he wanted to develop, and his companies, NeXT, Pixar and of course Apple which he founded in April 1976. Far from the caricature of the man obsessed with financial success and profitability – unlike managers, shareholders or investors – he viewed money only as a means to an end. The Innovator and the entrepreneur, share one obsession: making, creating and developing their new service or product. No amount of financial success, glory, or even failures, can satisfy their hunger for entrepreneurship, whatever the sector in which they operate. As an entrepreneur, Richard Branson has undertaken just as much in music and book stores as in sodas, in air and rail transport, as well as mobile telephony or space travel! The same applies to Elon Musk, whose renown and financial success with PayPal meant he had the privilege of leading a very idle existence, free from obstacles or annoyances. However, he set out to build the world's first electric car factory with the Tesla brand, to develop and market launchers and thrusters for astronautic and space flight projects with SpaceX, and to completely reshape modes of transport with his Hyperloop project. These contemporary examples are, in fact, a continuation of the entrepreneurial and innovative spirit which we find with Jeff Bezos (Amazon), Larry Page (Google), Bill Gates (Microsoft) and many, many others, and which was already very strong in the United States in the 19th century, with individuals such as Cornelius Vanderbilt who built a maritime and railroad empire, or John Rockefeller and his empire in oil, automobiles and aviation, or Henry Ford in automobiles. This entrepreneurial spirit has a universal quality, and in France, Xavier Niel, can be seen as continuing the American entrepreneurship ideal, initially with the Minitel, and today in telephony, the media and education with école42. Another example is Gérard Mulliez, who opened his first Auchan hypermarket in 1961 and a few decades later is at the head of a constellation of several dozen companies ranging from sports (Decathlon) to car parts (Norauto), DIY (Leroy Merlin) or mail order (les 3 Suisses) and clothing stores (Kiabi). Or in the 19th century, it was the utopian socialist Jean–Baptiste Godin who founded the eponymous company, an entrepreneur who knew how to combine the quest for profit with the well-being of his employees; or the great innovators in the automobile industry with Citroën or Renault. Let us end this series of innovators with Asia, where, as in the rest of the world, the individuals who dedicate their lives to the development of their ideas are legion. For example, Tokuji Hayakawa in Japan, the founder of Sharp, or Sakichi Toyoda, who built the

Toyota empire. While entrepreneurship and innovation were particularly restricted in China during the communist era at the beginning of the 20th century, today they dominate the Asia of innovation, with its emblematic innovators such as Jack Ma, who founded Alibaba and operates in distribution and in cinema, navigation systems or even electronic sports and virtual reality, or Zhang Zhidong, who developed Tencet in the late 1990s, a real equivalent of the flagship companies of Silicon Valley with WeChat, QQ, etc.

This series of borderless and wide-ranging examples shows how the Innovator, like the philosopher, are a relentless worker, obsessed with the development of ideas. This dedication, however, should not be confused with passion, the driving force of musicians, sportsmen or artists. Unlike the latter, entrepreneurs and philosophers do not work (only) for themselves. They work to disseminate their ideas; they believe that what they do is valuable for others, can solve the issues faced by their fellow citizens, whether this is how to manage their passions, their desires, understanding the way the world works, or meeting the needs of society, from driving cars, getting around quickly, using a computer or communicating reliably.

Solitude

Being an innovator and doing philosophy are similar in both being heroically lonely occupations. Philosophers carry within a belief which they transmit, orally, in writing, through their disciples. They develop their thinking alone, through their books, observations and analyses, they confront others to evaluate the validity of their arguments, and to convince. For the Philosopher, when the "other" is not the subject of thought, this "other" is either an opponent or a disseminator. Since the Philosopher challenges the status quo of knowledge, they are met with a great deal of resistance along the way, in the face of which they refine their intuition and solidify their arguments. Once this other has become sufficiently knowledgeable, they can become the conduit for the ideas of the Philosopher. The sounding board of the Philosopher is their audience, their listeners, their disciples and students. The image of the philosopher meditating alone as immortalised by Rembrandt is not a caricature, it is a reality. The Philosopher needs to find themselves, to think in solitude, at length, to weigh and measure the accuracy of their arguments. They are not – or at least no longer – necessarily staring at a skull, a candle in a study or wandering in the wilderness. Today, they may be sitting at their computer, wandering through the corridors of a subway station or sitting in a café to meditate. For the modern-day philosopher, the dissemination of ideas still lies mainly with their audience of students, but they can also use other media such as social networks, or more traditional such as newspapers or radio for example.

Even when surrounded by a large team, the Entrepreneur also works in solitude. While they may have support from their entourage, or may benefit from a nourished ecosystem which they needs in order to develop their organisation – banks, consultants, suppliers – it is indeed alone that they make the ultimate decision, it is alone that they must develop the concepts they wish to propose. Just like the Philosopher, eager to challenge the status quo, the Entrepreneur will also be met with opposition and their entire work consists in listening to the challenges levelled against their idea, observing and analysing customers and potential customers, integrating their remarks so as to refine their offer to be the best possible. Their sounding board is the market; will they find customers interested in their offer? Where the Philosopher evaluates the impact of their ideas through their acceptance by others, by rallying support for his proposals, the Entrepreneur evaluates their success in terms of the dissemination of their products or services and the acceptance by customers of what they propose, as well as their loyalty to their company. The only satisfaction of the Entrepreneur, the only compensation for their solitary work, their ideas, can come solely from the recognition of the market, and despite successes and failures, they will always be alone when it comes to making new proposals. Steve Wozniak, Bill Gates, Richard Branson or Elon Musk are among the most famous entrepreneurial personalities who have expressed their solitude when devising a new idea, announcing a new product, a new proposal, the success of which is obviously never guaranteed.

Ego

The solitude of the hero needs to be put in perspective with their ego, their narcissism. The Philosopher and the Entrepreneur are driven by the strong belief that they hold the truth. Whether it is Heidegger and the belief in the supremacy of Germany, St. Augustine or St. Thomas Aquinas in the existence of God, the Stoics for whom being happy means accepting destiny as it presents itself to us, or the Epicureans who are convinced that the Gods have no effect on us since they are in the inter-worlds, philosophers have always considered that they hold the truth. This is a veritable paradox because after a life of questioning, challenging, observing, analysing, there comes a time when they believe they hold the truth – even if they sometimes claim otherwise. They will defend their arguments tooth and nail, sometimes at the cost of having to withdraw from society, and becoming a recluse, the stereotypical image of the Philosopher as a lonely and misunderstood thinker. The Philosopher publishes books and articles, they present their research at conferences and symposiums, or sometimes even in the media, or on stage in front of their students or in public. The philosopher is commented on, filmed, recorded, broadcast, and the more their ideas are spread, the more the Philosopher will continue to develop and refine them, the more they will continue to have disciples who will come to listen to them, to question them, to interrogate them. Take, for example, Michel Foucault who changed his schedule at the Collège de France so as to ensure that he had the most motivated listeners attending his lectures, or Gilles Deleuze's classrooms full, overflowing, his desk covered with voice and tape recorders, or Alain Badiou who needed a theatre to accommodate all the people who wished to attend his seminars. This success, whether it takes place at the Academy, the Garden or the Lyceum, is inherent in the support for the ideas fathered by philosophers. It is not enough to be right, it is important for these ideas to resonate, to find an audience. The philosopher thus ensures their proposals are fairly sweeping so as to garner sufficient audience, without, however, them being too broad, so as to avoid falling in the trap of clientelism, of an undemanding, popular philosophy. The philosopher is therefore constantly in a dynamic tension between the promotion of his ideas, philosophical rigor and the quest for recognition.

The entrepreneur, too, has an oversized ego. They too feel they hold a certain truth, that they have the intuition to know what customers want, so much so that when they fail to convince the general public, they feel misunderstood, just like philosophers, or consider they are ahead of their time. This was the claim made by Apple's founder after the failure of the Newton Pad, the ancestor of the famous iPad: customers were not yet ready for the tablet, whereas he "knew" what they needed. The Innovator is, by definition, someone who seeks to solve problems, once they succeed in finding a solution, they quickly consider that it is *the* solution, the one and only, and that they are right. However, just as in philosophy, where the control of passions can be approached in different ways, where the question of beauty, aesthetics or justice can be studied from different perspectives, the one and only solution may not be the preferred solution, or even the most relevant one. What characterises the ego is that it is individual, it is unique to each individual and if it is so excessive as to replace the opinions of those who are potential customers, then it can even be an obstacle to entrepreneurship. At the same time, the Innovator needs a strong personality to develop their idea, their intuition, to convince others. In order to assert that their ambition is to "organise world information" on the Internet, entrepreneur Sergei Brin needs an ego that is well above that of the average citizen. In the 1960s, while still a student at Yale, Frederick Smith wrote a paper imagining an overnight delivery service. He was 18 years old at the time, and he had already imagined the beginnings of what FedEx would become. The company would officially be established a few years later. Now recognised as the world's leading express delivery company, among the most respected for its integrity, respect for its employees and performance, the company would never have been what it is without the strong personality of its founder, who had intuited, before most people, a way to deliver at the fastest rate at the best price throughout the world. The same can be said about Herb Kelleher, the founder of Southwest Airlines, who alone, without even holding a pilot's licence, without even having acquired basic knowledge about the airline industry – he is a lawyer by training – succeeded in 1971 in challenging traditional companies in the sector such as American Airlines, Delta Airlines or Continental Airlines and his company became the leading airline company in just a few years. We can only imagine that the ego of the man who is considered the greatest innovator of all time, Thomas Edison, with over 1,000 patents in his name, must have been particularly significant. In fact, many of his inventions are controversial because they are also individual struggles for the recognition of the real authorship, as in the case of electricity, cinema, the light bulb or sound recording. Contemporary France has its fair share of entrepreneurs with strong convictions. For example, Alain Afflelou, who at the age of 24 opened his first opticians, and quickly became a leading name in the French optical landscape. And 19th century France saw the birth of many entrepreneurs, innovators who wanted to revolutionise an industry, a way of life. We have already mentioned several of them, but there is also Aristide Boucicaut who, in 1852, founded modern retail with the notion of the department store, with the introduction of innovative concepts: free entry and price display; dedicated periods for high-selling items (toys in December); sales periods; the possibility to exchange and return goods; worldwide catalogue sales; and the construction of the Lutetia hotel to welcome wealthy foreign customers. He was followed by Ernest Cognacq for La Samaritaine, and Xavier Ruel for the Bazar de l'hôtel de ville. We can add to this list Louis Hachette who, in addition to being one of the first French publishing houses, also innovated in terms of marketing and sales model. For instance, he was the first ever to offer booksellers the opportunity to send copies of all their publications, with the possibility of returning them if they were not sold. Alongside this, he also had the idea of setting up points of sale in railway stations.

Whether it is through the desire to bring electricity to every home, to make fast deliveries accessible to all, to contribute to the dissemination of knowledge through publishing or to organise the distribution of goods or global information, the Innovator must have a unique personality, driven by the belief that they are the only person who can do what they do and that they have *the* solution to a given problem. This is carried by their strong personality, their ego, their narcissism. They themselves do not necessarily want to be in the limelight: they want the focus to be on their proposal, their product, their service in the same way that the Philosopher wants the focus to be on their ideas. Without this deep belief, an *élan vital* to quote Bergson, the Innovator and the Philosopher would certainly not have the psychological resources to complete their mission. While their ideas are innovative, there is no saying if they were the only ones to ever have had them. However, they were the only ones who were driven by a desire so strong to succeed, to accomplish this mission, regardless of whether others before them have failed, of whether it does not make money, or even if it ends up costing a lot of money, what is important to them is that they have made a difference. They have contributed to the world, to progress, and they alone are the authors of this progress.

Irrepressible creativity

It is impossible to satisfy the ego. Like the barrel of the Danaids, it is a bottomless pit; as soon as it is filled it empties. As soon as a philosopher successfully puts forward an idea, which is accepted as a definitive truth, what will they do if they do not work on it again, if they do not work tirelessly to convince others? They will start again on a different theme. The Philosopher cloaks themselves in their supposed ability to tackle all subjects, all themes. Philosophy is universal. Aristotle wrote on almost every subject: biology;

physics; metaphysics; logic; poetics; rhetoric; economics. Plato wrote as much about politics as ethics, but through Socrates he addressed justice, passions, aesthetics among many other themes. Montaigne's *Essays* is a universal book, a series of questions, reflections and thoughts on wide ranging topics, from cannibalism and learning about death, to religion and justice, politics or education. In the contemporary space Michel Foucault tackles the issue of the abnormal as much as the issue of prisoners, knowledge as much as the issue of sexuality. Sartre was interested in Marxism as much as in existence, in freedom as much as in the soul, and it did not matter the medium on which his ideas were developed: an editorial; in a long essay; in a newspaper article; in academic journals (such as *La Nouvelle Revue Française*); in plays or in films; in an auditorium; or in the street.

The philosopher seizes whatever is available, they pick and choose what they like, or seize the opportunities of their time, select among the events unfolding before them. It is not about a particular subject; it is about a method. Sometimes it is not even a matter of being drawn to a particular field or a personal interest this may generate, but rather the challenge it represents, the difficulty: that is what the philosopher clings to. In other words, the Philosopher likes philosophy in and of itself, just as the Innovator likes innovation in and of itself. It is the taste for innovation, risk, discovery and development which stimulate them. This is the case of personalities like Richard Branson, Xavier Niel or Jack Ma, who have developed a galaxy of innovations which are almost limitless. Today Google is developing just as much in the field of the Internet as that of self-driving vehicles, artificial intelligence and navigation systems. Often, these innovators invest in other areas to take on new challenges, which is often how they end up delving into politics. As a country, the United States is particularly sensitive to this aspect, and its 45th president follows this tradition of entrepreneur-politician, and he is definitely not the first: Rudolph Giuliani, the former mayor of New York, is a well-known entrepreneur; so too was Mitt Romney, who was in the presidential race against Barack Obama; and more recently, the CEO of Starbucks, who, worried about the political trends of his country, expressed his ambition to get involved in this field.

Philosopher and Innovator: One lifestyle

There are many similarities in the temperament of the Philosopher and the Innovator: the need to satisfy their ego, the quest for progress, the solitude of the hero, being creative, questioning existence, delving into all topics, being a hard worker, etc. It may seem surprising that we can establish such a link between the Entrepreneur and the Philosopher: one is viewed as a speculative thinker, whose work does not contribute much, while the other is generally reduced to the predatory quest for profit at all costs. But when you analyse them closely, it is easy to see how such a view is reductionist and that there are, in fact, many ways in which philosophers and innovators are similar. The common characteristics which we have just established between these two types of individuals are indispensable, immutable, fundamental for anyone who is or aspires to be a Philosopher, or an Entrepreneur. Philosophers and entrepreneurs from all time periods, all continents, all industries and on any subject, share these distinctive characteristics.

This is not to say that the Innovator and the Philosopher are one and the same at all levels. These common traits should not obscure their singularities. Both are driven by a desire to accomplish something strong, deliver something unique so as to making life simpler in one way or another. However, the end purpose is not the same. For the former, this takes the form of new products, services, offers which make life materially more comfortable. The latter also seeks to make life simpler, but through the work of the mind, through the acquisition of wisdom and love. And this may be the crux of the matter. In the face of the major innovations which have been developing before our very eyes over barely a few decades, given the recent innovations which are disrupting mankind, humanity and the environment, given the almost uncontrollable nature of the developments under way, should it not be the responsibility of the Innovator to also take on in their endeavours a quest for wisdom and love? What if the work of the mind was also a duty, a criterion for the Entrepreneur in addition to their responsibilities? While there is no need for the Philosopher to acquire the spirit of the Innovator, even though some already possess it, we have an obligation to demand that the Innovator acquires the spirit of the Philosopher.

It is not a question of asking innovators to stop being who they are, it is a question of ensuring that the Innovator understands the consequences of their actions, that they understand that they can no longer act without the necessary discernment, without the responsibility to take care of themselves and others. Expertise, analysis, science, hypotheses and deductions are often the decision tools of the Innovator. However, they in no way remove the uncertainty of the offers they put on the market. There is an increasing need to take into account the risks which innovators themselves take – and those which they oblige their customers and sometimes society as a whole to take – in their decisions to launch their innovation. Such oversight cannot be achieved only through testing, or by surveys or studies. By its very essence, innovation surpasses their innovator. Social networks have long slipped out of the control of their creators; the now fast and inexpensive sequencing of DNA is in the hands of countless organisations and not just the scientists behind it; and that the early stages of cloning are now present on almost every continent. And it is not a question of waiting for new laws or regulations to govern innovation. Innovation comes before legislation, that is a fact. If neither legislative regulation nor scientific foresight has any influence on our future, how, then, should we proceed if we want this future to be humanely sustainable?

The Philosophical Choice of a Humanely Sustainable Future

Do we want a humanely sustainable future? More precisely, how is a humanely sustainable future preferable to one we do not know and which we condemn out of principle? Artificial intelligence frightens us because it has the potential to surpass our knowledge and intelligence. Cloning and transhumanism scare us because we are afraid of losing our identity. Big data disturbs us because we fear the end of our freedom. The same applies to the environment. We see global warming as a threat, the disappearance of species as a catastrophe and the melting of glaciers, the rise of oceans and the increase in greenhouse gas emissions as something terrifying and which should be avoided at all costs. Such a view, however, is somewhat conservative, or characterised by a certain degree of selfishness and anthropocentrism. Over the last 4.5 billion years, several million species have appeared on Earth. They developed, sometimes they became the majority, sometimes they became dominant, and then the same species disappeared. In fact, there is a very high likelihood that a very large number of species, whether plant or animal, existed at one point in time, but we simply have no trace of them, no fossils to prove it. Homo sapiens is but one of these multiple developments. This species to which we belong, along with 8.7 million other living species on Earth, is very recent: it is approximately 200,000 years old. To a certain extent, we can consider it is a dominant species since it has managed to conquer all territories, is developing massively and is more or less taking control of nature. Does that mean this species is immortal? That it is worth protecting over others? That it should not evolve, change, or rather, adapt to its environment, that is, innovate in the Latin sense of the term? Our species appeared some 200,000 years ago as a result of a long evolutionary process, which took us from being small algae, fish, simple vertebrates, to being mammals, before the first hominids emerged approximately 7 million years ago. More precisely, palaeontologists consider that the *Sahelanthropus tchadensis* are the first species of the human lineage, probably very close to the divergence between the *Panines* – including chimpanzees – and the *homo genus* – including humankind – with the emblematic Toumai. Since that time, several species of hominids have disappeared, such as the Neanderthal, the *homo floresiensis* or the Denisovans – an Asian group. This means we are currently the last survivors of the human race. This state of fact, however, is in no way definitive, because like these other species, in the more or less long term and no matter what we do, our species too will disappear or evolve into another form. This is one of the major ideas emphasised by Darwin in *On the Origin of Species*: species are not immutable; they continuously evolve according to their environment and their needs. This is something Aristotle had already argued, in particular in *On the Parts of Animals*, where he stated: *nature never makes anything superfluous or in vain*,[10] which clearly means that nature, according to Stagirite, adapts itself for a reason, through a teleology of the continuity of progression, of advancement.

In the last centuries, the human species has extended its life expectancy, our bodies have grown taller, major bodily changes have taken place, and all of this happened so that we could continue to survive. Why should this stop now, just to stay with the form we know? What could possibly justify this, other than our desire to keep things the way they are, our reluctance to change, our arrogance in considering that what we have experienced and what we currently experience is necessarily good and better than what could happen. Is it not fear which drives us to act this way? Is it not our pathological anthropocentrism which leads us to such conclusions? We want to have children, grandchildren,

---

[10]Aristote, *Les Parties des Animaux*, II, 691b Aristotle, *On the Parts of Animals, III*. Translated to English by William Ogle. Retrieved from http://classics.mit.edu/Aristotle/parts_animals.3.iii.html.

great-grandchildren who look like us, we want for all our descendants to be like us. This stems from our fear of our own disappearance, the fear of our individual death, which we end up accepting out of resignation – even if investments in health and transhumanism seem to indicate the opposite. The ultimate resistance we seem to demonstrate, which we strive to show in the face of death, is that at least our species will survive, with the infinite hope that with it, a small part of us will live on and that, by proxy, this will make us immortal. Nature does nothing in vain, as Aristotle reminds us, but this does mean that it does things "for us", humans. It does what it must do for its own survival as a living organism within a living cosmos.

In what way is the body we have today so preferable to the one we might have in several millennia when it will have adapted completely to the environment in which it exists? If, through adaptation, we have one organ less or more, limbs which are one shape rather than another, or a brain developed according to some characteristics rather than others, why would that be particularly troublesome?[11] Who are we to condemn or judge nature's own evolution? Of course, over and over again, species will disappear. However, every year, scientists discover an average of 16,000 new species, and it is estimated there are still between 8 and 30 million species yet to be discovered. The International Union for Conservation of Nature reported that every year, 25,000 living species of animals and plants disappear. We must humbly acknowledge that we are part of this evolution, this very evolution which, paradoxically, we admire, but condemn whenever it concerns us as a species.

This begs the question, why should we have to rethink innovation and its consequences? Why not adopt an approach of "laisser-faire", let mankind and nature be as they are, by accepting the Darwinian *struggle for existence*? If we finally accept that the evolution and adaptation of life are permanent – as opposed to our current desire for the immutability of the young *homo sapiens* species alone – and if we believe that we will adapt in one way or another, which is quite honourable, why, then, struggle to protect our species in vain? In order to attempt to answer this, we need to change our point of view, looking at the theory of evolution as a fact, but also as a contingency. The point of view to adopt would be that of Sirius,

---

[11]As such, the works of the artist Agatha Haines, in which bodily transformations are imagined according to the evolution of the environment, can be seen as absurd, disturbing or prospective.

the second brightest star in the sky after the sun, that is to say, with as much height as light, with as much benevolent generosity as wisdom. What is our species from the point of view of this star? Henry David Thoreau states that: *Indeed, could one examine this beehive of ours from an observatory among the stars, he would perceive an unwonted degree of bustle in these later ages. There would be hammering and chipping in one quarter; baking and brewing, buying and selling, money-changing and speechmaking in another. What impression would he receive from so general and impartial a survey. Would it appear to him that mankind used this world as not abusing it?*[12]

Of course, our species is only a young species which will undoubtedly become extinct, and will not be missed. Nevertheless, the reality of our existence, the very opportunity we have to exist, is the result of a long process, a convergence of conjunctions thanks to which we can live, enjoy, love, move, learn, play, if only for a few years, if only for a few tiny moments on the scale of time. This opportunity given to us, albeit as a result of chance developments, should not be wasted. Not so much for the human species as for all the species. In other words, our inevitable disappearance as a species does not necessarily mean that we must destroy everything in our path and despise the continuity of nature, even if this continuity is different from what we know. Yet, this is exactly what we do. While there have been millions of species since life began on Earth, overall, the human species is that whose damage and consequences constitute a very real threat for the planet and for the continuation of life in general. The human species has played with nature at the risk of destroying it. In fact, we can take this one step further: who are we to destroy which made us what we are? To what extent do we own the place from which we emerged. It is not about assigning blame, moralising or sentimentalizing when we say that we borrow Earth from our children and grandchildren. Nobody truly takes this into account since it is difficult to project oneself into what we do not know, or cannot see. As Dominique Bourg points out, our senses tell us nothing about environmental problems and

---

[12] Henry David Thoreau, *L'Esprit commercial des temps modernes et son influence sur le caractère politique, littéraire et moral d'une nation*. French translation by D. Bazy, Le Grand Souffle, 2007. p. 28. Henry David Thoreau, *The Writings of Henry David Thoreau, Volume VI, Familiar Letters*, F. B. Sanbonrn (ed.). Copyright 1865 By Ticknor And Fields, Copyright 1894 and 1906 By Houghton, Mifflin & Co. Retrieved from http://www.gutenberg.org/files/43523/43523-h/43523-h.htm.

ecosystems.[13] The challenge lies elsewhere, and it is twofold: on the one hand, to respect what we are and to enjoy being what we are; and on the other, considering that other species – even if not exactly ours, or not exactly the same – may have the right to enjoy it just as we enjoy it today. Certainly, with such an approach, our own species could probably extend its existence by only a few centuries, perhaps even stretching that to a few millennia, but this is not what really matters, because what is at stake here is the future of an ensemble of things which we inherit, and which we in turn will pass on. This is why the consequences of our actions during our time on Earth are so significant. Another, much more selfish, reason to adopt a more responsible attitude concerns our here and now. Of course, our desire to offer our descendants a world identical to ours in the future is salutary – even though, as already mentioned, nothing tells us that the one we live in today is preferable to a different, future world – but the question also arises for us, in the here and now, for the next few years, whether talking about 50 or 100 years. While the innovations of today and tomorrow may, hundreds of years from now, bring about a life very different from the one we know, they also have an influence in the here and now. In other words, the fact that exposure to WiFi waves may affect the human brain and change it in one way or another in the very long term in a definitive – and perhaps even beneficial – way, is one thing; refusing it because in the short term, in the now, it is harmful to oneself is quite another. It is likely that in the long term, our bodies will adapt to the ingestion of genetically modified organisms and will be able to consume them without any problem; however, it is our right not to accept to be the guinea pigs who are on the front line, who will be the first to get sick before our species adapts and can accept such foods. Of course, DNA sequencing offers obvious benefits insofar as it can help us anticipate medical conditions, enable us to adapt our diet, protect us against certain health risks, and maybe even totally eradicate diseases in the future. But today, in the here and now, should we accept blindly the fact that only a portion of the population can benefit from these developments because they have the means to access them? Does this mean that the future of mankind will be continental, tall and white? The issue of big data raises a similar quandary: what this data can lead to in the long term, with its beneficial effects which we do not question, but also the extent to which these can be harm-

---

[13]Dominique Bourg, COP21 – Climat : le thermomètre et le philosophe – Spécial 2° avant la fin du monde.

ful here and now. What we are arguing here is that innovation is not only uncertain in its overall effects, but that, for any given innovation, there can be major, fundamental differences between its long- and short-term effects. Accepting the evolution of our species, our own evolution, our adaptation and even our disappearance does not mean we have to blindly accept a here and now laden with disease, suffering and inequality.

Whether it is for short-term reasons like the ones we have just outlined, whether it is out of respect for what was given to us and what we need to do to ensure the continuity of species in general, or even whether it is to extend our own species for a few centuries, we need to take a new look at what we are doing in terms of innovation. We need to think about our responsibility. More particularly, the Innovator, who is tasked with the progress of the world, needs to think about this responsibility. In order to achieve this, the Innovator needs help, guidance, to question who they are, on the assumption that they do not know it himself. For centuries, the Innovator has been making, shaping. The first hominids used a stone as a tool, referred to as primary tools. Then emerged secondary tools, which were shaped by using another tool. This, for example, is the case of the flint knife which was a tool sharpened by being struck with a stone. For Bergson, this marked the beginning of Homo faber, who sees in this a link with the development of intelligence: *intelligence, considered in what seems to be its original feature, is the faculty of manufacturing artificial objects, especially tools to make tools, and of indefinitely varying the manufacture.*[14] What is the computer today if not a more sophisticated tool, developed by the hand of man, what Aristotle would describe as *the tool of tools.*[15] The Innovator is therefore a tool machine, a machine which produces the tool of tools. The Innovator makes, solves problems, but does so without considering the consequences of their actions. To continue our metaphor, they are not programmed to integrate a form of wisdom, of benevolence. However, this is necessary. And so, if we question who they are, their role, this is tantamount to "reformatting" them, so that its "processor" integrates this dimension of wisdom.

---

[14] Henri Bergson, *The Creative Evolution,* Translated to English by Arthur Mitchell, p. 139. Retrieved from https://www.gutenberg.org/files/26163/26163-h/26163-h.htm.
[15] Aristotle, *Treatise on the Soul*, Book II, Part I, Chap. VIII, 431b20 Aristotle, *On the Soul*, Translated to English by E.M. Edghill. Retrieved from http://homepage.westmont.edu/hoeckley/Readings/Phil%20texts/Aristotle/aristotle_anima_final.pdf.

Philosophy seems to be the preferable way to help the Innovator to become a benevolent innovator, and the Philosopher, therefore, is best equipped to help them in this evolution. Like a guide, a master, the Philosopher is the one who can enable someone to become someone else, help them to see who they are and how to act differently. In order to understand this, let us look back at the role of the Master in Ancient philosophy. The role of the Philosopher is to guide his disciple correctly towards knowledge and understanding, towards a form of savoir-faire and correct behaviour, to help his disciple answer the question: how else can I behave? The master's mission is to guide the disciple out of his state of *stultitia*. This is a fundamental notion of Stoicism and can be found in particular in Seneca's *Of Peace and Mind*.[16] *Stultitia* comes from *stultus*, meaning a person "who does not take care of himself". Therefore, *stultitia* is the condition of the person who fails to take care of themselves, before undertaking philosophy.[17] Seneca tells us that a *stultus* is a person blown about by every wind, who simply lets their mind accept whatever they experience, without evaluation or analysis.[18] With no memory or recollection of their actions, the *stultus* constantly changes their mind and lets life drift by without ever taking care of themselves.

In order leave this state, Seneca continues, the *stultus* has to have the desire to access the self. The difficulty, however, is that what characterises *stultitia* is precisely the inability of the *stultus* to rise out of this state, because they do not want to. *Stultitia* is defined precisely by this non-realisation of the self. If this realisation of the self is to succeed, it can only do so with the help of external guidance. The external individual will polarise the desire of the *stultus* to come out of this state *stultitia* and help them to become the master of themselves. The individual causing this self-realisation, the "operator" of change of the self, is the Philosopher. Whether among the Epicureans or the Stoics, only the Philosopher is capable of helping others by guiding them: *the philosopher is indeed the*

---

[16]Sénèque, De la tranquillité de l'âme, II, 6-15, trad. R. Waltz, cité par Michel Foucault, *L'Herméneutique du sujet*, Cours au Collège de France (1981–1982), Gallimard-Seuil, 2001, p. 126. Seneca, *Of Peace of Mind* (1900), Translated to English by Aubrey Stewart https://en.wikisource.org/wiki/Of_Peace_of_Mind From: L. Annaeus Seneca, Minor Dialogs Together with the Dialog "On Clemency"; Translated by Aubrey Stewart, pp. 250–287. Bohn's Classical Library Edition; London, George Bell and Sons, 1900.
[17]*Idem.*
[18]*Ibid.* II, 37-4, quoted by Michel Foucault, *L'Herméneutique du sujet, Op. cit.*, p. 127.

teacher and leader of men in all the things which are appropriate for men according to nature.[19] Philosophers guide in the understanding of how to behave and also how to guide others. Summarising the role of philosophy, Foucault states that philosophy *is a set of principles and practices which allow for the proper care of the self and other.*[20]

The Innovator does not know how to get out of their exclusive state of "producer of new proposals". As a result, they do not duly consider what they are doing, they are in a state of *stultitia* which blinds them. They are entrenched in a certain form of analysis which enables them to discern new ways of doing things, of acting, of progressing, of evolving, but they by no means integrate a benevolence which is foreign to them. And it is not just a matter of telling them to build responsibility, care, wisdom and respect into their innovations: they will hear such a request without knowing *how* to do what is asked of him. It is their education which needs to be reconstructed, it is their entire thought model which needs to be rethought, starting from the fundamentals, whose roots can be found in philosophy. The Innovator must die to re-emerge as the benevolent Innovator, the movement of creative destruction brought about by innovation must apply to the Innovator themselves, they must disappear in order for a new form of Innovator to emerge: the Innovator of the 21st century.

Understanding Philosophy

What is philosophy? This is certainly one of the oldest and most complex questions there is. The purpose here is not to address this question, and less still to attempt to formulate an answer. However, in the same way that we sought to rigorously explore the fundamental meaning of innovation, it seemed necessary to go back to the historical fundamentals of philosophy in order to evaluate what it is as well as its role and, consequently, its relevance for the Innovator. Philosophy is not subjective, abstract or vaporous. It is steeped in history and developed in a structured way.

---

[19]Musonius Rufus, fragment 15: "*hêgemon tois anthrôpois esti tôn kata phusin anthrôpô prosêkontôn*", Reliquiae, ed. O. Hense, p. 71, quoted by Michel Foucault, *L'Herméneutique du sujet, Op. cit.*, p. 130. Musonius Rufus, The Roman Socrates Lectures and Fragments, Translated to English by Cora E. Lutz.

[20]Michel Foucault, *L'Herméneutique du sujet, Op. cit.*, p. 131.

Knowing philosophy, understanding its fundamental principles show us its possible effects, but this is not enough. Philosophy is first and foremost an activity which should be practised in order to be fully effective.

The Greek origin of philosophy

As demonstrated by Jean–Pierre Vernant, the Messianic current appeared in the 6th century BC. Through Thales, Anaximander and Anaximene, emerges, as a revealed truth, what is referred to as the *Greek miracle.*[21] The term "philosophy" did not yet exist, as it only appeared in the 5th century BC, known as the *century of Pericles,*[22] with the adjective *philosophos*[23] in Heraclitus, as well as with the word *philosophia.* However, it is only with Plato and Aristotle that philosophy truly came into being. Plato defined the term in the 4th century BC, time at which "philosophy" was a very technical term. In the Neoplatonic commentaries to Aristotle's works, Plato defines philosophy firstly as what is, insofar as it is; secondly as *the knowledge of things divine and human*; thirdly as *the exercise of death*; fourthly as *the assimilation to God*; fifthly as *the art of the arts and the science of the sciences*; sixthly and lastly as *the love of wisdom.* These different definitions fell into three categories: the category of "theoretical" definitions for the first two; the category of "practical" definitions for the next two; and the category of "mixed" definitions for the third, fourth and sixth.[24]

The very notion of "philosophy" for Plato had a polemical connotation, because at the time, being a "philosopher" meant defying the Milesians, who limited themselves to the analysis of nature. To call

---

[21] Jean-Pierre Vernant, *Mythe et pensée chez les Grecs*, La découverte, 1996, p. 406. Our translation.

[22] It should be noted that, for Hadot, "the pre-Socratics of the 7th and 6th centuries BC, Xenophanes or Parmenides, and even probably, despite some ancient but very debatable testimonies, Pythagoras and Heraclitus, knew neither the adjective *philosophos* nor the verb *philosophein*, let alone the word *philosophia*" (Our translation). Pierre Hadot, Qu'est-ce que *la philosophie antique*, Gallimard, 1995, p. 35.

[23] Jean-Pierre Vernant, *Mythe et pensée, Op. cit.*, p. 404. Our translation.

[24] Definitions used by Elias, "Proleg. Philos" in *Commentaria in Aristotelem Graetica*, XVIII, 1, pp. 7, 26–29, quoted by Juliusz Domanski, *La Philosophie, théorie ou manière de vivre, controverse de l'Antiquité à la Renaissance*, Éditions du Cerf, 1996, p. 11. Our translation.

oneself a philosopher also meant distinguishing oneself from *sophos*, "sage", or *sophistēs*, "sophists", branded by Plato as masters in persuasion, with so-called universal competence.[25] This distinction stirred up difficulties and controversies, as we can see in the work of Jean-François Balaudé. Indeed, contrary to Plato's position, the fact of being a philosopher (*philosophos*), of formulating philosophical proposals (*philosophein*), was not initially conceptualised as being in opposition to wisdom, *Sophia*.[26] In order to understand this, we can turn to the research of Walter Burkert, who demonstrated that the word *philosophos* is composed of the root *phil-*, which does not mean love or the search for something lacking, but rather emphasizing the fact of "being acquainted with", having a connection with something present.[27] This would mean that there is no initial opposition between *philosophos* and *sophos*, contrary to what can be observed in Plato who, in *Phaedra* and *The Banquet*, places philosophers between knowledge and ignorance, as opposed to gods, who need not resort to philosophy, since they are already wise.[28] Burket's etymological interpretation opens up a positive dimension because, when combined with *Sophia*, the root *phil-* would indicate a type of knowledge. *Philosophia* would therefore suggest a certain "practice of knowledge". This is important, and opens up a rift between Socrates and Plato. For the former, the action of philosophising, *philosophein*, is geared towards self-improvement; the latter, however, proposes a program of knowledge.[29] Whereas, for Socrates, there is both a human sophia and a divine sophia, Plato *sets divine knowledge as the standard reference for human knowledge which leads to the distinction between philosophia and Sophia*.[30] Consequently, there is in Plato a kind of desire, a form of admiration for what one does not have, what is more, for what one cannot possess

---

[25]Nevertheless, it cannot be argued that there is no filiation between Milesian thought and philosophy. Aristotle sees in Thales, for example, "the initiator of this type of philosophy [materialism]". Aristotle, *Metaphysics*, 983 b 20, quoted by Jean-Pierre Vernant in *Mythe et pensée chez les Grecs*, *Op. cit.*, p. 405.

[26]Jean-François Balaudé, *Le Savoir-vivre philosophique*, Grasset, 2010, pp. 37–39.

[27]Walter Burkert, "Plato oder Pythagoras", *Hermes*, 88, 1969, pp. 159–177, analysed here by Jean-François Balaudé, *Le Savoir-vivre philosophique*, *Op. cit.*, p. 41.

[28]Plato, *The Banquet*, 204 a-d, trans. Léon Robin, Gallimard, *Bibliothèque de la Pléiade*, 1950, pp. 737–738.

[29]Jean-François Balaudé, *Le Savoir-vivre philosophique*, *Op. cit.*, p. 44.

[30]*Idem.* Our translation.

because it is accessible only to the gods. However, as Jean–François Balaudé summarises, for both of these philosophers the challenge remains *the achievement of the best in man, as a practical accomplishment which revolves around the quest for knowledge: for Socrates, knowledge of oneself and of what has value; for Plato, knowledge of the complete truth. For both, a knowledge to which humankind can but aspire.*[31]

Going back to the role of the Milesians in the origin of philosophy, it should be noted that their major contribution is the disembodied reading of myths. Relying on the immanence of nature, Milesians seek to go beyond the appearance of things, the permanent principles. Even though certain myths live on in thought and speech, there are no supernatural beings, and the elements such as water, earth, lightning, thunder, etc., are conceived of in positive terms. For Milesians; nothing exists, nothing has happened or will ever happen that is not found in *physis*.[32]

According to the Milesian school analysis, nature is perceived as a true reality, and the paths to understanding this reality must be revealed by the philosopher and their meditations. As Vernant said, this is the moment when philosophy supersedes religious thinking[33] while operating in the same frameworks of the invisible, of the contrast between the divine and the human, between mortal and immortal. The philosopher accesses the truth through an elitist initiation[34]; however, the philosopher's aim is not to preserve the ineffable, but rather to shed light on the questions of existence through dialogue and debate.

The history of the emergence of philosophy is also reported by Cicero in the introduction to Book V of *Tusculanae Disputationes*.[35] He explains that "philosophers" were originally called "wise men", *sapientes*. The famous Seven Wise Men of Ancient Greece were called *sophoi, sapientes* by their contemporaries, until Pythagoras. Heraclides Ponticus reported that tyrant Leonidas, astonished at the wisdom of Pythagoras, had asked him what his trade was. He replied that he had no profession, that he was a philosopher. Leonidas did not understand the meaning of the word, so

---

[31] *Ibid.*, p. 45. Our translation.

[32] Jean-Pierre Vernant, *Mythe et pensée chez les Grecs, Op. cit.*, p. 406.

[33] *Ibid.*, p. 409.

[34] *Ibid.*, p. 410.

[35] Cicero, *Tusculanes*, V, 3, 7–9, French translation by Émile Bréhier, Gallimard, 1962, Book V, § XVII. Cicero, *The Tusculan Disputations of Cicero*, W. H. Main, Leopold Classic Library, 2016.

Pythagoras replied metaphorically that human life is like the Panhellenic games in which three kinds of men participate: those who come to win glory; those who come to do trade; and those who come to watch. The latter are fewest in number, but are the noblest, as they seek neither glory nor wealth. Philosophers, Pythagoras then explained, are those who have come to this life from another life, not to gain glory and money, but with contempt for these so-called goods. Philosophers seek the nature of things, reality itself. As their name suggests, they "tend toward wisdom". Their nobility lies in the fact that their interest is solely to understand and contemplate the nature of things.[36]

Cicero points out that the evolution of the term "philosopher" was profoundly marked by Socrates, the first philosopher to divert philosophy from its interest in nature. Socrates re-introduces philosophy into the human environment, reducing it to ethical problems, with openness to the world as his primary concern. It is in this openness to the world which we can also read the origin of philosophy according to the Socrates-Platon dyad. For it is wonder which is the basis of philosophy. Socrates of the Theaetetus declares that *philosophy begins in wonder*,[37] for "*owing to their wonder that men both now begin and at first began to philosophise*".[38]

By departing from myths, and instead by being astonished, by aiming for the wisdom proposed by Pythagoras, philosophy becomes an attitude, a behaviour, a way of being. The contemplation of nature, the search for reality itself, the refusal of glory and wealth are all attributes which make anyone who devotes themselves to this a philosopher.

Philosophy, therefore, is the result of an evolution, of the many developments which have made it what it is today. However, looking back at its origin as we have just done, we can already identify some important notions relevant to the subject which concerns us here. As can be seen in

---

[36] Anne-Marie Malingrey, *Philosophia. Étude d'un groupe de mots dans la littérature grecque, des présocratiques au IVe siècle après J.-C.*, coll. « Études et commentaires », Klincksieck, 1961, pp. 29–30, cité par Pierre Hadot, in *Exercices spirituels et philosophie antique*, Albin Michel, 2002, p. 71.

[37] Platon, *Théétète*, 155d, trad. Léon Robin, Gallimard, "Bibliothèque de la Pléiade", 1950, p. 103. Plato, *Thecætetus*, Translated to English by Benjamin Jowett. Retrieved from http://www.gutenberg.org/files/1726/1726-h/1726-h.htm.

[38] Aristote, *Métaphysique*, 982 b 13. Aristotle, *Metaphysics*, 982 b 13. Translated to English by W. D. Ross. Retrieved from http://www.documentacatholicaomnia.eu/03d/-384_-322,_Aristoteles,_13_Metaphysics,_EN.pdf.

Pythagoras, philosophers are individuals who cultivate a contempt for wealth and material possessions, and who devote their life to finding the true nature of things, reality and truth, and tend toward wisdom. It is for these historical reasons, positions and foundations that philosophy still today is considered as detached from material goods, as a discipline of asceticism. This stands in stark contrast to entrepreneurs, who are not engaged in a quest for truth but rather in the production of ideas, goods which may generate profit in order to survive. That being said, as we have pointed out multiple times, such a view of the Innovator would be reductionist. The Innovator is not merely an individual focused on producing and increasing merchandise, they operate in many ways and fields, whether it is in politics, non-profit organisations, in religion or even in philosophy.

The fact that Socrates is careful to place philosophy in a human environment, and not simply as a contemplation of nature, is particularly relevant here because it shows the importance of ensuring philosophy does not stand alone, disconnected from the world of the common man. It is not the exclusive prerogative of a fringe of the population, but on the contrary, it takes hold in the real world. Like Socrates, who went to markets to meet others, the Entrepreneur is fully involved in everyday life, they are interested in real life. More precisely, we know that philosophy is above all a way of life, a permanent way of being. What we are advancing here is that the Innovator is also in a similar permanent way of life, but that the Innovator must also behave in a way which reconciles thought and actions, which is not necessarily the case today. Philosophy, for its part, has always revolved around thinking and doing in a singular way, which can be said of the spiritual exercises that we will detail later and which are perhaps key to the future of benevolent innovation.

The practice of philosophy: Articulating theōria and praxis

Philosophy is a way of life, which means that it has a direct hold on the world and does not exist only in its speculative form. However, while wonder is what led the first thinkers to philosophical speculation, this does not explain what said speculation is, and, even more importantly, its consequences.

The act of "doing philosophy" can only become a reality with its two facets, *theōria* and *praxis*. Since Plato, Domanski points out, there has been a *communis philosophorum opinio* which considers that, in order to be a true philosopher, it is certainly important to know how to lead one's life, but it is just as indispensable to live in full accordance with this knowledge: *The life of the philosopher, his behaviour, his personality thus constitute the fulfilment of the complete and integral notion of philosophy.*[39] Pierre Hadot also specifies that: *philosophical discourse is to be understood in the context of the lifestyle for which it is both the means and of which it is the expression. Consequently, philosophy is above all a way of life, but one which is intimately linked to philosophical discourse.*[40]

Theōria and *praxis* are two dimensions which are completely inextricable from philosophy, even if practice is what logically predominates since *in fine*, the goal is to know the best way to behave. Philosophy, therefore, is less of a discursive form than it is a way of life, as expressed by Socrates who, when asked for a definition of philosophy replied: "Rather than professing it, I express it through my actions".[41]

Theory is predominant and even necessary in philosophy, namely for the master who must teach, convey to their disciples the best way of being. Theory does not deal with the dogmas of the school of the Master, because these are indisputable, but rather with theoretical elaborations, which can be disputed.[42] Above all, there is a continuity between lifestyle and philosophical discourse. In fact, theory itself seems to be a practice. Discourse is an integral part of the way of life, it contributes, when the Master exposes it, to the inner transformation of the disciple who hears it, thereby helping their spiritual transformation.[43] Foucault highlights the use of texts as spiritual exercises which have a real effect – whether in the form of speeches, notes or interviews. He says, these texts are *written for the purpose of offering rules, opinions, and advice on how to behave as*

---

[39] Juliusz Domanski, *La Philosophie, théorie ou manière de vivre? Les controverses de l'Antiquité à la Renaissance, Op. cit.*, p. 11. Our translation.

[40] Pierre Hadot, *Qu'est-ce que la philosophie antique, Op. cit.*, p. 19. Translated to English by Michael Chase in Pierre Hadot, *What is ancient philosophy? Harvard University Press Chase. paperback edition*, 2004, pp. 2–4.

[41] Xénophon, *Mémorables*, IV, 4, 10, trad. L.-A. Dorion, « Collection des universités de France », Les Belles Lettres, 2003. Xenophon, *The Memorabilia: Recollections of Socrates*. Translated to English by H. G. Dakyns. Retrieved from http://www.gutenberg.org/files/1177/1177-h/1177-h.htm#link2H_4_0006.

[42] Pierre Hadot, "L'histoire de la pensée hellénistique et romaine. Leçon inaugurale au Collège de France", in *Exercices spirituels et philosophie antique, Op. cit.*, p. 275.

[43] Pierre Hadot, *Qu'est-ce que la philosophie antique, Op. cit.*, p. 22.

one should: "practical" texts, which are themselves objects of a "prac-
tice" in that they were designed to be read, learned, reflected upon, and
tested out, and they were intended to constitute the eventual framework of
everyday conduct. These texts thus served as functional devices that
would enable individuals to question their own conduct, to watch over
and give shape to it and to shape themselves as ethical subjects.[44] Note
here the use of the notion of "ethical subject", which is articulated with
"ethical substance", "ethical work" and is defined and developed in
History of Sexuality.[45] This "ethical subject" is particularly relevant with
our articulation of *theōria* and *praxis*, for it is the element, the component
of the individual which must be subjected to modification, work and
transformation. "Ethical work", then, is the form of the activity which the
subject carries out on himself. This work, in Greek and Roman philosophy, is expressed through, *enkrateia*, an activity of mastery of the self.
This ethical subject, in the Hellenistic and Roman period, is evidence of
an ethic which favours the sovereignty the self can have over itself.

This articulation between *theōria* and *praxis* enables us to understand
that the philosophers of Antiquity, up to a certain period – which is still
subject to debate – did not consider philosophy as a conceptual system but
above all as a practice.[46] Hierocles of Alexandria, for example, specifically articulates the necessary relationship between theory and practice so
as to enable a progression of the self, or more precisely, an elevation:
Practical philosophy [praxis] *has the power to generate virtue; contem-*
plative philosophy [theōria] *has the power to give us the truth* […]. *One*
must therefore first become man and only after want to become God.[47]

---

[44]Michel Foucault, "Usage des plaisirs, techniques de soi" in *Dits et écrits II, Op. cit.*,
p. 1365. Michel Foucault, *The Use of Pleasure, Vol 2 of The History of Sexuality*, Vintage
Books. A Division of Random House, Inc., New York, 1990, p. 13. Translated to English
by Robert Hurley. Retrieved from https://monoskop.org/images/a/a3/Foucault_Michel_
The_History_of_Sexuality_2_The_Use_of_Pleasure.pdf.

[45]Michel Foucault, *Histoire de la sexualité II. L'usage des plaisirs*, Gallimard, « Tel »,
1984, pp. 127–183. Michel Foucault, *The Use of Pleasure, Vol 2 of The History of
Sexuality*, Vintage Books. A Division of Random House, Inc., New York, 1990, p. 13.
Translated to English by Robert Hurley. Retrieved from https://monoskop.org/images/a/
a3/Foucault_Michel_The_History_of_Sexuality_2_The_Use_of_Pleasure.pdf.

[46]Pierre Hadot, "La philosophie antique : une éthique ou une pratique", in Paul Demont,
Problèmes de morale antique (dir.), université d'Amiens, 1993, pp. 7–37.

[47]Hiéroclès, *In Aureum Pythag. Carmen Comment, Prolog.*, 3, p. 6, 11 köhler. Traduction
de M. Meunier, in Hiéroclès, *Les Vers d'or*, Guy Trédaniel, 1925, (rééd. 1979), p. 41, cité

This interlinking of the two inseparable components of Ancient philosophy should help our understanding of the classic Greek philosophers, even if it is itself fraught with complexity. The texts which have been handed down to us cannot be read through the prism of conceptual philosophy, as they have been. Ancient philosophical writing cannot be transposed to the model of modern philosophical writing without the risk of error or misinterpretation. For this reason, although modern philosophical texts are now coherent, structured, articulated, this is not what one should look for in Ancient philosophy, where the written word is to be compared rather to a sum of themes and variations.[48] In order to fully comprehend classic thought, it is fundamental that it be situated in the living *praxis* from which it originated. In other words, as Hadot says: *In the background of Ancient philosophical writing, there is the life of a school, that is, the community of disciples to which the philosopher speaks; and there is a philosopher who speaks, not primarily to build up an edifice of concepts, but to form this group of disciples, either through discussion with them or through a lecture.*[49] Classic Greek philosophers are neither teachers nor writers, they are men with a certain lifestyle – which they have chosen voluntarily – and who live *among* their fellow citizens without however living *like* them. Their behaviour, their morals, their outspokenness, the way they eat and dress are singular. Merleau–Ponty, whom Hadot sees as a contemporary philosopher implementing a practical philosophy, also states that, *In order to understand the total function of the philosopher, we must remember that even the philosophical writers whom we read and who we are have never ceased to recognise as their patron a man who never wrote, who never taught, at least in any official chair, who talked with anyone he met on the street [...], we must remember Socrates.*[50]

Moreover, the Ancient writings which we are exploring here are to be read through the prism of teaching, and must necessarily be associated with the spoken word: *With regards to philosophical teaching, writing is*

---

par Juliusz Domanski, *La Philosophie, théorie ou manière de vivre, Op. cit.*, p. 16. Our translation.

[48] Pierre Hadot, "La philosophie antique : une éthique ou une pratique", *Op. cit.*

[49] *Idem.* Our translation.

[50] Maurice Merleau-Ponty, *Éloge de la philosophie*, inaugural lesson at the Collège de France, Gallimard, 1960, p. 39. Maurice Merleau-Ponty, *In Praise of Philosophy and Other Essays*, Translated to English by John Wil and James Edie, Northwestern University Press, p. 34.

only a reminder.[51] Philosophy is above all oral, real teaching is oral, because only the spoken word allows for dialogue and discussion. Disciples can discover the truth only through the game of questions and answers with their Master, who adapts their discourse according to their disciples, according to the questions they raise. Moreover, philosophical writings are often only an extension of oral teaching, sometimes merely as *aide-mémoires*. The image often used for understanding how these writings ought to be used is that of the "toolbox" (or "dagger"). The individual must build up their own toolbox of precepts, dogmas and principles by themselves. This toolbox inherently personal, shaped by each individual according to their fears, what haunts them and the obstacles they dread, in order to master it, to better understand it, use it. They should carry it with them at all times, always keeping it in mind, so that they can use it in their everyday life, whenever the circumstances call for it. They can "pull it out" and choose the right tool when faced with a particular challenge. This image of the toolbox being useful in the face of difficulties can be found in various forms, through various metaphors, in each of the Ancient schools, be they Stoic, Epicurean or Cynical.

Classic Greek philosophers refused to consider philosophical activity as intellectual, theoretical and formal. For them, it was above all else a practice which is determined through spiritual exercises, as we will discuss later. This is important because it should be noted that philosophy, in its essence, is a practice, an implementation. What matters is not so much philosophical speculation as the actions we carry out on a daily basis. More explicitly, we do not ask of a human resources director, a politician, an innovation manager, a head of department in a hospital or a CEO to quote a philosopher, to have philosophical knowledge or to have graduated in philosophy; we expect this person to act according to his area of competence. We ask that his behaviour, his personality, be in accordance with philosophy, a quest for wisdom. In other words, to paraphrase the "father" of philosophy, within an organisation, anybody who wants to or claims to be "responsible" or "caring" must demonstrate this through actions.

Anyone can claim to be responsible, benevolent, and that they care for others, but one cannot claim they are endowed with these characteristics without showing this through actions, without establishing themselves, Foucault tells us, as an ethical subject with rules. In the defence of those

---

[51]Pierre Hadot, "L'histoire de la pensée hellénistique et romaine", *Op. cit.*, p. 275. Our translation.

who do not act in this way, and contrary to the Classic Greek philosophers, there are no precise rules to follow, no guidance telling them how to behave, no master to bring them back to the right path.

What is also useful in this understanding of philosophy, in the articulation between *theōria* and *praxis*, is the constant back and forth between theory and implementation. For it is not a question of acting without knowing, of being responsible only according to what one believes to be responsible. It is to conform to established knowledge, rules, theories and ideas. This means that anyone who has the ambition to carry out a responsible activity must constantly be influenced and nourished by knowledge which enables them to act "correctly". And it is often the Master who plays this role.

The Challenge of Spiritual Exercises

If we understand the origin of philosophy through the "Greek miracle", with the wonder of the first men destined to understand the world that was taking shape, philosophy as a path to wisdom should in no way be detached from everyday life. There is a fundamental dimension of practice, of implementation. This was a challenge for classic Greek philosophers: how to associate *theōria* and *praxis*? How to make philosophy practical in everyday life? But most importantly, how can it help us forge better lives? The answer lies in what Pierre Hadot called spiritual exercises.

Spiritual exercises: The essence of philosophy

Ancient philosophy as a whole is a spiritual exercise, an expression which designates any practice intended to transform, in oneself or in others, the way of living, of seeing things. It is both a discourse, whether internal or external, and a practical application. It is in these terms that Pierre Hadot describes the philosophy of Antiquity which, in the tradition of classic Greek philosophers, he considers is as a discipline designed to help people lead better lives, to become better, to enjoy what they are experiencing rather than living subject to their passions which will never be fulfilled.[52]

---

[52] First published in the *Annuaire de la Ve section de l'École pratique des hautes études*, vol. XXXIV, 1977, pp. 25–70, then reprinted in the journal *Études augustiniennes*, 1981,

This notion of spiritual exercise was developed within the different schools of Antiquity, mainly among the Stoics, but also the Epicureans and Cynics, who developed techniques and methods in order for everyone to achieve a greater state of being. All of them take as their central focus man and his serenity, man in harmony with the awareness that life is short and that life is uncertain, that existence is punctuated daily with woes, ailments and hurdles and it is a question of knowing how to overcome them.

The practice of philosophy as a spiritual exercise flowed through Antiquity, from the Hellenistic period until the advent of Christianity, when philosophy was partly taken over by religion and became a discipline at the service of God. Pierre Hadot, as well as Michel Foucault, show in particular that Christianity did not forge its own spiritual exercises until the dawn of the second century, when it sought to establish itself as a competitor to Greek philosophy. However, and as a direct result of this "confiscation", an alternative to religion developed for *those who cannot or do not want to live according to a religious way of life: the possibility of choosing a purely philosophical way of life.*[53]

In order to grasp the full significance of the term "spiritual exercise", it is important to examine each of the two terms which make up this expression. The word "exercise" finds its etymology in the Latin *exerccitium* and means "the act of training someone to something" or "developing a skill". Classical definitions of this word show that exercise can be about the body – exercising your body to do something, a walk, stretching, etc. – or the mind – doing a memory exercise, for example. The notion of exercise is intimately linked to the notion of work, practice, repetition, and also learning. These elements are important, because "repeating", "training", "learning", are the fundamental actions, the very pillars of the implementation of spiritual exercises. Nevertheless, "practising", "exercising" must, like all occupations, have a meaning, a purpose. Before you even begin to practice something, you have to define the end, the why, justify what you want to be or become through said exercise.

---

pp. 13–58. This article was later published in Pierre Hadot, *Exercices spirituels et philosophie antique*, Albin Michel, 2002, pp. 19–74. We will refer to this latest edition later on. See also Pierre Hadot, *La Philosophie comme manière de vivre*, Albin Michel, 2001, p. 149. Pierre Hadot, *Philosophy as a way of life*, translated by Michael Chase, Blackwell, 1995.

[53] *Ibid.*, p. 70. Our translation.

As the Stoic Epictetus said, whether speaking about a "distance runner", a "carpenter" or a "blacksmith", there must always be a relation between what is being done, and why it is being done.[54]

The term spiritual is a little more complex to define. The notion of spiritual pertains to the immaterial, the soul, the nature of the spirit. It is an activity of the mind, where there is no mention of reason, yet it is not excluded. It becomes one with our sensory perceptions, and at the same time with our metaphysical concerns, from the self to its environment, others, the world. Religion, particularly Christianity, used the term "spiritual" early and extensively to refer to the relationship of the spirit, the soul, with God. However, it must be remembered that the relationship to the soul is not exclusively determined by religion or by God.

All which is spiritual is also free. In fact, Churches have always been suspicious of spirituality, confiscating it from men, as Paul Lombard reminds us.[55] It is precisely because spirituality means freedom, both individual and subjective, that religions have wanted to control it. It can lead to God, just as it can lead to ignorance of God's existence. This freedom gave rise to religions without God and, clearly, there can be spirituality without a God.[56] From there, the notion of spirituality is neutral with regard to that of "faith in God"; spirituality is the exploration and questioning of one's own individual, inner-life. In that sense, then, it is dissociated from religious faith, which is external because it refers to a transcendent God, as Pastor Alain Houziaux explains: *Spirituality is a preoccupation of the inner and private life, whereas faith, referring to a transcendent God, is extroverted, reaching for a transcendental force.*[57]

Spirituality, therefore, seems to be something unknown, but not for the self. Spirituality is knowable by the self and through the self, it is not based on anything external to the self; it is a subjective experience which is lived from within. This distinguishes it from religions, which manifest

---

[54]Épictète, *Entretiens*, in *Les Stoïciens*, trad. Émile Bréhier, Gallimard, « Bibliothèque de la Pléiade », 1962, p. 1015. Epictetus, *Discourses, Fragments, Handbook*, translated by Robin Hard, Oxford University Press; Critical ed. Edition, 2014.

[55]Paul Lombard, "Existe-t-il une spiritualité sans Dieu?", in Alain Houziaux (dir.), *Existe-t-il une spiritualité sans Dieu?*, Éditions de l'Atelier, 2006, p. 48.

[56]Numerous articles explore this, see journal *Esprit*, "Le temps des religions sans Dieu", No. 233, June 1997.

[57]Alain Houziaux, "La mort de Dieu et le renouveau de la spiritualité", in A. H. (dir.), *Existe-t-il une spiritualité sans Dieu?*, *Op. cit.*, p. 15. Our translation.

themselves in external rites, myths and dogmas. Religion is, in fact, the externalisation of gestures, behaviours, conventions. Spirituality is individual, sensitive to emotions, eccentric in relation to itself, but always internal, and it is this dimension which is crucial. Spirituality, moreover, is firmly rooted in life, which clearly brings it closer to the notion of "living the best life possible", for it can accept, even demand, a form of discipline, a form of asceticism with the aim of living life as fully, as intensely as possible. *If [spirituality] accepts a form of discipline and sometimes even asceticism, it is to better explore all the possibilities of existence with its affects, contradictions and passions* explains Houziaux.[58]

These remarks show that the association of the words "spiritual" and "exercise" suggests that these are "exercises" which require work, practice; and that this is 'spiritual" work for the soul. For classic philosophy, this relationship to the soul is orchestrated through work on the self but seeing this as human. For religions, this relationship to the soul serves only one objective: God. However, there are many more possible stances: the soul, the spirit and spirituality are not the preserve of religions and originally do not in fact appear in any religion.

Spiritual exercises seek to address two important issues: the importance of taking care of oneself on the one hand, and preparing for what may happen on the other. Spiritual exercises are therefore intended to help us to live better, enjoy life more, or to endure life as best we can. By associating discourses which can be internal or external with a practice, they work to ensure that what is of concern to mankind can be resolved.

Elevating one's existence

It is important to keep in mind that spiritual exercises are only tools, they are not an end in themselves. The end is to evolve towards inner freedom, a state in which the self depends only on itself. An "I" who has taken care of self in order to reach this point, and who continues to take care of self in order to elevate itself. In order to understand this, we must understand that the self exists on three levels.[59] The first is that of the sensory

---

[58] *Ibid.*, p. 19. Our translation.
[59] Pierre Hadot, *La Philosophie comme manière de vivre, Op. cit.*, p. 140.

consciousness, which comprises one single entity with the body. The consciousness and the body merge in a way which ultimately leads to the spirit being forgotten or even denied. For example, this is the case of infants who, when hungry, start crying until they are fed. They have no capacity for resistance, no capacity for reflection allowing patience. The second level of the self is the awareness of the soul, and so of the self's capacity for reflection. This is the acknowledgement of a first distinction, a first separation of the elements which make up the individual. This level opens the way to a first contact between the self, the mind and the body. We could say here that it is the ordinary person who is aware that they have a capacity for reflection, that they are not just a body. While the infant is only a "body" which seeks to grow and develop, older children, adolescents and adults are capable of thinking, of contemplating and discerning things around them. The third and final level is that of spiritual consciousness. The self fully understands that over and above the distinction between spirit and body, there is also a form of transcendence which transcends the self and yet at the same time of which the self is aware. The individual is aware that they can work on themselves, there is a transcendence to which they aspire. In no way does understanding the existence of this transcendence limit a certain form of immanence of the body, of the mind, and of the individual in general. Immanence and transcendence are not opposed to each other, and it is at this third level of "self" that this can be grasped. First there is becoming aware of one's own consciousness and understanding that this has multiple dimensions, and thereafter comes the understanding of the possibility of working on and having an influence on these dimensions.

The essential thrust of philosophy, and of spiritual exercises, is to elevate individuals from the first to the third level. Spiritual exercises provide a number of techniques and methods for achieving this, and will enable the ordinary person, naturally unaware of their own complexity, to reach a certain level of spiritual maturity. Progressing from the path of self-ignorance, this level of maturity will lead to the path of self-realisation. For this realisation of self to succeed guidance is required. This was the role of the Master, whose role is to guide the disciple towards knowledge and understanding, to a form of know-how and behaviour. The Master's mission is to guide their disciple out of their state of *stultitia*.[60]

---

[60] Sénèque, *De la tranquillité de l'âme*, II, 6–15. Seneca, *Dialogues and Essays*, translated John Davie, Oxford University Press, 2009.

With no memory or recollection of their actions, the *stultus* constantly change their mind and lets life drift by without ever taking care of themselves. They are all around us, they are not capable of forming an opinion for themselves, fail to develop a critical mind with regard to what they hear or see. Such individuals vote because they are told to without questioning this act, or rush into work for hours on end without ever contemplating that life could be otherwise.

At what level does the "self" of the Innovator lie? Are they not like the infant, not yet capable of questioning themselves, who do without thinking about the consequences? The hungry infant throws themselves on their bottle without thinking about whether or not it is good for them. Even when overweight or suffering from diabetes, for example, a baby will continue to want to eat as much as possible and will cry if something which could fill him up is taken away. Is this not similar to the Innovator who, without thinking, endlessly continues to innovate, to launch products and services, as long as it is possible. Irrespective of environmental issues, irrespective of the social consequences, the Innovator feels compelled to generate maximum profits, collect as many subscriptions as possible, garner as many votes as possible, etc. Most innovators are currently at this stage. For the Innovator, the second level would be to become aware of what they are insofar as how they relate to a body: the organisation to which they belong. Whatever its form, it is a social body, a political body, and it needs to recognise itself as such in society because it acts, interacts with others and must take them into account in its daily relations, its consequences and its endeavours. Finally, the third level of the Innovator's self, the level we aspire to here, is a state which enabled us to understand that innovation has a determining role in society, that it plays the role that no other discipline, no other "technique" plays, and consequently confers rights, but above all duties and responsibilities. The Innovator must therefore imagine how to succeed in getting raising out of their *stultitia* which confines them to the first level of the self, so as to enable them to reach a decisive role in the second and third stages. They must be able to become aware of their actions, to act responsibly. This is a form of transcendence which allows the Innovator to elevate themselves, to gain perspective on the issues they can solve or address with the innovation they are developing. In this, the Master plays a decisive role, as does education. However, the Innovator must first and foremost understand that they need to take care of themselves.

The need to take care of self

Taking care of self is a determining expression in philosophy because while the techniques and methods provided by spiritual exercises are key to living a better life, we must never forget that, above all else, primary target of these exercises is our attitude to self. To understand this idea, we must twist the common notion of what we mean by knowing ourselves. *Know thyself* is not so much a matter of knowing oneself but rather a matter of care of self, *epimeleia heautou*, to care for oneself, which is a fundamental notion in Greek culture as a whole.

Taking care of oneself is the act of taking care of the self. This notion has been obscured by that of *gnôthi seauton*, "know thyself",[61] Foucault, Courcelle, Roscher, Defradas and Vernant all agree that *"know thyself"* might not have had a philosophical meaning, but rather was a demand for self-awareness on the part of those who came to consult a god or the oracles of Apollo. This was to be understood as a rule, a guidance stemming from the very essence of the consultation. This formula means that we must remember that we are mortals and not a god, and that we should not overestimate ourselves *vis-à-vis* ourselves as well as the deities. But it did not go any further. Taking care of self, on the contrary, is a way of being, a way of life.

Nevertheless, a connection can be established between "know thyself" and "self-care"[62] insofar as both imply being concerned with self. This does not mean learning to know oneself, nor is it introspection, but rather it is assuming self as agent, understanding I am the subject of action in response to outside events or my environment. Caring for self does not mean disconnecting oneself from the world and from others. Quite the contrary, it means accepting our responsibilities through our actions. Therefore, Epictetus is talking about "self-care" when he discusses the need to question what might be one's responsibilities at home as a father, or in society as a citizen.[63] This phenomenon reflects the co-existence of the importance of knowing oneself as an agent engaged in the life of an organisation, and of taking care of oneself in order to fulfil the missions of that organisation.

---

[61] Michel Foucault, *L'Herméneutique du sujet, Op. cit.*, pp. 3–20.
[62] *Idem.*
[63] *Ibid.*, p. 56.

The concern for self in Antiquity is a way of life, a form of life, which one follows throughout one's life, because, for classic Greek philosophers, *"one must be for oneself, and throughout one's existence one's own object"*.[64] Epicurus therefore advocates philosophising throughout life to take care of oneself, and the Stoic Musonius Rufus or Galen also explains that: *"To become an accomplished man, each individual needs to exercise, as it were, his whole life through,"* even if it is true that it would be better *'to have looked after his soul from his earliest years.*[65] This is reflected when Socrates recommends to Alcibiades to take care of himself while he is still young, because, at 50 years of age, it would be too late.[66] Indeed, Socrates is the one who encourages others to take care of themselves, to be concerned with themselves rather than in knowing themselves. He says: *Oh my friend, why do you who are a citizen of the great and mighty and wise city of Athens, care so much about laying up the greatest amount of money and honour and reputation, and so little about wisdom and truth and the greatest improvement of the soul, which you never regard or heed at all? Are you not ashamed of this?*[67]

This concern for self did not appear spontaneously in Greek philosophy; rather, it is what is called a common principle. This concern for self was at the centre of Ancient Greek culture stemming from a Lacedemonian sentence, as Plutarch reports. Alexandride, a Lacedemonian, who was once asked: *Alexandridas, the son of Leo, ... when asked why they let their Helot slaves cultivate the fields, and did not take care of them themselves, replied, "Because we acquired our land not caring for it but for ourselves".*[68]

---

[64]Michel Foucault, « Le sujet et le pouvoir », *Op. cit.*, p. 1175. Michel Foucault, *Critical Inquiry* 8(4), 1982, 777–795. https://www.jstor.org/stable/1343197?seq=1.

[65] Michel Foucault, *Le Gouvernement de soi et des autres, course at the Collège de France, 1981–1982*, Gallimard-Seuil, 2008, p. 44. Michel Foucault, *Ethics: Subjectivity and Truth: Essential Works of Michel Foucault 1954–1984*, Edited by Paul Rabinow, Translated to English by Robert Hurley and others.

[66]Platon, *Alcibiade*, 133c.

[67]Platon, *Apologie de Socrate*, 29d Plato, *Apology*, 29d, Translated to English by Benjamin Jowett http://classics.mit.edu/Plato/apology.html.

[68]Plutarque, Œuvres morales, t. III, trad. F. Fuhrmann, Paris, Les Belles Lettres, 1988, pp. 171–172. Plutarch, "Laconic apothegms", in *Plutarch's Morals*, translated by several hands. Corrected and revised by William W. Goodwin with an Introduction by Ralph Waldo Emerson. Boston, Little, Brown and Co. (based on 5th ed. of 1718), Volume 1.

It should be noted that the concept *epimeleia heautou* is fundamental throughout all Hellenistic and Roman philosophy: among the Epicureans who advocate that every man, night and day, and throughout their life, must take care of their own soul[69]; among the Cynics or the Stoics – Seneca, for example, for whom the Latin notion of *cura sui* is capital throughout his Letters. Taking care of self, then, leads to undertaking a certain number of acts that one exercises on oneself: meditation, memorisation, examination of consciousness – with a view to self-modification, purification or transformation.

It is important to re-introduce the philosophy of spiritual exercises into the heart of society, at the heart of organisations in all the forms these may take. And the issue of concern for self is a demonstration of this. The philosophy of yesterday and that of today alike are not only found only in gardens and Acropolis or high schools and academies. It must be permanently present in all strata of society. Epicurus, Musonius and Socrates warn very clearly about the importance of caring for self, of caring about oneself. Because if you do not take care of yourself, then you cannot develop, there can be no reflection on what is being done. And this is true throughout all stages of life. Through spiritual exercises, practices such as meditation, examination of consciousness, memorisation, among many others, we can begin to take care of self through this necessary introspection. As Epictetus points out, the idea is not to remove oneself from the world, but on the contrary, to understand what role to play in the world. What are the duties the Innovator must understand in order to be able to carry them out? This question is only possible with the awareness of the need to take care of self.

Caring for others

This notion of self-care does not always have a very positive connotation, because of how it places the individual's self at the centre of its own existence. The individual obviously exists in the group and the collective, but the group must not annihilate the individual. This is illustrated in the words attributed to the Cynic Diogenes of Sinope: *When you worry about*

---

[69]Épicure, *Lettres et Maximes*, trad. M. Conche, Éditions de Mégare, 1977, chap. 122, p. 217. Epicurus, *The Essential Epicurus: Letters, Principal Doctrines, Vatican Sayings, and Fragments*, Prometheus Books, 1993.

another, then you neglect yourself.[70] It is a question of bringing to the fore the individual as it relates to the existence of different entities which make up a group. This is quite different from the egoist, who only defends their own good. An interesting example for understanding individualism is the motto of the Comédie–Française troupe *Simul et singulis*,[71] be together and be oneself. There is the troupe, the group; there are actors, a multiplicity of individuals, a multiplicity of "selves". Within this group of "selves", there can be no egoist, an individual thinking only of his own interests, because this would jeopardise the balance of the troupe. There cannot be an individual who thinks only of themselves and their own success because the very principle of the troop is obviously joint success. Nevertheless, each individual actor, all actors, must exist in and of themselves in order to live and develop fully. It is not a question of erasing the individuals and only bringing out the notion of the troop because these individuals are precisely what make up the troop. If the troop is only considered as an entity, the individuals which comprise it feel diminished or even non-existent, considered as equivalent to any other. Individualism not only has its place, but is a fundamental path to a perfect balance between self and others, self and community.

Epimeleia is also about taking care of someone. It is a certain form of solicitude, and this applies as much to the shepherd towards his flock as it does to the shepherd towards his family. This is the case of the doctor who is *epimeleisthai* in his recommendations, in his advice, in his care. It is also about taking care of oneself, it is the goal of Socrates who takes care of others so that they can learn to take care of themselves.[72]

It is above all through dialogue that concern for others can emerge, for it is through dialogue that we can become aware of a point of view other than our own. When dialoguing, we must go beyond our own vision to submit to the requirements, to the objectivity of the reason which emerges from discussion. What is fundamental in dialogue, and therefore in the interaction with others, is not so much the result obtained as the journey of the different actors, between the disciple and the Master, for example.

---

[70]Léonce Paquet, *Les Cyniques grecs, fragments et témoignages*, Le Livre de Poche, 1992. p. 114. Translated to English by Robin Hard in *Diogenes the Cynic: Sayings and Anecdotes*, London, OUP, 2012, Saying 275, p. 63 (Stobaeus 2.31.61: G315).
[71]https://www.comedie-francaise.fr/en/the-pillars#.
[72]Platon, *Apologie de Socrate*, 29d, Plato, *Apology of Socrates*, 29d.

The challenge of dialogue is above all to achieve common progress, through successive agreements between interlocutors, as does Socrates.[73]

It is also important to note the possible shift from dialogue with others to dialogue with oneself, by speaking to oneself aloud for example, which is what the Sceptic *Pyrrho does*. In doing so, he said he was practicing being useful.[74] It is also the case of Cleanthes, who criticised himself aloud.[75] Epictetus, for his part, proposed as an exercise to walk alone and therefore be able to converse with oneself.[76] In this practice, once again, the aim is to reach an objective universality, to distance oneself from the self, to talk to oneself in order to gain a better understand of this self.

What the relationship to others, care for others, demonstrates is the need for the care of self in order to establish a relationship with others. Without the first principle, the relationship with others can be neither true nor good. This has daily consequences, for example, the Stoic Musonius questions the concern for the other at the time of marriage, because in this event, the concern for oneself engages the concern for the other, it is a process of extension of the relationship that one has with oneself towards the other. If we are not engaged in a regular process where we care about ourselves, then establishing a relationship with others will be all the more complicated.

While the Innovator can be alone, solitary in their will to change the world, they are not alone in their actions. All innovations have consequences, as we have pointed out with responsible innovation. If they have to take care of themselves, it is also because they have to take care of others. In fact, they take care of themselves by taking care of others who are part of their own community of human beings, of their ecosystem among living beings. And they must of course understand that their

---

[73] Michel Foucault, *Histoire de la sexualité III. Le souci de soi*, Gallimard, "Tel", 1984. Michel Foucault, *The Care of Self*, Penguin Books, Limited, 2006.

[74]Diogène Laërce, *Vies et sentences des philosophes illustres*, IX, 64, trad. Jacques Brunschwig, Le Livre de poche, 1999, p. 1101. Diogenes Laërtius, *The Lives and Opinions of Eminent Philosophers*. Translated to English by C. D. Yonge.

[75]Diogenes Laërce, *Lives and Sentences of Illustrious Philosophers*, VII, 171, trans. Richard Goulet, *Op. cit.*, p. 894. Diogenes Laërtius, *The Lives and Opinions of Eminent Philosophers*. Translated to English by C. D. Yonge.

[76]Épictète, *Entretiens*, III, 14, 1, *Les Stoïciens*, trad. Émile Bréhier, Gallimard, « Bibliothèque de la Pléiade », 1962. p. 990. Epictetus, *The Moral Discourses of Epictetus*, translated to English by Elizabeth Carter.

primary action is to dialogue with those around them. It is because they will speak with those which make up their community that the Innovator will understand the demands and needs of their community, but also become aware of possible risks and concerns. The Innovator must constantly be in a Socratic process of discussion and dialogue with others. Once more, it is not about being right, but rather to seek agreement, mutual consent between risks and opportunities. Today, the lack of dialogue between the Innovator and society results in a form of recklessness, a lack of concern, when what is needed is a shared path so as to ensure the best innovations for all, for the benefit of all.

The need to ready oneself

The purpose of spiritual exercises, then, is to help mankind to live better in the face of the obstacles it may come up against by means of dialogues, techniques and methods. This is entirely consistent with the objective of taking care of self, for taking care of self is also intended above all to prepare oneself, the *paraskhuê*, which Seneca translates as *instructio*. The idea is to be prepared for external events, the hazards of life. "What is it to be a Philosopher? Is it not to be prepared against Events?" asks Epictetus.[77]

Whatever the philosophical school you belong to, you "prepare", "ready" yourself by following a number of dogmas. Strictly speaking, this is the philosophy of the school to which we belong. For the Stoics, one of the main issues is self-control in all circumstances: learning to master one's passions such as accepting everything which happens as conforming to a universal order which is that of nature, in other words, accepting that some things depend on us and others do not. Epictetus puts it this way: *Seek not that the things which happen should happen as you wish; but wish the things which happen to be as they are, and you will have a tranquil flow of life.*[78] The Stoics consider it is necessary to prepare for what may happen in order not to be destabilised by it, thus Marcus Aurelius announces: *When you wake up in the morning, tell yourself: the people*

---

[77]Épictète, Entretiens, III, 10, 6, 1, Les Stoïciens, *Op. cit.*, p. 982. Epictetus, *The Moral Discourses of Epictetus*, translated to English by Elizabeth Carter.
[78]Epictetus, *Handbook*, Chap. VIII. Translated to English by George Long. Retrieved from http://pioneer.chula.ac.th/~pukrit/bba/Epictetus.pdf.

I deal with today will be meddling, ungrateful, arrogant, dishonest, jealous and surly.[79] This, of course, is to prepare for death, having it before our eyes every day to tame it, not fear it, and remember that we are going to die.

For Epicureans, it is a matter of "readying oneself" to take care of one's soul, in order to bring about a better life. In order to achieve this, it is necessary to follow several proposals. One of the most fundamental of these articulates that life is based on the pleasure and the avoidance of displeasure, ataraxia – dietary frugality in particular. For Epicureans, pleasure is easy to obtain, because it is a matter of having very few needs: to provide only for the natural and necessary desires to live happily – to eat and drink with simplicity, to have a modest dwelling, to dress soberly. This is in contrast to natural and unnecessary desires – including sexual activity – and to unnatural and unnecessary desires – such as the search for power, for example. Another important proposal found in Epicurus is the *tetraphamarkos*, the "four-part remedy". He explains that four principles are to be observed in order to live happily: do not fear god; do not worry about death; what is good is easy to get; what is terrible is easy to endure.

Finally, for Cynics, taking care of self goes through self-sufficiency. For them, pleasures and passions are deceptive, harmful and ephemeral, and therefore should be avoided. One must also beware of fortune, power and property which are elements to be handled with care so as to ensure a life free from worries. Cynics consider that we should not aim for happiness, but rather for apathy. Apathy lies in the will to find oneself in a sufficiently serene state to face the hazards of life, of daily life without experiencing suffering. In order to achieve apathy, the Cynics tell us, we must comply with two orders: the animal world and the divine world. The gods have no needs and therefore we should strive to act like them. The same is true for animals, their very limited needs should be a source of inspiration.

Once these foundations have been laid, disciples must train themselves to follow these principles so that they are steeped in them, so that they understand them and practice them. This requires having methods, exercises, of which there are many: meditation; correspondence

---

[79]Marc Aurèle, *Pensées pour moi-même*, VIII. Marcus Aurelius, *Thoughts for Myself*, VIII. Our translation.

and reading; writing, and physical exercise; exploring our consciousness; nutrition; and of course, the guidance of a Master.

For the Innovator, this preparation is key. By this we do not refer to preparing for the possible failure of the idea which is being developed, but rather in the sense of readying oneself for the effects of the innovation which is being implemented. In other words, the Innovator must think in terms of actions and consequences. It is not a matter of thinking about the innovation on the one hand and how to implement it on the other. It means continuously putting oneself in the position of thinking about action. This applied also to responsible innovation, which dictates that the consequences of innovations be considered. However, the spiritual exercises from the three schools of Antiquity outlined herein also provide fundamental wisdom which underlines the importance of accepting one's destiny, a destiny which can bring glory as well as death, success as well as failure. It is also important to understand that for Epicureans, what matters is not the quest for pleasure but possibly the absence of displeasure; or that passions are deceptive, harmful and ephemeral. Among other dimensions, these spiritual exercises must make the Innovator understand why they do what they do. Of course, we have described an Innovator who wants to change the world, who wants to improve it; but the question is also at what cost? Are they able to control themselves? Are they in a position to ask themselves whether or not they should do something and why? What does the Innovator ultimately look for? Money? Fame, that ephemeral situation as described by Marcus Aurelius, and if so, at what cost? The philosopher emperor gives us the answer to this question: at the cost of compromises, arrangements, of betrayals. Are there not, to use the Epicurean classification, unnatural and unnecessary innovations which are ultimately not worth developing? Especially when these can be harmful to the environment and to individuals? This may be the case for certain sports cars or off-road vehicles for example. Ought not a natural and necessary innovation such as a vaccine be a priority in terms of human and financial resources? What could make this happen if not the will, the spirit of the Innovator? Do they not have an obligation to be inspired by the Cynical philosophy of apathy, taking their inspiration from animals and Gods?

The issue here is clear: innovation as it stands today increasingly calls into question the foundations on which humanity was built, whether through transhumanism, posthumanism or the exploitation of nature, for example. The choice of a humanely sustainable future as we have developed it requires us to question who we are, what we do and what we want; this is the only way. This forces us to think about the life we want to lead in the here and now, and what we want to leave pass on and leave behind us. It forces us to renounce what we have learned, to give up what we usually do without thinking. This requires pruning the branches which made the Innovator what they are today in order grow new branches from the cuttings. We are the fruit of the innovators of the 1960s, 1970s, 1980s, 1990s and even 2000s, a span of five decades in which the possibilities for innovation were nothing close to those we have today. Our current approach to innovation is the same as when DNA sequencing or organ transplants were in their infancy, or when the Internet did not exist, when robotisation was at its beginnings, the speed of information itself was not comparable, nor is globalisation, which has since continued to develop. In other words, the innovators of today act with a spirit shaped by those who never had to face exponential innovations which could tip the human being from one situation to another. These paradigmatic innovations are profoundly and lastingly changing humankind, and while this has been the case in the history of the human species, never before has it been so profound and so rapid. Should innovators continue to be crushed by their own hand or should they reformat their "processor"? Or the spirit of innovation as a whole?

Innovation methods, laws, legislations, sanctions will not change this. Innovation always emerges before the legal framework which can control it, and processes are constantly circumvented. This means nothing can be done with certainty unless it comes from the Innovator themselves. Spiritual exercises are a possible path, what else is there since everything has already been tried? There is an imperative need for the Innovator to question their "self", what they are and what they do, for the Innovator to care about themselves in order to constitute themselves as an ethical subject, and take care of themselves and others. No law, sanction or framework allows for this. This need is imperious because it concerns the person who shapes the world. Of course, it is important that each and every one of us behave like a philosopher and practice spiritual exercises. In the case of the Innovator, however, this is a priority and a determining factor insofar as it impacts everyone.

Caring for self and others, practicing spiritual exercises and readying oneself require that the individual be ready to undertake a profound and radical change, to bring about a radical transformation of the self, which could be called a conversion, that is, a new way of being. The objective of a new way of being, a new way of thinking is simply to bring about a new way of acting. In other words, it is impossible for us to change how we act if we do not change how we think. Therefore, there is a need for a radical change, a disruption within the self. The notion of conversion is certainly the most appropriate because it conveys the idea of profound change, of moving from one state to another.

Converting Oneself

Etymologically, *conversio*, "conversion", has two meanings in Latin: on the one hand, a "change of orientation", implying a new exploration of the self; and on the other hand, a "change of thought", including the idea of transformation and rebirth.

Conversion was initially linked to political conversion as Plato imagined it in his desire to change Society by transforming mankind.[80] In Antiquity, conversion did not refer to religious conversion, but political, and was used to describe the act of modifying, changing the of a political opponent through discussion and methods of persuasion. It is not uncommon for rhetorical techniques, the arts of persuasion, to be used to change the mind of one's interlocutor. In the context which interests us here, conversion refers to the act of changing one's own mind, of changing course to attain the good, of striving for the best for oneself, for others and for Society at large. The Philosopher is the one person who is capable of bringing about this change. Only the Philosopher is capable of transforming others, for they themselves are a "convert".[81] The Philosopher succeeded in turning their gaze away from the shadows of the sensitive world to turn instead to the Good, as Plato explains with the myth of the cave.[82] Plato argues that if we let philosophers govern Society, they will convert Society to the idea of the Good. This proposition is less prevalent among the Stoics and Epicureans, whose aim was for the conversion of individuals rather than that of the Society.[83]

Conversion, here, is achieved by radically changing one's way of being, whether it be in terms of morals, food or clothing. It takes place in

---

[80]Pierre Hadot, *Exercices spirituels et philosophie antique*, *Op. cit.*, p. 225.

[81]Plato, *The Republic*, 518c.

[82]*Ibid*, 515c.

[83]Pierre Hadot, *Exercices spirituels et philosophie antique*, *Op. cit.*, p. 225.

the immanent structure of the individual, in the here and now, and not in the perspective of a possible *post-mortem* salvation, unlike Christian-type religious conversions. Indeed, while Christians conversion is a form of rebirth, it is done in a very different perspective from philosophical conversion: it is about joining the people of God, following God, and placing one's faith and future in his hands. This type of conversion, which is often the common meaning attributed to this notion, has a radical and totalitarian aspect, and should not be confused with philosophical conversion. Religious conversion is guided by an exclusive faith in God, and requires from the faithful an all-encompassing and unwavering adherence. It is an abrupt shift towards God, a fracture of the self, which has to die in order to be reborn. In fact, what religious doctrine demands is a renunciation of self, since its focus rests exclusively on the divine.

In Ancient times, however, philosophical conversion was above all a return to oneself, to one's essence, a transcendent self, on which we have the possibility to work for an objective which is the here and now. Philosophers insist that the only possible transformation of mankind is philosophical conversion,[84] because it is the only way to make the individual, their soul, go from one state to another, from frustration to well-being, from anguish to serenity, from fear to mastery, from darkness to light. As Clement of Alexandria says, conversion is *"the soul taking a turn to what is better, and a change from a kind of nocturnal day"*.[85] In other words, *conversio* seeks to enable the individual who is in a state of discomfort, worry, stress and anguish, to build a place of peace, serenity, a secluded place within oneself, which is protected from the outside.

This focus on self through conversion is achieved through spiritual activity, whose prime purpose is to tear oneself away from everyday life. However, the end result of this uprooting is a return to the world, but to a world which has now been converted, that is to say, an original, authentic world. Conversion takes place somewhere between this uprooting from the ordinary world and the return to what is true, and is made possible through elevation. This elevation is implemented through techniques found in the great schools of Antiquity, whether among the Stoics, Epicureans or Cynics, spiritual exercises: the acceptance of the Epicurean

---

[84] *Ibid.*, p. 234.
[85] Clement of Alexandria, *Stromates*, IV, VI, 27, 3. Translated to English by William Wilson, in *Ante-Nicene Fathers*, Vol. 2. Alexander Roberts, James Donaldson, and A. Cleveland Coxe (eds.), Christian Literature Publishing Co., Buffalo, NY, 1885.

tetrapharmakos; the experience of the Socratic dialogue; the will to know oneself; it is also the following of dogmas such as understanding what depends on oneself and what does not, understanding that passion is to be fought or that pleasure is neither useful nor good. These dogmas, techniques and methods which aim to transform us while elevating us must be implemented, experimented and tested. It is the practice of these spiritual exercises which makes self-transformation possible; and for philosophers who pursue wisdom, true transformation can only be achieved by practicing the exercises which make conversion possible.[86]

Spiritual exercises push us toward the ultimate goal, which is conversion. You convert to a philosophy in the literal sense, you become someone else. *Conversio* seeks to build a place of peace, serenity, a secluded place within oneself which is protected from the outside, a sense of immensity. It is a transformation of the self, achieved through the practice of the different spiritual exercises, and which makes it possible to exist in a world which is no longer quite the same, since it has been "converted". There is no turning back. This is why spiritual exercises are somewhat elitist: although they are available to all, only a limited few can really access them. Their apparent simplicity masks the need for an extraordinary willingness to implement them in order to benefit from their effects. Similarly, the wide dissemination of philosophical propositions, whether in a market place, under a Stoic Portico or in an Epicurean Garden, does not mean that spiritual exercises have become popular, far from it. On the contrary, it is precisely because they are rare, laborious and elitist that classic Greek philosophers sought to be heard by as many people as possible. While the desire for access to wisdom, to a better life is universal, the complex paths leading to it discourage the vast majority. When asked how many individuals Socrates had managed to convert to philosophy, he answered: not even one in a thousand.[87] As a result, it is imperative we convert as well and as quickly as possible those whose conversion will have an impact on the greatest number: for Plato this was rulers; today it is innovators.

---

[86] See the two volumes published on these themes: Xavier Pavie, *Exercices spirituels. Leçons de la philosophie antique*, Les Belles Lettres, Paris, 2012 and Xavier Pavie, *Exercices spirituels. Leçons de la philosophie contemporaine*, Les Belles Lettres, Paris, 2013.

[87] Seneca, *Interviews*, III, 1, 18–19 quoted by Michel Foucault, *L'Herméneutique du sujet*, *Op. cit.*, p. 115.

The conversion of the Innovator

To what should the Innovator convert? And why must they do so? In Antiquity, the Philosopher wanted to convert rulers, those who governed, those who did and acted in society. They so wished because in their capacity as Philosopher, they were aware that politicians are able of acting according to Good or Evil, exercising democracy or authoritarianism. And since rulers are unable to discern what they should do, because trapped in a state of *stultitia*, it is the Philosopher who is to guide them out.

Today, the purpose of the Philosopher is to help the Innovator to act for the greater good, to convert them to something other than what they are used to doing, to orient them towards other types of behaviour and actions. The goal for the Philosopher is not to change the Innovator for the Innovator's benefit: as with the rulers, the ultimate goal is to effect change at the level of Society as a whole. As a player in the world, the Innovator has the power to direct the world, and this is precisely what the Philosopher fights for: that society, the world in the broadest sense of the term, may move towards benevolence and wisdom rather than towards exploitation and degradation. This is why it is indeed philosophical conversion which is needed here, because other types of conversion do not focus on the transcendence of the self in the here and now.

In order to convert, the Innovator must first of all tear themselves away from everyday life through the practice of spiritual exercises, so as to break out of the habits which they may have, change their reflexes, those they have always used. They have to leave behind the ordinary world so that they can start thinking differently. The Innovator is constantly subject to a wide range of competitive pressures, from shareholders, the ecosystem, management, partners, customers, members, supporters, patients, suppliers, and the list goes on. The Innovator never has the possibility to leave the sphere in which they are required to operate, exclusively dedicated to the continuous production of new offers, new ideas, new services intended to ensure survival, at any cost. One cannot change their perceptions, behaviours in the blink of an eye. This cannot even be achieved in a few hours, days or weeks. It is a veritable asceticism which the Innovator is to implement in hopes of arriving at a new way of being. This requires a voluntary disconnection from everyday life, of everything which currently makes up their world. In order to achieve this, they must practice spiritual exercises, meditation, ready themselves for what may happen, consider the *tetrapharmakos*, but also engage in the exercises of the classic Greek philosophy which are reading, writing, recollection. If the Innovator exercises their spirit, they transform it. Through the work of the mind, the exercise of their consciousness, through introspection, the Innovator becomes someone else, they are converted to philosophy and its attributes of seeking wisdom and goodness. The overarching goal is obviously to return to the world, the much-needed involvement of the Innovator in everyday life. The practice of spiritual exercises is not an end in itself, and while they lead to conversion, this is only so that the Innovator can act in a different way once they return into society. In other words, the converted Innovator must have learned to behave differently. It is important to stress here that what happens here is a conversion, not merely a change in behaviour, a posture. This is why the notion of "ethics" seems ill-suited, the Greek origin of this expression reminds us that ethics refers to the idea of right behaviour which could perhaps make sense in the context of innovation. However, it is not so much a question of acting in an *ad hoc* way, in a temporal way on a specific question, a specific issue, a specific point, a specific challenge. Rather, it is a way of being which must be attained, a way of life which only a conversion to philosophy through spiritual exercises can bring about.

In practical terms, an individual who practices spiritual exercises, who reflects on the interest of glory and power for example, on what does or does not depends on them, who practices meditation, who practices introspection to question themselves, who remembers their deeds and records them in the form of *hupomnemata*[88] – those little personal notebooks Ancient Greeks always carried with them and which were used not only for taking notes, but also for noting down quotes, including excerpts from books, narratives, writing anecdotes, aphorisms and reflections so they could reread them and meditate on them – becomes different, but above all, acts differently. This does not mean that they should isolate themselves from the world: they extracted themselves from the world out of necessity, in order to modify himself, only to return to the world a better version of themselves. Of course, once this conversion is attained, these converted individuals should not abandon their position and duties

---

[88] Foucault focused on this notion in Ancient Greece in many articles, as well as in "Les techniques de soi", Michel Foucault, "Usage des plaisirs et techniques de soi", in *Dits et Écrits II Op. cit.*, p. 1602. Michel Foucault, "L'écriture de soi" in *Dits et Écrits II, Op. cit.*, p. 1234; Michel Foucault, "À propos de la généalogie de l'éthique" in *Dits et Écrits II, Op. cit.*, p. 1443.

because of the risks these present. This would be tantamount to rejecting the world. Quite the contrary, because others, less well-intentioned people, will take their place if it is not filled. What is needed is not the disappearance of innovators, but rather the emergence of a new form of innovators, of the benevolent, caring Innovator.

The reign of Emperor Marcus Aurelius was marked by complexity both from a political and personal point of view. As a philosopher, he never gave up despite the difficulty of making battles and wisdom coexist. As soon as he took power, he found himself faced with the resurgence of wars on all fronts. For the emperor, reigning was above all about plugging the breaches which were opening up in the borders of an immense Empire which was under attack from all sides. He fought, he killed, and his reign was marked by violence, namely against Christians who suffered severe persecution. Alongside this, he wrote his *Meditations* which became universal, in which he meditated, reflected on Stoic techniques and exercised his mind. In addition to his important legislative work, he also carried out a great many actions in the field of education, notably with the establishment of the first chairs of philosophy. Ancient and current historians alike are unanimous in their praise of this figure and admit his great moral rigour without denying the many hardships his reign brought on.[89] He is the epitome of spirituality, complexity and responsibility in action.

In the same way, the Innovator will continue to accomplish their mission. By continuously practicing spiritual exercises, the Innovator will always be at work philosophically. No one can prevent – nor should they, perhaps – a political leader from launching a new, innovative proposal, a doctor from proposing a new form of operation, a charity from finding a new way of attracting members, an entrepreneur from devising services or products which their competitors have not yet imagined. However, perhaps a politician, doctor, entrepreneur or leader, trained in the practice of spiritual exercises, will consider this innovation in a different, benevolent way, and if it could present risks – for them as an individual or for their ecosystem – will consider it afresh, defer it so as to improve it, or maybe even forego it altogether.

The Innovator must convert to themselves, to the individual they are. They convert to the humanity for which they are responsible and of which they must take care. Are there other choices than this conversion, this practice, if we are to preserve a humanely sustainable future?

---

[89] Pierre Grimal, *Marc Aurèle*, Fayard, 1991.

The conversion of the Innovator through spiritual exercises is not one path or proposal among many, it is vital, fundamental, if not compulsory. No other path seems to allow for a benevolent consideration of the fate of humanity than one which builds on the fundamentals of philosophy for today's society with its many actors, its codes and its ecosystem.

The burning relevance of spiritual exercises

From its origins, philosophy has been a spiritual exercise: its predominant challenge is to work, to exercise the soul, the spirit, so as to live as well as possible in the face of the obstacles which life necessarily brings. When practiced, spiritual exercises enable one to take care of their soul. They act as a form of medicine, of therapy, so that whoever uses them can live as well as possible. And this focus on the care of self is neither solitary nor selfish; it is done with, by and for the community. While this practice is discussed here for the population of innovators, it is just as important and vital for all.

In theory, discourse and practice, spiritual exercises run through all Hellenistic and Roman philosophy, all schools combined. These exercises persisted beyond Antiquity, as the teachings of Ancient philosophers as a whole gained universal reach. And it would be naive not to understand just how topical and necessary spiritual exercises are for our modern times. Whatever the school – Stoic, Epicurean or Cynical – the proposals still resonate very definitely with contemporary needs. As Pierre Hadot clearly pointed out: *In my opinion, the model of Ancient philosophy is still current, which means that a quest for wisdom is still current and still possible... I would only say that there are, it seems to me, universal and fundamental attitudes of the human being when seeking wisdom.*[90] It would be a mistake to consider Pierre Hadot's thoughts only as they pertain to philosophy, for philosophy does not exist for itself alone. This is the case of some philosophies, but definitely not those which emerged during Antiquity and certainly not the philosophies whose essence is to find the best way to live, the best possible way of life. If the universal and fundamental attitudes referred to here by Pierre Hadot – the quest for current wisdom – are addressed only to philosophers, then philosophy is on

---

[90] Pierre Hadot, *Exercices spirituels et philosophie antique*, *Op. cit.*, p. 376. Pierre Hadot, *Philosophy as a way of life*, translated by Michael Chase, Blackwell, 1995.

the brink of ruin. Philosophy must be practiced in the world. We can even wonder whether philosophy might not have been overpowered in the last few decades, because its discourse is not audible and carries no weight in the face of questions such as artificial intelligence, big data, DNA sequencing, human genetic modifications, etc. Has not philosophy deserted the fields of innovation and progress? At the beginning of 2017, a team of Chinese researchers succeeded for the first time in editing the genome of viable human embryos. Philosophical discourse and action seem nowhere to be found today in the face of these issues which are paradigmatically changing the human species. What does philosophy deal with today? Banalities and minor news? Political commentary? And when philosophy is relevant and rigorous, where does it speak? At university, i.e. only with young disciples? What about the rest of the population? It is imperative that philosophy take hold in everyday life, the public space. This is all the more necessary in the field of innovation.

It was Ancient philosophy which first developed spiritual exercises, however, these evolved and developed beyond this period.[91] They continued to exist in the philosophy of the Middle-Ages, the Renaissance, the Classical and the Modern era. This is a key element because, to a greater or lesser degree or in ways which were more or less recognised, Montaigne, Descartes, Shaftesbury, Kant or even Rousseau all had an impact on contemporary philosophers. Obviously, this filiation with Ancient spiritual exercises does not end there. Our contemporary era, which we can count as beginning toward the end of the 19th century, is just as affected by the influence, not to say the presence, of Ancient spiritual exercises. Thinkers ranging notably from Emerson to Wittgenstein, Peirce, Foucault or even Thoreau all contributed, in their own way, to maintaining the tradition of spiritual exercises, given that they continue to see philosophy as a way of life. Emerson, whom we have already discussed to help us understand the development of entrepreneurial thinking in the United States, could be considered as the founding father of spiritual exercises in contemporary philosophy. Whether it concerns reading, writing, the aesthetics of existence or meditation, Emerson took up the teachings from Ancient philosophy, which he then passed on to Thoreau,

---

[91]Xavier Pavie, *Exercices spirituels et philosophie contemporaine*, Les Belles Lettres, 2013.

who in turn, passed it on to great American thinkers such as Hilary Putnam, Stanley Cavell, Richard Shusterman, among others.[92]

The choice to innovate

The question, then, is not whether or not to innovate, but rather how to innovate? And the practice of spiritual exercises for innovation seems to be the only way. This path, however, is not the easy road. It is always simpler to be content with innovating without looking at the consequences of our actions, without taking care of others. To what extent will the innovator of today, who is confronted with the necessity to radically transform themselves, have the courage, the strength to accept this need to rethink themselves? The Innovator needs to be the paragon of a new world, and must embody the courage of thought in order to act, even if this is by challenging centuries of blind innovation. *Sapere aude*! Dare to know! Horace tells us in *The Epistles*.[93] Kant in his text on the Enlightenment in 1784 explains that *Sapere aude* is *Enlightenment is the emergence of man from his self-imposed immaturity. Immaturity, that is, the inability to use one's understanding without guidance from another. Self-incurred is this immaturity when its cause lies not in lack of understanding, but rather a lack of resolve and courage to use it without direction from another. Sapere Aude! Dare to use your own mind! Thus is the motto of Enlightenment.*[94] The Innovator must have the courage to understand what they are doing, through insight, reason and intelligence, in order to act with a view to a humanely sustainable future. The Innovator is the only

---

[92]*Idem.*

[93]Horace, *Epistles*, I, 2, 40 *in Works*, French translation by François Richard, Garnier-Flammarion, 1993. Horace, *Satires and Epistles*, translated by John Davie, Oxford University Press, 2004.

[94]Emmanuel Kant, *Beantwortung der Frage : Was ist Aufklärung? (« Réponse à la question: « Qu'est-ce que 'les Lumières'? »)* publié en décembre 1784. Traduction de Stéphane Piobetta in *La Philosophie de l'Histoire*, Éditions Gonthiers, Montaigne, 1947, revue Par Cyril Morana in *Qu'est-ce que les Lumières?* Mille et une nuits, 2006.

Emmanuel Kant, *Beantwortung der Frage: Was ist Aufklärung? ("Answer to the question: What is enlightenment?")* published in December 1784. Translated into French by Stéphane Piobetta in *La Philosophie de l'Histoire*, Éditions Gonthiers, Montaigne, 1947, review by Cyril Morana in *Qu'est-ce que les Lumières?* Mille et une nuits, 2006. Our translation.

one who knows what they are doing, why they are doing it and how they are doing it, so the Innovator is the only one who can have the courage to use their own discernment to know what to do. Neither legislation, processes nor sanctions have any real, relevant effect. Legal considerations always occur in the wake of innovation, processes are not endowed with an ability to think, sanctions are always handed out after the fact, when it is already too late. This responsibility, therefore, inevitably falls upon the Innovator.

The Innovator, therefore, is confronted with a choice: they can either decide to change themselves in order to change the world; or they can carry on as if nothing were amiss, and in so doing give up on a future which is humanely sustainable, or opt for a future which is perhaps not to be condemned but which is not the one known in recent centuries. The dilemma with which they are faced can be understood through the notion of *bivium*, a notion first expressed by classic Greek philosophers. Hesiod expresses this in his poem "Works and Days", in which he reflects on the life choices available to us: *Badness can be got easily and in shoals: the road to her is smooth, and she lives very near us. But between us and Goodness the gods have placed the sweat of our brows: long and steep is the path that leads to her, and it is rough at the first; but when a man has reached the top, then is she easy to reach, though before that she was hard.*[95] In other words, it is easy to innovate in the traditional way, to continue to do what we have been doing for decades, but it is much more complicated to choose a path which presents new obstacles, new hardships which force us to question ourselves, and demands of us that we behave in a new way.

Pythagoreans symbolised this alternative between two life choices, between decisions to be made, with the letter Y[96]; it was even the sign of the sect. This Y represented a fork in the road, the choice that each disciple had to overcome in order to be able to join the community, abide by its rules, and in so doing become divine. This idea of life paths can also be found in the Sophist Prodicus, who explained how, on entering manhood, *having reached that season in which the young man, now standing upon*

---

[95] Hésiode, *Les travaux et les jours*, pp. 287–290, trad. P. Mazon, Paris. C.U.F, 2002, p. 97. Hesiod, *Work and Days*, translated to English by Hugh G. Evelyn-White, Dodo Press, 2008.

[96] Franz De Ruyt, "L'idée du 'Bivium' et le symbole pythagoricien de la lettre Y", in *Revue belge de philologie et d'histoire*, t. X, fasc., Jullien, 1931, pp. 137–145.

the verge of independence, shows plainly whether he will enter upon the path of virtue or of vice.[97] Already, in the 8th century BC, philosophers formalised the notion of a crossroads in life, which has now become fundamental to human existence, between a path which is broad and easy to access but leads to shame, and a steep and difficult path, which leads to honour, peace and freedom.

The Pythagorean allegory of the letter Y resurfaced among calligraphers from the Middle Ages.[98] They made the left branch of the letter Y long and the other branch a short, broad branch. This is based on the same idea: on the one hand, there is the narrow path of virtue leading to glory which is somewhat tortuous and challenging; and on the other, the easy path to pleasure, where the Spirit ultimately dies. Many artists, such as Carrache, Matteis, or Soggi, to name but a few, tried to express this life choice, this dilemma, this Y letter in their works depicting "The Choice of Hercules", with a choice between a life of debauchery and easy pleasures, without examination, or a life of work, honour and purpose.

It goes without saying that the idea of the *bivium* in Ancient philosophy is intended for life choices, and spiritual exercises are intended to advance on the complex path which leads to wisdom. These proposals are not so far removed from the idea developed here for Innovators. What life choice do they want to pursue? Will they be more inclined to choose the easy way to innovate with the consequences which one can imagine, or will they prefer a way of life adapted to the continuity of a humanely desirable development? It is likely that the Innovator who becomes aware of their actions, of the risks to which they are consciously or unconsciously exposing society, will choose the sinuous path of spiritual exercises which will lead them to pursue a caring innovation policy. Today, how does the Innovator achieve this? What enables the Innovator to implement a responsible innovation policy? How are they aware of the impact of their work? What guides their reflection? Absolutely nothing. Today, there is no tool, no method, no guidance, nothing to steer the activity of the Innovator towards this notion of care. The Innovator can choose to innovate by freeing themselves from the constraints of philosophy of

---

[97]Xenophon, *Memorabilia*, I, 21–34. Translated to English by H. G. Dakyns.
[98]Baldine Saint Girons, "The heroic character of Shaftesbury and Vico: Hercule et le trouble de mémoire de Shaftesbury", in *Shaftesbury, philosophie et politesse* (actes du colloque de Nantes, 1996), M. Malherbe et F. Brugère (eds.), Champion, Paris, 2000, pp. 135–173.

the spiritual exercises, as innovators have been doing for centuries, by taking responsibility for their actions as actors of society. Just as they can choose to practise spiritual exercises which will enable them to question themselves, to know how to control themselves, in particular to master their passion to continue to "create" at all costs, to question themselves about the glory or the success which they are seeking and to what end. The long and winding road will certainly discourage many, and probably even the vast majority of innovators, because the practice of philosophy deters most people, which is why Socrates only managed to convince one person in a thousand to convert to philosophy. The effort this demands is daunting, discouraging those who need it the most because they are in charge of the State and its future. For this very reason, it is fundamental to integrate these considerations into education.

Teaching spiritual exercise to Innovators?

Plato says *there is no one [...] who desires evil*,[99] justifying that if someone acts maliciously towards others, it is because of a lack of education, lack of instruction and lack of knowledge. For knowledge is the key to the world, if it can be accessed, that is. The acquisition of knowledge for its own sake is not an end in itself. And reasonably well-informed individuals know that global warming is spreading, have heard about the accelerated disappearance of animal species, are aware of the consequences of human activities on the ozone layer, for example. However, what matters is not so much the acquisition of knowledge, as how this knowledge is used. Not to mention that most of the time it is possible to think that we are doing the right thing when we are not. In other words, the use of knowledge must enable us to act as much as to question what we believe to be true, to modify what we used to take for granted, to get as close as possible to the truth. From the moment we are born, when we are in a raw state, we forge certainties. It is incumbent upon us to work to unravel them. The new born is certain that they need more milk despite the risk of being overweight, just as the young child is certain that there is nothing harmful about playing video games hours on end. Whether we are in our teens, in adulthood, we are full of certainties. Because we were convinced, because we found the argument appealing, because it is easier not to dig deeper so

---

[99] Platon, *Ménon*, pp. 77a–78b. Translated to English by Benjamin Jowett.

as to avoid hearing what we do not want to, because a given argument may change our minds. Only knowledge and education can challenge our most entrenched certainties. This is why education, even though it must be present throughout our lives, is all the more critical during early stages of life, when intellectual "kneading" is easiest and most necessary. Education should begin from the youngest age: that is when we can learn to learn, learn how to approach knowledge. The Socratic postulate that the only thing we know is that we know nothing, is something which should live within us until we die. Nikolai Frederik Severin Grundtvig, the "father" of lifelong learning, was convinced that everyone should enjoy a meaningful education throughout life, comprising not only concepts, but also civic responsibility, and aimed at personal and cultural fulfilment. Two aspects warrant closer analysis: the teaching of spiritual exercises and the teaching of innovation.

The practice of spiritual exercises may seem complex, abstruse, nebulous or even unsuitable or useless. This is because of a lack of awareness of its many strengths and qualities, despite its 3,000 years of history – if we consider the first spiritual exercises in Homer[100] – but above all, because it is not what we are used to. It can certainly be challenging for an adult to spontaneously decide to meditate, to write down their thoughts, their reflections and those of others. It is not common practice to reflect on what does or does not depend on us, or to prepare for the evils or troubles which may arise. Caught up in habits which are rarely those of introspection, the common man is often in the habit of rejecting this kind of practice which can be described as "useless", "theoretical" or "speculative". For this reason, this habit must be taught from youth.

The Innovator, and we cannot stress this enough, is the person who develops an idea, with more or less success, whatever the field of activity, whether in the world of business, health, charities, politics, education, etc. Not everyone is an innovator, far from it, but innovators can come from any background, which is why education in benevolence, in care for self and for others, in short to spiritual exercises, must begin at the youngest age possible, in kindergarten, where learning about the relationship to oneself and to others starts. Traditional education models glorify those who have the best grades in discipline-based teaching, rather than those

---

[100]Homère, *Odyssée*, XX, pp. 18–23, translated to French by. R. Flacelière and V. Bérard, Gallimard, *Bibliothèque de la Pléiade*, 1955, p. 673. Homère, *The Odyssey*, HardPress Publishing, 2019.

who take the best care of others, for example. Of course, it is easier to score mathematics, languages or sports than to evaluate good behaviour. In the current system, a student who does not have time to finish their own assignment because they took time to help a classmate receives no recognition. By focusing exclusively on marks, this system promotes academic success, and in so doing crushes those who behave well and caringly toward others.

It is common to have dedicated "quiet times" in classes for younger pupils, often at nap time, but also so that they can rest in order to work better afterwards, and not be overexcited because they are too tired. Important as this moment may be, it is just as important to take a moment to teach children to meditate, even if only for a few minutes, to encourage them to think about their body, the sensations they feel, and to think about nothing else – without falling asleep. This need not be only for younger pupils. Older pupils, teenagers perhaps, are in even greater need of resources to calm their mind and refocus on themselves for a few minutes a day. Nevertheless, a 17-year-old will not practice meditation if they have not been used to practicing in the 10 years prior. The same applies to higher education: an individual who has gotten into the habit of meditating for a few minutes at 5, 10 or 15 years of age will have no difficulty getting into this disposition at 25 and will not find it at all absurd.

What we demonstrated with this simple example of meditation applies to spiritual exercises: learning to accept what does or does not depend on us, learning to write down one's thoughts, learning to control oneself and to weigh what we call success and failure, glory and defeat, our relationship to money, etc. All these learnings ought to be acquired from a very young age in order to be able to benefit from them as an adult. Above all, knowing that spiritual exercises are not an end in themselves, this practice will enable the individual, throughout their adult life, to practice introspection and ensure that they act as wisely and justly as possible. The question is not whether or not we should learn to practice philosophy from an early age. The answer to this will always be yes. However, philosophy today is particularly far removed from spiritual exercises. It consists in learning concepts and methods, such as how to structure thought in essays, for example. Therefore, it is not a question of being ambitious, but rather of being realistic and pragmatic in order to achieve a goal which concerns us all. If from the age of three the criteria for success are defined by excluding vainglory and the accumulation of goods, for example, if we learn to act always with a view to the preservation of a humanely sustainable future, reflexes will undoubtedly change. Of course, there will always be some individuals greedy for money and for futile and ephemeral fame, nevertheless this "success" would be lessened by the disdain of a part of the population which will have learned different values.

This proposal can, of course, be called into question. An education in spiritual exercises for a better innovation in the face of the globalisation of education and innovations may seem dangerous. This could lead to a loss of competitiveness, productivity, which are necessary to increase market shares and profits (as far as business is concerned). However, the question can no longer be asked in these terms, because these ideals are what characterised recent decades, with the harmful consequences that we now know. Moreover, a benevolent innovator is not necessarily "lesser" from a performance point of view. It is not because they care for their environment that their ideas will be less relevant. Perhaps this way of being is what will enable such an innovator to draw together a greater number of players around him, a greater number of partners, who will trust him more, who will prefer to work with him rather than with an innovator hungry for money and glory.

At no extra cost to pupils and students, and without expensive training for teachers, we need to reconsider how we teach the "way of being", starting with little children. This means learning introspection and writing to oneself, so as to build up one's *hupomênatas* from a very young age; it means learning to speak aloud as Cleanthes did to listen to himself; it means learning to dialogue, and that dialogue is not necessarily winning the argument *over* your interlocutor but rather of being right *together*; it is learning that we must act on what depends on us and not try to control what does not depend on us; it is learning to read, not by a "simple" concern with increasing our knowledge, but meditating on these readings, for example the texts of the Ancient philosophers; it is learning to consider what we eat, and not eating by reflex; it is learning to take care of our body by exercising, feeling and experiencing it.[101] There is no lack of activities enabling young children to begin the practice of spiritual exercises. These exercises are rich, varied and enable them to learn about the world, the environment, themselves and others. The acquisition of these reflexes will become a habit and, like the philosophers of Antiquity, a way of life. It is, in all likelihood, a path which will enable future innovators

---

[101] Xavier Pavie, *Exercices spirituels. Leçons de la philosophie contemporaine*, *Op. cit.*, p. 165.

to develop a way of being respectful and caring for themselves and others.

The question of the Master

Spiritual exercises, therefore, are an important path for the education of innovators. However, we still need to bring about this change, this conversion, and this is the role of the Master. The Master is who will guide us out of our state of *stultitia*, that state of blindness about ourselves and which prevents us from changing our relationship to the world. Entrenched in our certainties from a very young age, in our education, in our environment, only the intervention of others can help us change our vision. This external individual will help us see in a new light our confinement and its limitations, our obstinacy and its risks, our ignorance and its dangers.

While we need this "other" who can guide us for our own enrichment and ultimately help us to see the world differently, this person can also be much more than that for us. They can also be the one who leads us towards conversion, the transformation we must undergo. We need to have a guide, someone to lead us towards our conversion, someone who cares for the universal good. The Master in Antiquity is the one who helps us sift through what is good for us and what is not: what readings are suitable for us; the arts forms we should explore; how to meditate so as to improve ourselves; what bodily or dietary regimens we should observe; what teachings we should follow. From Plato to Montaigne, from Aristotle to Marcus Aurelius, all great philosophers had masters.[102] This is true also for other eras, and other fields. Having a Master to help us see "the light" in companionship is a common principle. The reason we need a Master, and particularly when we decide to change our perspective, is because we acknowledge, consciously or unconsciously, that we find ourselves in a context which requires that we change. This may not always be particularly clear, we may not always be able to formulate precisely what we do not like, what we do identify are the effects: situations in which we are uncomfortable; relationships which stress us; difficulties which we cannot overcome; obstacles which block us in our everyday lives.

---

[102] Marc Aurèle, *Écrits pour lui-même*. Tome I : Introduction générale. Livre I, translated to French by Pierre Hadot, Les Belles Lettres, 1998, pp. 1–3.

When an innovator finds themselves under great pressure from shareholders and their managers, whose obsession is to make a profit as quickly as possible by launching non-compliant products, it is understandable that the innovator may find the situation difficult. They may not be aware of the reason of this malaise, they may also be so entrenched in their environment that all they can do is comply with the demands of shareholders without considering what they do in their day-to-day life, without the discernment which it would be necessary to have. When an innovator at a car manufacturer violates the *Clean Air Act*,[103] they are caught in a spiral from which they cannot extricate themselves. They need someone from the outside to help them see reality with a fresh perspective, to help them look objectively at what they are doing, to make them realise that they are blinded by the system in which they are trapped, and that they need to find both wisdom and truth for the common good.

Unable to see our own limitations, the certainties in which we are trapped, unwilling to step back and question our beliefs, we need an outside, experienced and caring eye to help us. This is the role of the Master: they are the one who can show us the way. The Master is someone who can help us because they have experienced similar situations or, thanks to their experience, knows how to address this challenge. The master shows a path which enables us to heal from the ills which prevent us from acting for our own good and that of others. In other words, to receive the guidance of a Master is a method of personalised education in which the Master suggests a pattern of behaviour to the disciple. This is why masters are elders, who do not necessarily need to be philosophers. Even in Antiquity, a Master could simply be a middle-aged man, a friend or a lover. Their role today is unchanged: they pass on knowledge, principles, know-how, with the aim of helping people to elevate themselves from a state of ignorance to one of knowledge.

Establishing a relationship with a Master means having the opportunity to surrender, to express freely all our anxieties, our weaknesses, and the desire to resolve them. It is about building an intimate and unique relationship which does not require the commitment of a romantic relationship, which is not confronted with the judgment of family or childhood friends, which is not as intrusive as psychoanalysis. It is simply someone other than oneself to whom we can tell everything, so that

---

[103] https://www.epa.gov/clean-air-act-overview.

this person can help us to direct our consciousness, to understand our sensations and impressions. This relationship is not confined to discussions, the role of the Master is to encourage, to show, to explain, to influence. The disciple, on the other hand, confides in the Master in order to be changed. The Innovator is alone in facing their responsibilities and doubts, especially since there are many phases in the development of an innovation where they are alone in their discovery: a molecule; a novel use of a database; a unique genetic modification; a way of circumventing a law; etc. Alone, the Innovator does not necessarily know how to act and cannot easily confide in colleagues, let alone competitors, customers or shareholders, because all these stakeholders will all judge only based on their own interests or disinterests.

Marcus Aurelius had decided to confide in his Master on all aspects of his life, as much on the food he ate as on his current readings, his dreams, his discussions with his mother.[104] By confiding in his Master, Fronton, about each of these subjects, he exposed himself to the objective criticism of his Master and genuinely wanted his opinion on all matters. Does what he eats keep him healthy? Are his readings relevant to the duties he has to face? How should he interpret his dreams? It is not a matter of blindly relying on someone – or indeed following all their advice – but rather of them having a watchful eye over us.

The fusional relationship which arose from these discussions resulted in Marcus Aurelius speaking words of fundamental truth, and revealing his true self. He told him everything, confessed everything to him in every detail. By committing himself to this task, above and beyond all else, it is with himself that he is becoming being honest, hiding nothing and, as a result, he can work towards his own improvement.

Accepting to have a Master is to accept to listen, an ability which is decisive for spiritual exercises. We talk, we communicate, we discuss, but listening, that is active, in-depth listening, the ability to auscultate what we hear, is perhaps the most valuable of them all. Based on the Latin verb *auscultare* (from which the French verb *écouter* is derived), this means "to listen", "to lend an ear", "to examine by listening".

Listening, understood here as a form of attentiveness, is the key to acting in a caring way, as it requires a genuine commitment on the part of

---

[104] Armand Cassan, *Lettres inédites de Marc Aurèle et de Fronton*, A. Levasseur, 1830, t. I, livre IV, lettre 6, pp. 249–251.

the listener. It is a manifestation of the will of the listener to come and look for something, a path to follow, a voice to hear and possibly follow. Whenever you get involved in a dialogue, when you exchange views with someone, you have to do so with this objective of modification of the self through listening in mind, and therefore create the necessary conditions for it to work: attention, concentration, diligence. The challenge of listening is to grasp and memorise what we hear, the message, so that we can embrace it, make it our own let it become an integral part of ourselves. It also means hearing what we need to do and practising introspection in order to assess where we stand in relation to what we hear.

The Innovator, therefore, must integrate listening into their daily spiritual exercise. Of course, this means listening to the word of the Master, and listening to those to whom their own message is destined. But it also means listening to their ecosystem, to their environment, or to the people who are indirectly affected by their message, to their partners, to those with whom they work every day or less regularly. The Innovator should act as a sponge, and absorb all these messages so as to produce something which takes account of and respects all these stakeholders.

We learn little by speaking, by listening to our own voice; we learn mostly by listening to the one we have chosen to hear and who can, like the Master, be the custodian of a certain wisdom which enables us to make progress, advance. It is state of mind which we are not necessarily used to because it implies accepting advice without contesting it, letting a discourse penetrate our being because this is what is good for us and what will transform us. When we know how to listen correctly – Pythagorean novices were required to remain silent for 5 years so as to learn how to listen – we open up within ourselves a predisposition towards others. We must, however, be careful with our sense of hearing, as this is the most passive of all. In *On Listening to Lectures*, Plutarch explains that hearing is also the only sense which can lead us to virtue[105] because other senses can be misleading, whether through an error of taste, sight or touch. In order to achieve virtue, the author continues, we must

---

[105] Plutarque, Comment écouter? in *Œuvres morales*, tome I, 2e partie. Traités 3–9, Trad. R. Klaerr, A. Philippon, J. Sirinelli, Les Belles Lettres, 1989. Plutarch, *Moralia On Listening to Lectures*. Translated to English by F. C. Babbitt. (The work appears in pp. 201–259 of Vol. I of the Loeb Classical Library's edition of the *Moralia*, first published in 1927) Retrieved from: http://penelope.uchicago.edu/Thayer/E/Roman/Texts/Plutarch/Moralia/De_auditu*.html.

train our listening skills, teach this sense to sift the wheat from the chaff. We must hone our ability to listen by challenging our hearing with discernment. We must train this sense to hear and listen to things which are good for us, because, due to the passive nature of hearing, we will always be bombarded with things which are useless to us. Practicing listening means challenging what we are told, so that we can grow and change, with great speeches as well as relevant lectures, modern courses as well as classical texts. There are many possibilities for training our ears to listen to reason as well as wisdom. Of course, the choice of who and what we listen to is important. As such, the choice of who we accept as our masters, who will influence us, is equally important. The Innovator must keep in mind that whomever they chose as their master must resemble the ethical and responsible mission they have *vis-à-vis* society. In other words, the Innovator should not listen to whoever promises fame, success, money and power, but rather to the person who shows them the way towards a society which is as prosperous as it is benevolent. If this does not come from one person alone, then it is upon the Innovator to confront perspectives, to constantly shift their gaze so as to make sure that they take due account of the many points of view which will enable them to forge their own.

The Innovator must question who they want as their Master, where they can find them. Maybe this Master is already part of their circle but they have not yet realised it? What can they expect from them? And of course, they must ask themselves this important question: am I ready to listen to them? Will this person help me to see my limitations, my shortcomings and my failings, and overcome them? These questions are necessary for anyone who wants to innovate with a full awareness of their actions. It is not only about working with a Master – whose rigour, moral conscience and rectitude are the building blocks –, but also engaging with the whole of what constitutes the development of the mind. This is why being able to truly listen is a requirement for becoming a "great" Innovator. By listening to patients and voters, customers and members, students and professors, scholars and philosophers, colleagues and fellow citizens, the Innovator forges their own mind by absorbing the needs, expectations and behaviours of the world. By listening, they make themselves available to others and ready themselves to meet the needs of others with discernment, which means not meeting all needs, and most importantly, not at all costs, but looking out for the rest of the community.

Deconstructing the Way We Teach Innovation

The traditional innovation process

Teaching innovation as a discipline is relatively recent, and was introduced only approximately 20 years ago. While in engineering and management schools there have been courses on research and development or courses on the development of new products for a long time, the term "innovation" was relatively rare. Even more surprising is the fact that courses on innovation are still restricted to management and engineering schools, even though innovation – as we have seen – is by no means confined to these exclusive fields. Developments in medicine through transhumanism are proof of this, as are innovations in politics, sports, economics or social sciences. Innovation is everywhere; yet it is taught almost nowhere. This is all the more true since, when you take a closer look at business enterprises, innovators of new products or services do not necessarily come from schools where this discipline is offered. There is nothing to prevent a geography or humanities student from developing an innovative product or service. In other words, on the one hand, learning spiritual exercises from an early age would be beneficial, whatever the individual may do later on in life; and on the other, the issue of innovation and the teaching of innovation in all its aspects needs to be considered far beyond the spheres of business and managerial. Let us look at how education on innovation is delivered in existing education models.

Historically, innovation has been offered mainly in technical courses, and consequently, has remained confined in the study of methods and processes. Traditional courses on innovation cover the emergence of ideas to the market launch, considered through the lens of marketing, financial, commercial and technical perspectives, and in so doing offer a perspective closer to project management methods, and fails to address topics such as content or the type of ideas. Overall, it is more concerned with the process itself, commonly referred to as Innovation Process Management. Students are therefore initiated into the rudiments of the methods which enable them to find ideas, to know how to evaluate costs, how to communicate about something new, to learn how to manage a new way of producing products, how to get a new product accepted within an organisation, how to succeed in distributing this new product in its ecosystem, what is the pedagogical approach to ensure consumers understand its usefulness, etc.

As explained above,[106] the innovation process revolves around five main phases: ideation; feasibility; capability; launch; and post-launch. It is at the heart of each of these different phases which responsible innovation can be integrated.[107]

Today, teaching innovation is about providing students interested in innovation with a detailed understanding of the process as a whole. Over time, the syllabus has been expanded to make it more precise, more effective, more up-to-date for each of the phases. However, there is no chapter dedicated to the "qualities" of the Innovator as an individual, nor any course explicitly devoted to the question of introspection which the Innovator should regularly practice. What is implied is that anyone can be innovative, if they surround themselves well (creative, technical, marketing, financial and sales, etc.) and follow proven processes. Of course, many innovators wonder about what they are doing, and the essence of responsible innovation is to help them ask these questions. However, nothing is really done to make us question the purpose of the innovation that we, as innovators, wish to have in order to guarantee a humanely sustainable future.

The innovator I want to be

There is a need to rethink how we teach innovation, so as to frame it no so much from the perspective of the *processes* but rather of the *individual* behind innovation. Innovation processes are efficient and are constantly improving, particularly in recent years, and are increasingly integrating the aspect of responsibility. What is needed today is to deconstruct how innovation is taught, by helping innovators to question themselves, their practices and their motivations. Helping students to ask themselves why they want to become innovators is an important preliminary question. Is it for money and/or fame? Do they want to innovate to help poor populations? Is their willingness to innovate linked to a personal experience? What is their own relationship with innovation? Do they feel compelled to always own the latest "hype" product? Or do they tend to let innovations grow in the marketplace before purchasing them? The next important

---

[106] See the section describing the innovation process on page 29 of this book.
[107] See the section describing the process of responsible innovation on page 98 of this book.

question is to help them analyse how they view innovators. Do they consider them as being representatives of the business world? Or do they think that innovators can come from the world of sports, associations, or politics? Then, to ask with whom they identify. Is there a glorification of the innovator, seen as a hero in whose footsteps they want to follow, or on the contrary, does the innovator come second to the innovation? These fundamental questions should be used as the starting point for any course on innovation because they will challenge students to think about what they want for themselves, and what they want for society, decide whether they want to be more passive or active, or if they want to guide innovation or be the ones to propose it. Over and above innovation, these initial considerations help students situate themselves in their own professional and even personal life path, even if this will evolve over time. In other words, these questions help students to position themselves on the *bivium,* and to choose between a life as a pioneer, innovator, entrepreneur and a life as a user of innovation, a guide or even a challenger. One of the key challenges of these questions is to better understand the "why" which drives them. Without making value judgements, it is important to frame the issues of innovation starting with the intrinsic motivations of individuals.

Relearning how to dialogue

Once these initial questions have been explored, a new approach to the teaching of innovation should then enable students to practice the spiritual exercise of dialogue. As stated above, dialogue as a spiritual exercise does not so much seek to persuade or to convince the interlocutor, as to provide an opportunity for a discussion in order to be right together. This is precisely what the Socratic approach proposes. Through a succession of questions, Socrates leads his interlocutors to expose and acknowledge their ignorance, but also, and above all, to provoke sufficient turmoil in them to force them to call into question their knowledge, sometimes even their whole life.[108] In Plato's Socratic dialogues, this crucial moment, this turning point, occurs when the Socratic interlocutor loses confidence and, as self-doubt grows, becomes discouraged. The dialogue could even end with Socrates' listener just leaving or giving up on the conversation. But

---

[108] Pierre Hadot, "La figure de Socrate" *in Exercices spirituels et philosophie antique, Op. cit.*, p. 111. Pierre Hadot, *Philosophy as a way of life, Op. cit.*

Socrates systematically identifies this moment and maintains a form of tension, through which he demonstrates that he is partly to blame for the possible failure of the discussion. He turns the dialogue its head so that his interlocutor does not feel humiliated, but rather supported in adversity, and this adversity is ultimately not Socrates as an individual, but rather pseudo-knowledge, false convictions, errors of judgement, mistakes, etc.

When the interlocutor leaves, they do so having acquired a form of ˙knowledge, that of the activity of the mind, that is a method for accessing knowledge, which is not, however, knowledge itself. This is the very essence of the maieutic method, that is, enabling interlocutors to question their knowledge in order to acquire a new and different, methodological knowledge. Paradoxically, it is in this tension of dialogue that Socrates takes care of others. Dialogue is a form of cooperative, joint progress, through successive agreements between the interlocutors. Through dialogue, they submit to the requirements of rational coherence, and in so doing elevate from their individual point of view to a common point of view.[109] It is through dialogue that the concern, the care for others emerges. It brings about an awareness of the existence of a point of view different from one's own. Similarly, those involved in innovation must go beyond their individual perspective in order to surrender and submit to the requirements of the objectivity of reason. The care of self, here, means going beyond one's own individuality in order to reach an objective universality.[110]

This is what students of innovation need to learn: to learn to dialogue with others in order to overcome their own subjectivity. Talking with others is a fundamental exercise which every innovator must learn to do. By this we do not mean talking to customers or potential customers in order to identify what they need and propose a corresponding innovation. It is rather a matter of encompassing those who will experience said innovation directly or indirectly into their thought process. When an innovation such as nanotechnology, genetically modified organisms or artificial intelligence emerges, it is more than necessary to ask questions about the perception, desirability and interest of such proposals, which will undoubtedly change the world in the more or less long term. The aim of the dialogue we propose here is obviously not to convince others of the

---

[109]Michel Foucault, *Histoire de la sexualité III. Op. cit.* Michel Foucault, *The Care of Self*, Penguin Books, Limited, 2006.
[110]*Idem.*

merits of innovation, but to work with others in order to ascertain how and to what extent this innovation can benefit everyone. A possible innovation such as universal income should not be decided on unilaterally by any given person or political party. This should only happen as a result of discussions with representatives of the population, with those who would be directly impacted by it, as well as those not directly affected. In the same way, it is not a question of forcing or imposing the idea of universal income, but of defining jointly with all interlocutors who should benefit from such a system, how, for how long, why, so as to weigh its consequences, benefits and risks. In other words, it is through dialogue that we can make society evolve towards a shared, desirable outlook. For example, when a doctor decides to collect stem cells after a child is born and implant them in another child to enable that child to survive, this raises important questions, both in terms of practice and consequences for society. This also raises issues of cost and of equality, which cannot be resolved simply between a doctor and a patient. It is society as a whole which is affected by this initiative and therefore it must be discussed in order to determine whether it has been accepted, modified or rejected.

Dialoguing is a skill to be learned, it also requires learning a different appreciation of time as well as new listening skills. The Innovator should act as a mediator between scientists, scholars, discoverers and inventors, engineers and civil society. They must also be a conciliator, so as to put an end to the traditional schism between those who do, who "create" on the one side, and those who receive on the other. For society to advance, different players need to come together. While everybody engages in dialogue, few people are really trained in its art and know how to set it up properly: identifying the dialogue to be had; taking the time to listen and discuss; learning empathy so as to better define the position of the other; knowing how to reformulate in order to ensure arguments are understood properly; and finally knowing how to help one's interlocutor as well as knowing how to be helped by him so as to reach a common agreement.

Learning to meditate: A phenomenology of innovation

The term "meditation" can take on different meanings, all the more so today when the term is increasingly used and publicised. The meditation to be considered here is "philosophical meditation". The term "meditation" is derived from the Greek word *melete*, which means "to practice". Philosophical meditation can mean very simply practicing to love wisdom, but in the context of spiritual exercises, meditation takes on a unique place and is characterised by its desire to be in the moment, in the present, in everyday life. Philosophical meditation can and must be applied to the here and now.

The goal of such an exercise is to ensure our well-being in the face of our environment, in the face of hardships which may arise, in the face of the complex situations which we constantly come up against. Philosophical meditation helps us to deal with these complexities by working along two paths. The first, by meditating on the acts we know we must carry out or potential actions we could take. It is a question here of anticipating our future behaviour according to the way we want it to be. In this context, the preliminary meditative question is: how do I want to behave in the face of this action which is about to happen? In other words, meditation precedes action, whether it takes place in the very near or distant future.

It is important that students learn to think about what they want to do before doing it. That, through meditation, they learn to think about the innovation they are developing or would like to develop, to imagine its uses, its consequences, the reaction of individuals, how they would feel about it if they were in the place of the users, the customers, the people concerned by it. This is close to a phenomenology of innovation, since it is a question of succeeding in thinking about it, suspending one's judgement, analysing it in all its dimensions in order to understand it better. It is also the opportunity to practice another spiritual exercise: doubt, that is, to question again and again the benefit and relevance of innovation through doubt. What if we do not launch this innovation? What if we defer it in order to improve it? What if we initiated a dialogue with our competitor so as to set some standards which are less polluting? What if we explained to customers, partners and members that this need should not be met for very good reasons? Doubt is a pillar of meditation because it is during its practice that we can, with time and benevolence, question our certainties.

The second path of philosophical meditation consists in putting into perspective acts which have been carried out. For this path, then, meditation takes place after the fact. It is a reflection on an action which has already taken place, a past experience, and which must be analysed anew, enlightened by hindsight, to learn for the future. The *a posteriori* meditative act will look into the chronology of events, question the behaviour which was adopted, the preconceptions and reflexes. For example, in our relationship with others we must ask ourselves whether there has been a loss of self-control. Was there any denigration of self or others? This form of meditation has only one objective: to analyse the consequences on our deepest self, our conscience, our spirit.

For students of innovation, it is then a question of reflecting on innovations they themselves may have endured or experienced. Did they feel disturbed by this new innovation? How did they experience a change brought about by the arrival of the innovation, regardless of whether it was technological, in the field of sports or in the school curriculum? The challenge is to get students to reflect on the perception of innovation from the point of view of the recipient of innovation. This enables us to acquire a more humble approach, in which we are no longer actively working towards bringing forward new proposals, but rather passively subjected to innovative decisions made by others. This enables students of innovation to question: did these innovators act the right way? What caused friction? What caused discomfort? What were the sources of satisfaction?

The ultimate goal of philosophical meditation is nothing less than a change in behaviour towards the actions we perform by questioning them, by pausing to analyse them. That is why it is so important future innovators be trained in this practice. This meditation is a direct modification of the Innovator, before taking action in order to anticipate, or just after, to understand. It is also an indirect modification since, as the meditations progress, the individual naturally becomes ready to understand what to do in the face of certain reactions. In a way, then, over time, they acquire new reflexes.

What depends on the self

Dialogue and meditation constitute the fundamental pillars of spiritual exercises for our proposed new approach to teaching innovation. In addition to these, other spiritual exercises would be equally relevant. Let the students learn from Marcus Aurelius that glory is fleeting, that taking care of oneself should be our main concern, that we must take care of what depends on us and not of what does not. The latter notion is particularly relevant for innovators. It is in the doctrine of Epictetus, which takes up the classical Stoic categories, that we find the famous quote: *Of things some are in our power, and others are not*".[111] It is essentially the

---

[111]Épictète, *Manuel*, trad. J. Pépin *in Les Stoïciens*, *Op. cit.*, p. 1111. Epictetus, *A Selection from the Discourses of Epictetus With the Encheiridion*. Translated to English by George Long. Retrieved from http://pioneer.chula.ac.th/~pukrit/bba/Epictetus.pdf.

beginning of this sentence which must not only be understood but embraced by students of innovation. Through the innovations we propose, we must work on what depends on: the environment, the care of others, the future of humanity, respect for others. Innovation depends on the Innovator, even when it is intentionally diverted from its initial purpose. This is the classic example of firearms, where the innovator must understand that a very large number of situations depend on them, and cannot ignore the fact that the uses of their innovation can be devastating, even though this was not the innovator's intention or how they intended the innovation to be used. If this type of tool is to be put on the market – which the innovator may question – to what extent should the innovator not also propose the sale be conditioned on user training, regular psychological monitoring, a chip enabling the weapon to be traced, i.e. a great many elements intended to guarantee, insofar as possible, the "acceptable" uses of the innovation, such as shooting sports, for example? It is incumbent upon the Innovator to consider the overall life of the idea they bring to market.

Processes such as responsible innovation should help the Innovator understand what is "in their power", the questions this process raises help the Innovator to think about what they ought do. However, responsible innovation alone is not enough: the methodological considerations of a process maintain a distance between the Innovator and their innovation, a cool, objective distance, which is of course necessary, but which does not allow for the development of an understanding of innovation in all its aspects, and it is this distance which must be bridged. Only through meditative introspection, by calling into question their role and what they do, by entering into a dialogue with others as well as with themselves, can the Innovator develop an intimate relationship with innovation, a relationship with the role of this innovation in society, everyday life, in the life of the individuals who will be on the receiving end of their innovation.

These techniques are the only way for the Innovator to understand their role, and they will only succeed in applying them if they are adequately trained in them, if the learning of innovation processes is framed by an initiation to spiritual exercises. The classroom must become a place of heightened awareness and benevolence for these innovators in the making. During their studies, they must live and experience for themselves the care and caution they are to implement for this desirable future. The only way they can acquire the capacity to question their actions according to this future which must be caring towards themselves as well as their entire ecosystem is through the practice of spiritual exercises. At the same time, the understanding of the world which they need to acquire can no longer remain shackled in silos, limited strictly to the disciplines they know, be it management, politics, philosophy, art, physical education. The Innovator must be able to understand that transdisciplinarity in and outside the classroom must be part of their everyday life.

Transdisciplinarity for Understanding the World

Aristotle tells us that the first quality of philosophers is their ability to wonder, because this quality is fundamental for those who want to direct their existence towards wisdom. The ability to open up to the world, to be astonished by what it offers, to always observe the world anew helps to change how we see things, to modify our point of view which filled with certitudes and habits. The young child is easily surprised. The infant is less so, but awakens to curiosity: a ball, an animal, a fruit, a tune. This develops hand in hand with their imagination, and they imagine themselves entering the toy they are having fun with, they are ready to swallow a raw vegetable when it is time to cook it, their parents' bed becomes an ocean, or sometimes even an Olympic trampoline.[112] In the current education system, there are many objects which arouse curiosity: subjects, teachers, classmates. However, the form in which these are proposed is not conducive to developing learners' imagination: sitting on a chair for several hours a day, ingesting material by reading and listening passively. From the beginning, we kill imagination and curiosity, creativity and dreams. Secondary school and high school are not places where imagination can flourish spontaneously. This is truer still if higher education. Whether in law, philosophy, management or mathematics, students are required to study a given subject at length, which they discover only through the voice of their Professor, books and other exercises. Students' imagination is constantly being stifled by discipline. There is no room for imagination, curiosity (apart from that necessary for the subject) or creativity: cramming and other rote learning methods are often the sad pillars of teaching.

---

[112]Michel Foucault, *Le Corps utopique, les hétérotopies*, Lines 2009, pp. 24, 39 and 61. Michel Foucault, *Of Other Spaces: Utopias and Heterotopias* translated by Jay Miskowiec. (Retrieved from http://web.mit.edu/allanmc/www/foucault1.pdf).

Ode to transdisciplinarity

Transdisciplinarity is nourished by imagination, an inherent quality which we all possess spontaneously, but which needs to be nurtured and protected, otherwise it disappears. How do you stay curious? How can our imagination be sustained? The most obvious path is that of transdisciplinarity. It is incumbent on all students to imagine the world in the long term, from different perspectives, in order to make it humanly respectable and humanely sustainable: politics, health, entrepreneurship, lifestyles, education, etc. Students' educational journey, whoever they are and whatever that may be, must lead them to formulating concrete answers about the world as it should be according to them. This can only be achieved by tearing down the walls which separate disciplines. Students must be regularly exposed to scientists – whether these are palaeontologists or astrophysicists – artists – whether these are punk singers or cellists – or artisans – chocolate confectioners or jam makers. By observing and understanding a living and breathing cyborg, students can rekindle the seed of imagination which lives within them; by listening to a Fields Medal winner, they embark on a captivating mathematical adventure; by watching an artist perform before their eyes, they reconnect with their inner-child and marvel, eager to express themselves in a similar way; by listening to an astronaut, their eyes, brain and heart are in a state of turmoil. It is by exposing them to all these individuals, all these disciplines, all these sciences and all these art forms that students can become curious again, can learn to ask questions again, can (re)experience the wonder so dear to Aristotle.

Transdisciplinarity does not claim to be a discipline, but it wants to link them all. Unlike multidisciplinarity (the juxtaposition of different expert views) and interdisciplinarity (dialogue between disciplines), transdisciplinarity wants to make the most of its ecosystem as a whole. *The Transdisciplinarity Manifesto*[113] indicates that transdisciplinarity, as the prefix "trans" transdisciplinarity concerns that which is at once between the disciplines, across the different disciplines, and beyond each individual discipline. Its goal is the understanding of the present world, of which one of the imperatives is the overarching unity of knowledge.

This manifesto clearly explains that we have all been formatted by disciplines, and that from the point of view of classical thinking, there is

---

[113]Basarab Nicolescu, *La transdisciplinarité*, Manifesto, Éditions du Rocher, Monaco, 1996. *Manifesto of Transdisciplinarity*, State University of New York Press, 2002.

nothing across and beyond disciplines. This means we have to think across several levels of reality, all independent from one other, neglecting the spaces between disciplines. Disciplinary research concerns, at most, one and the same level of reality. In fact, in most cases, it concerns only fragments of one and the same level of reality. Transdisciplinarity, on the other hand, concerns itself with the dynamics generated by the activation of several levels of reality at the same time. The discovery of this dynamic necessarily requires disciplinary knowledge. Transdisciplinarity, is not a new discipline or a new hyperdiscipline; it is nourished by disciplinary research, which, in turn, is informed in a new and fruitful way by transdisciplinary knowledge. In this sense, then, disciplinary and transdisciplinary research should not be viewed as antagonistic but rather as complementary.

The three pillars of transdisciplinarity are the levels of reality; the logic of the included third; and complexity. Together they determine the methodology of transdisciplinary research. Even though this is obviously only possible with a hint of indiscipline.

Over 20 years ago the Manifesto of Transdisciplinarity established the Charter of Transdisciplinarity.[114] was established during the first World Congress of Transdisciplinarity in Portugal, one of whose spokespersons was Edgar Morin. This Charter promotes values such as rigor, respect and tolerance. It is unfailingly vigilant in recognising the different realities before us, and obliges us in some way to open up a dialogue with all sciences, art, literature, poetry and spiritual experience. It promotes the dignity of the human being as a citizen of the world, and views education as the authentic path to the development of intuition, imagination, and sensitivity of the body. Finally, this Charter is grounded in strong ethical principles which postulate that the economy must be at the service of the human being and not the other way around.

Today's students are heirs to this Charter of Transdisciplinarity and they have the responsibility, along with teachers, to bring it to life and make it tangible. The world of tomorrow cannot be built with the brains of yesterday, relying on educational methods which have outlived their relevance. Entire generations have been raised in the mentality of disciplines; therefore, it may be necessary to shatter the normative structures of education by paving the way to transdisciplinarity.

---

[114] Charter of Transdisciplinarity, adopted at the First World Congress of Transdisciplinarity, Convento da Arrábida, Portugal, November 2–6, 1994.

Our everyday life is an ecosystem of transdisciplinarity

Transdisciplinarity is above all a question of behaviour and attitudes, a transformation of the self so as to accept the many facets of the world. While many profess their curiosity and open-mindedness, most of us are put off by the tediousness of trying to understand what is being said, done, communicated. It is easier to listen to the speech of a politician from the party we support than to try to understand in depth and objectively that of an opponent. If the vast majority of children follow their parents' religion, this is partly because of religious conditioning but also because converting to another religion requires extensive, dense study, learning and having to face unfamiliar practices.

Being curious and adopting a transdisciplinary attitude in order to understand and build the world means going to art galleries, which is within everyone's reach, or tasting a totally new cuisine. It is as much about questioning life as it is about understanding that life itself questions, and in every possible aspect: political, geographical, historical, sociological. Being faced with life experiences, disciplines and their forms of expression is a veritable way of life which is absolutely vital for students who are building the future, because in challenging their own status quo by confronting their brain, their mind, their intellect to what is unknown to them, they widen the scope of their knowledge, they feed off the disciplines which enable them to (re)model and (re)structure themselves. The brain is like a muscle. It is a matter which can be strengthened, refined and developed. But we still need to dare to shake up our intellectual comfort in order to give it the means to approach a new paradigm. It is so comfortable to stay entrenched in what we already know. It is easier for a rap singer to go to a rap concert, and for a music lover to listen to a symphony. However, it is easy to understand how much both of them would gain from venturing into uncharted territory if they want to think about the future of music, if they want to go beyond the boundaries of their musical territory, if they want to create a new form of music.

Our everyday life is surrounded by achievements stemming from transdisciplinarity: machine learning, which has been gaining increasing momentum in recent years, is a field of artificial intelligence which consists in conferring on a machine the ability to learn on its own and to enrich its database. There is no doubt that the creators of these "machines" relied on observations and discoveries of the human brain, on cognitive sciences and biology.

Steve Jobs, who had taken a calligraphy course at university, put into practice what he had learned in the development of the first Macintosh. As a result, he created variable fonts, which established a niche market for the product among graphic/web designers and corporate communication services.

The kingfisher is a bird which, unlike other birds, can very easily hunt fish because it dives into the water without losing too much speed thanks to its aerodynamic beak. This species inspired Japanese engineers who designed the nose of the Shinkansen (the Japanese high-speed train) like a kingfisher's beak to enter tunnels at 400 km/h with as little loss of speed as possible (10% faster, 15% energy saving compared to a conventional trains).

In the field of aeronautics, Crew Resource Management (CRM) was developed in the 1970s to improve the cooperation and speed of a crew in the event of an emergency. These checklist-based techniques were then adopted by the medical sector, what has now become the famous Medical Team Training (MTT) which is taught in flight simulators.

The aerospace industry often inspires medicine, and the Aerospace Valley and Cancer Bio Santé competitiveness clusters have joined forces so as to transfer algorithms developed in the aerospace industry to add augmented reality to medical imaging, thereby enabling doctors to interpret patient imaging more accurately.

Another example of the use of transdisciplinarity is the team of researchers at the French L'École Nationale Supérieure des Mines de Saint-Étienne[115] who developed an innovative textile which can be turned into an electrode. The objective is to control cardiac activity (without contact or wires). To achieve this, they used a kimono colouring technique called *yuzen*, which involves using rice to concentrate the dye on a specific area.

In the field of biomimicry, transdisciplinarity reigns supreme. For example, engineers have developed a robotic arm which can grasp objects, based on the gecko and its extendable tongue. When the silicon clamp, filled with air and water, touch an object, it causes a double chamber pressure, exactly on the same model as the reptile. Staying in this field, many engineers are working on different flight mechanisms for UAVs. Some people have had the idea of taking their inspiration from bats. Their wings

---

[115] Commonly abbreviated EMSE, it is a French graduate engineering schools specialised in industry-oriented research.

are very flexible, linked together, and their ears allow them to manoeuvre while at the same time remaining almost motionless.

Art is also a great source of inspiration. Willow Garage has collaborated with animator Doug Dooley of Pixar Studio to infuse personal robots with movements and reactions close to those of a living breathing being.

Literature, and science fiction in particular, pushes us to imagine things which seem unthinkable. What is less well known is that literature served as inspiration for many of the technologies used today. For example, the creators of Star Trek developed an entire graphical interface for the series called LCARS, which is said to have inspired Mike Kruzeniski, the designer of the Windows Phone 7. It is also believed that shape and name of the iPad was inspired by the Padd, a touch device from the same universe. Also inspired by Star Trek and its tricoder which allows you to find objects from a distance, Stanford University students worked on a device which detects hidden objects buried in the ground using ultrasound and microwaves.

Similarly, it is difficult to imagine that Elon Musk's Hyperloop, a supersonic train which would link San Francisco to Los Angeles in 30 minutes, was inspired by the electromagnetic-propelled gun, a missile propulsion system based on magnetic fields.

These few examples show us the power gained from mixing disciplines, and putting sectors as well as actors into perspective. The challenge is understanding that the construction of the world is done by multiplying dialogues among disciplines, by associating different fields of knowledge. It is by drawing from what we do not know, or know less, that we can create, that we can connect dots which were a *priori* not made to connected. The future will be built in the interaction and intersection of many fields and many players. Education, therefore, has no choice but to adapt and embrace transdisciplinarity. This does not require a significant investment or training elites, but rather the deployment of a new behaviour, for us to change our reflexes.

The Innovator of the 21st Century

Progress is the realisation of Utopias.

Oscar Wilde
The Soul of Man

When Kant asked the question *Was heisst Aufklärung?*[116] (what is enlightenment?) in 1784, he was asking his contemporary society and himself what was happening in that period. For him, the Age of Enlightenment was humankind's way out of its inability to use its own understanding. The individual now had the courage to know, *sapere aude,* to serve their own understanding.

The way in which Kant argues that we should serve our own understanding needs to keep resonating today. The times in which we are living, teeming with ideas, technologies, innovations, inventions, but which instead of creating an optimistic and positive feeling, is ushering in their own share of worries and doubts, This, as we have pointed out, is not unprecedented.[117] At the time of the Paris Universal Exhibition at the beginning of the 20th century many of the scientific and industrial advances which were exhibited also provoked dread and anxieties. This is exactly when Henri Matisse painted his famous *Bathers with a Turtle,* a work in which the artist astutely expresses our reaction to a changing world. It depicts three possible attitudes to change, which are still relevant today. Firstly, there is reluctance or fear, represented by the woman who is bathing at the far right of the painting. The central character has a neutral stance, that of a passive observer. Finally, there is the third bather to the left who is approaching what is unknown to them all, in this case a small turtle in the middle of the painting. What is to say she is any less scared? However, she is intrigued, and this drives her to get closer so as to learn more about this new discovery. We should approach innovation much in the same way: to tame it, domesticate it and not fearing it, nor letting it unfold without examining it. We cannot, as in the picture, simply refuse innovation, look away and pretend it does not exist; nor can we let it happen and simply sit idly watching it pass us by. The third behaviour is the one we must adopt, that is to say to take a closer look at innovation in order to understand it.

The reason philosophy has this obligation to think about innovation, to put it to the test, is not to oppose innovation nor to denounce it, less still to forestall it. That would be fallacious and counterproductive. On the contrary philosophy needs to take greater interest in innovation so as to evaluate its role, its actions, and to question how it can bring about a better life for all – a major concern of philosophy – and whether it can design a

---

[116]Emmanuel Kant, *Beantwortung der Frage: Was ist Aufklärung?*, *Op. cit.*
[117]See pages 71–73 of this book.

humanely sustainable and desirable future. Alongside such an evaluation of innovation itself, philosophy must also examine, analyse, and influence the figure and the behaviour of the Innovator. Clearly, innovators nowadays do not think; they do. As if crushed under the pressures of their ecosystem, they are no longer able to take the necessary distance to analyse what they are doing, why they are doing it and how they are doing it. Each and every Innovator must understand the responsibilities which lie on their shoulders, and if they cannot, then they should bow out of altogether. The Innovator is expected to be the paragon of exemplarity for what they do for the community, to be a thinking being who takes care of self as well as their ecosystem. The role of philosophy is to lead the Innovator out of their blindness and to help the Innovator adopt a benevolent vision.

Perhaps the innovator of today needs to disappear, and the concept of creative destruction, whose essence is to create something different, something better, learning from one's past, should perhaps apply to innovators. The 21st century needs the kind of Innovator capable of preserving the future and developing a caring and sustainable humanity – none of which will happen without philosophy. This will only be possible through the spiritual exercises as developed by Greek philosophers, such as Epictetus, Marcus Aurelius, Seneca, Epicurus or Diogenes, hundreds of years ago. The real mission of the Innovator is to take care of others, which is only possible by taking care of themselves. To take care of self is a genuine calling, it requires abnegation, a veritable labour of meditation, reading, writing and introspection. This is not something which can be learnt overnight, rather it demands lifelong education, which of course ought to be taught from a very young age, but also then should remain a daily practice throughout life. In other words, the Innovator who wants to be in a position to innovate must be ready and open to conversion: capable of becoming someone other than who their past environment has made them, to become an exemplary being who analyses, sees, surrounds themselves with others, who anticipates and cares. Of course, spiritual exercises for everyone and for innovators in particular will not solve all the problems of innovation. Then again, the law has not succeeded in solving these issues, nor have sanctions or rigorous process-based approaches. At the very least, this proposal raises the question of the practice of the care of self and of others by working directly on the Innovator, on who they are, on what they should be.

Dimensions such as these which focus on the individuals to bring about the Innovator of tomorrow should not, however, be the exclusive preserve of individuals involved in innovation. These philosophical devices are useful for innovators, but fundamental for all. We are all concerned, because individually, each of us is also called to question our relationship with innovations: where do we stand *vis-à-vis* innovation? How do we respond to innovations? When we as individuals, talk about being crushed by innovation, about being dependent on certain innovations or when we reject or glorify innovation, we are, in fact, talking about ourselves, not about innovation. In our current times, then, it is not innovation being put to the test of philosophy, but ourselves being put to this test: who are we and what do we want? This is the question raised by innovation, which is exactly the question philosophy has been asking for 2,500 years.

Bibliography

Able Emily K., Margaret. Nelson (dir.), *Circles of care. Work and Identity in Women's life*, Albany, State University of New York Press, 1990, quoted in Joan Tronto, *Moral Boundaries... Op. cit.*

Adam Smith, *An Enquiry into the Nature and Causes of the Wealth of Nations*, Random House, New York, 1937.

Alexandre Laurent, "Après l'homme réparé, l'homme augmenté?" in "Les Échos" on April 17, 2015.

Alexandre Laurent, *La mort de la mort*, JCLattès, 2011.

Alexandria Clement of, *Stromates*, IV, VI, 27, 3. Translated to English by William Wilson, in *Ante-Nicene Fathers*, Vol. 2. Edited by Alexander Roberts, James Donaldson, and A. Cleveland Coxe. (Buffalo, NY: Christian Literature Publishing Co., 1885.)

Alter Norbert, *L'Innovation ordinaire*, PUF, 2003.

Anders Günther, *The Obsolescence of Man*, Volume II: On the Destruction of Life in the Epoch of the Third Industrial Revolution.

Apology, 29d, Translated to English by Benjamin Jowett http://classics.mit.edu/Plato/apology.html.

Aristote, *Les Parties des Animaux*, II, 691b.

Aristote, *Métaphysique*, 982 b 13.

Aristotle, *Metaphysics*, 982 b 13 Aristot. Met. 1.982b.

Aristotle, *Metaphysics*, 982 b 13. Translated to English by W. D. Ross http://www.documentacatholicaomnia.eu/03d/-384_-322,_Aristoteles,_13_Metaphysics,_EN.pdf.

Aristotle, *On the Parts of Animals, III*. Translated to English by William Ogle http://classics.mit.edu/Aristotle/parts_animals.3.iii.html.

Aristotle, *On the Soul*. Translated to English by E.M. Edghill.

Aristotle, *Treatise on the Soul*, Book II, Part I, Chap. VIII, 431b20.

Aristotle. *Aristotle in 23 Volumes,* Vols.17 and 18, Cambridge, MA, Harvard University Press; London, William Heinemann Ltd. 1933, 1989. Translated to English by Hugh Tredennick.

Arntz M., M., T. Gregory and U. Zierahn (2016), "The Risk of Automation for Jobs in OECD Countries: A Comparative Analysis", OECD Social, Employment and Migration Working Papers, No. 189, OECD Publishing, Paris.

Baber Walter F., *Organizing the Future: Matrix Models for the Postindustrial Policy,* Alabama, The University of Alabama Press, 1983.

Balaudé Jean-François, *Le Savoir-vivre philosophique,* Grasset, 2010.

Bensaude-Vincent Bernadette, *Histoire de la chimie,* La Découverte, 2001.

Bergson Henri, *L'Évolution créatrice* (1907), Éd. PUF, coll. "Quadrige", 2007 (édition critique).

Bergson Henri, *The Creative Evolution.* Translated to English by Arthur Mitchell https://www.gutenberg.org/files/26163/26163-h/26163-h.htm.

Besnier Jean-Michel dans l'article « Post-humain » *in Encyclopédie du trans/ posthumanisme: L'humain et ses préfixes,* sous la direction de: Gilbert Hottois, Jean-Noël Missa et Laurence Perbal, Vrin 2015.

Besnier Jean-Michel, *Demain les posthumains: Le futur a-t-il encore besoin de nous ?* Fayard 2010.

Bostrom Nick and Anders Sanders, "The Wisdom of Nature, An Evolutionary Heuristic for Human Enhancement", in *Human Enhancement*, J. Savulescu and N. Bostrom (eds.), Oxford University Press, 2008.

Bostrom Nick, "A history of transhumanist thought", *Journal of Evolution and Technology,* 14(1), April 2005.

Bostrom Nick, "Transhumanism FAQ: A General Introduction, version 2.1", online: http://humanityplus.org/philosophy/transhumanist-faq/, 2003.

Bourg Dominique, COP21 – Climat: le thermomètre et le philosophe – Spécial 2° avant la fin du monde.

Bowen H. R. *Social Responsibilities of the Businessman,* Harper & Brothers, 1953.

Brundtland G. H., *Our Common Future – Report of the World Commission on Environment and Development,* United Nations General Assembly, New York, 1987.

Burkert Walter, "Plato oder Pythagoras", *Hermes,* 88, 1969.

Cancian Francesca M. and Y. Oliker Stacey, *Caring and Gender,* Thousand Oaks, Pine Forge Press, 2000.

Carson Rachel, *Silent Spring,* Mariner Book Edition, 2002.

Cassan Armand, *Lettres inédites de Marc Aurèle et de Fronton,* A. Levasseur, 1830.

Cavell Stanley, *Qu'est-ce que la philosophie américaine?* Translated by Sandra Laugier, Gallimard, 2009.

Chesbrough Henry, *Open Innovation: The New Imperative for Creating and Profiting from Technology*, Harvard Business School Press, 2003.

Cicero, *The Tusculan Disputations of Cicero,* W. H. Main, Leopold Classic Library, 2016.

Cicero, *Tusculanes*, V, 3, 7–9, French translation by Émile Bréhier, Gallimard, 1962.

Condorcet, *Esquisse d'un tableau historique des progrès de l'esprit humain*, édition dite Prior-Belaval, Vrin 1970.

Condorcet, *Outlines of An Historical View of the Progress of the Human Mind.*

Darwin Charles, *On the Origin of Species* (the complete title of the original edition is *On the Origin of Species by Means of Natural Selection, or the Preservation of Favoured Races in the Struggle for Life*), 1st edition 1859.

De Ruyt Franz, "L'idée du 'Bivium' et le symbole pythagoricien de la lettre Y", in *Revue belge de philologie et d'histoire*, t. X, fasc.

Demont Paul, *Problèmes de morale antique* (dir.), université d'Amiens, 1993.

Descartes René, *A Discourse on Method.* Translated to English by John Veitch https://www.gutenberg.org/files/59/59-h/59-h.htm.

Descartes, *Discours de la méthode*, in *Œuvres*, Bibliothèque de la Pléiade, Gallimard, 1953.

Diogenes the Cynic: Sayings and Anecdotes, London, OUP, 2012, Saying 275.

Domanski Juliusz, *La Philosophie, théorie ou manière de vivre, controverse de l'Antiquité à la Renaissance*, Éditions du Cerf, 1996.

Eberhard Christophe, *Traduire nos responsabilités planétaires. Recomposer nos paysages juridiques*, Bruxelles, Bruylant, 2006.

Emerson Ralph W., "Self-Reliance" in *Essays: First Series* (1841). *The Collected Works of Ralph Waldo Emerson*, ed. R.E. Springer, A. R. Ferguson, J. Slater, D. E. Wilson. J. F. Carr, W. E. Williams, P. Nicoloff, R. E. Burkholder, B. L. Packer, Cambridge M.A., Harvard University Press, 1971–2003.

Épictète, *Manuel*, chap. VIII.

Épictète, *Manuel*, trans. J. Pépin *in Les Stoïciens*, Bibliothèque de la Pléiade, Gallimard, 1952 p. 1111. Epictetus, *A Selection from the Discourses of Epictetus With the Encheiridion*, Translated to English by George Long http://pioneer.chula.ac.th/~pukrit/bba/Epictetus.pdf.

Epictetus, *A Selection from the Discourses of Epictetus With the Encheiridion.* Translated to English by George Long http://pioneer.chula.ac.th/~pukrit/bba/ Epictetus.pdf.

Epictetus, *Discourses, Fragments, Handbook,* translated by Robin Hard, Oxford University Press, Critical ed. Edition, 2014.

Epictetus, *Handbook.* Translated to English by *George Long.*

Epictetus, *The Moral Discourses of Epictetus*. Translated to English by Elizabeth Carter.

Épicure, *Lettres et Maximes*, trad. M. Conche, Éditions de Mégare, 1977.

Epicurus, *The Essential Epicurus: Letters, Principal Doctrines, Vatican Sayings, and Fragments*, Prometheus Books, 1993.

Ewald François, *Histoire de l'Etat-Providence*, Folio, 1996, p. 86. *The Birth of Solidarity, The History of the French Welfare State*, Ed. Melinda Cooper. Translated to English by Timothy Scott Johnson, Duke University Press.

Favaro Ken, Per-Ola Karlsson and Gary L. Neilson, "CEO Succession 2000–2009: A Decade of Convergence and Compression" for Booz&Co, *Strategy Business*, no. 59, summer 2010.

Faye E. *Heidegger, l'introduction du nazisme dans la philosophie: autour des séminaires inédits de 1933–1935*, Albin Michel, "Idées", 2005.

Ferenczi T. (dir.), De quoi sommes-nous responsables?, Éditions Le Monde 1997.

Foucault Michel, *Dits et écrits I*, Gallimard, "Quarto", 2001.

Foucault Michel, "The Subject and Power", *Critical Inquiry* 8(4), 1982, 777–795.

Foucault Michel, Essential Works of Foucault, 1954–1984, New Press, 2001.

Foucault Michel, *Ethics: Subjectivity and Truth: Essential Works of Michel Foucault 1954–1984,* Edited by Paul Rabinow, Translated to English by Robert Hurley and others.

Foucault Michel, *Histoire de la sexualité III. Le souci de soi*, Gallimard, « Tel », 1984.

Foucault Michel, *L'Herméneutique du sujet*, Cours au Collège de France. 1981–1982, "Hautes études", Gallimard-Seuil, 2001.

Foucault Michel, *Le Corps utopique, les hétérotopies*, Lines 2009.

Foucault Michel, *Le Courage de la vérité, Le gouvernement de soi et des autres II*, Cours au Collège de France. 1984, éditions Hautes Études, Gallimard-Seuil, 2009.

Foucault Michel, *Le Gouvernement de soi et des autres, course at the Collège de France, 1981–1982*, Gallimard-Seuil, 2008.

Foucault Michel, *Of Other Spaces: Utopias and Heterotopias* translated by Jay Miskowiec (http://web.mit.edu/allanmc/ www/foucault1.pdf).

Foucault Michel, *The Care of Self*, Penguin Books, Limited, 2006.

Foucault Michel, *The Hermeneutics of the Subject, Lectures at the Collège de France, 1981–1982*, F. Gros (ed.), Translated to English by Graham Burchell http://www.rebels-library.org/files/foucault_hermeneutics.pdf.

Foucault Michel, *The Use of Pleasure, Vol. 2 of The History of Sexuality*, Vintage Books, A Division of Random House, Inc. New York, 1990, p. 13. Translated to English by Robert Hurley https://monoskop.org/images/a/a3/Foucault_Michel_The_History_of_Sexuality_2_The_Use_of_Pleasure.pdf.

Friedman Thomas, *The World Is Flat: A Brief History of the Twenty-first Century*, Farrar, Straus and Giroux, 2005.

Gagnepain Laurent, "La climatisation automobile, Impacts, consommation et pollution" in *Repères* published by the French Environment and Energy Management Agency – Transport Technologies Department, 2006.

Garbarinoa Ellen, Michal Strahilevitzb, "Gender differences in the perceived risk of buying online and the effects of receiving a site recommendation", *Journal of Business Research*, 57, 2004.

Geoffrey Moore, *Crossing the Chasm: Marketing and Selling High-Tech Products to Mainstream Customers*, HarvardBusiness, second edition, August 2006.

Gilligan Carol, *In a Different Voice: Psychological Theory and Women's Development*, Harvard University Press, 1982.

Gilligan Carol, *Une voix différente, pour une éthique du* care (1982), French translation by Annick Kwiatek, reviewed by Vanessa Nurock, Champ-Flammarion, 2008.

Godin Benoît, "Innovation: The History of a Category", Working Paper, 2008, http://www.csiic.ca/innovation.html.

Grimal Pierre, *Marc Aurèle*, Fayard, 1991.

Guichard Renelle and Laurence Servel, « Qui sont les innovateurs ? Une lecture socio-économique des acteurs de l'innovation », *Sociétal* 52, 2006.

Güzin Mazman S., Yasemin Koçak Usluel and Vildan Çevik, "Social Influence in the Adoption Process and Usage of Innovation: Gender Differences", *World Academy of Science, Engineering and Technology*, No. 49, 2009.

Hadot Pierre, *Exercices spirituels et philosophie antique*, Albin Michel, 2002.

Hadot Pierre, *La Philosophie comme manière de vivre*, Albin Michel, 2001.

Hadot Pierre, *Philosophy as a way of life*, translated by Michael Chase, Blackwell 1995.

Hadot Pierre, Qu'est-ce que *la philosophie antique*, Gallimard, 1995, p. 35.

Hadot Pierre, *What is Ancient Philosophy?* Translated by M. Chase, The Belknap Press of Harvard University Press, 2004.

Hans Jonas, *Le Principe responsabilité. Une éthique pour la civilisation technologique*, Translated by J. Greisch, 1998. Paris, Flammarion, 1979, pp. 95–106.

Hans Jonas, *The Imperative of Responsibility: In Search of an Ethics for the Technological Age,* University of Chicago Press, 1985.

Hans Jonas, *The Imperative of Responsibility: In Search of an Ethics for the Technological Age,* University of Chicago Press, 1985.

Hart Herbert, Punishment and responsibility, Oxford University Press, 1968.

Hesiod, *Work and Days*, translated to English by Hugh G. Evelyn-White, Dodo Press, 2008.

Hésiode, *Les travaux et les jours*, 287–290. Translated by P. Mazon, Paris. C.U.F., 2002.

Hiéroclès, *In Aureum Pythag. Carmen Comment, Prolog.*, 3, p. 6, 11 köhler. Traduction de M. Meunier, in Hiéroclès, *Les Vers d'or,* Guy Trédaniel, 1925, (rééd. 1979).

Himanen Pekka, *The Hacker Ethic and the Spirit of the Information Age*, New York: Random House, 2001.

Homère, *Odyssée*, XX, 18–23, translated to French by. R. Flacelière and V. Bérard, Gallimard, "Bibliothèque de la Pléiade", 1955.

Homère, *The Odyssey*, HardPress Publishing 2019.

Horace, *Epistles*, I, 2, 40 *in Works*, French translation by François Richard, Garnier-Flammarion, 1993. Horace, *Satires and Epistles*. Translated by John Davie, Oxford University Press, 2004.

Houziaux Alain (dir.), *Existe-t-il une spiritualité sans Dieu?*, Éditions de l'Atelier, 2006.

Huxley Julian, "Transhumanism", *Ethics in Progress* 6(1), 2015, 12–16; doi: 10.14746/eip.2015.1.2y; ISSN 2084-9257.

Juliette Grange, "Au XIXᵉ siècle. La république sociale et ses critiques", *L'idée de République*, Paris, Pocket, 2008.

Kant Emmanuel, Beantwortung der Frage: Was ist Aufklärung? (« *Réponse à la question: « Qu'est-ce que 'les Lumières'? »*) publié en décembre 1784. Traduction de Stéphane Piobetta in *La Philosophie de l'Histoire*, Éditions Gonthiers, Montaigne, 1947, revue Par Cyril Morana in *Qu'est-ce que les Lumières?* Mille et une nuits, 2006.

Kant Emmanuel, *Foundation for Metaphysics of Morals in Metaphysics of Morals*, Translated to English by Thomas Kingsmill.

Kant Emmanuel, *Kant's Introduction To Logic, And His Essay On The Mistaken Subtilty Of The Four Figures*, Forgotten Books, 2018. Translated to English by Thomas Kingsmill Abbott.

Kant Emmanuel, *Fondation de la métaphysique des mœurs* in *Métaphysique des mœurs*, I, *Fondation, Introduction*. Translated by Alain Renault.

Kant Emmanuel, *Logique*, Vrin, 1965.

Kelley Thomas, *The Ten Faces of Innovation: IDEO's Strategies for Defeating the Devil's Advocate and Driving Creativity Throughout Your Organisation*, Broadway Business, 2005.

Korotayev A. V., L. E. Grinin, "Kondratieff Waves in the World System Perspective", in *Kondratieff Waves. Dimensions and Perspectives at the Dawn of the 21st Century,* Leonid E. Grinin, Tessaleno C. Devezas, and Andrey V. Korotayev (eds.), Volgograd, Uchitel, 2012.

Kurzweil Raymond, *Humanité 2.0: la bible du changement,* M21 éditions, 2007.

Kurzweil Raymond, *The Age of Spiritual Machines*, Viking Adult, 1999.

Kurzweil Raymond, *The Singularity Is Near: When Humans Transcend Biology,* Penguin books.

La Mettrie Julien Jean Offray de, *Man a Machine*. Translated to English by Gertrude Carman Bussey http://www.gutenberg.org/files/52090/52090-h/52090-h.htm.

La Mettrie, *L'Homme-machine*, édition présentée et établie par Paul-Laurent Assoun, Paris, Denoël, 1981.

Laërce Diogène, *Vies et sentences des philosophes illustres*, IX, 64. Translated by Jacques Brunschwig, Le Livre de poche, 1999.

Laërtius Diogenes, *The Lives and Opinions of Eminent Philosophers*. Translated to English by C. D. Yonge.

Lapied A. et S. Swaton, "Sélection naturelle ou volonté de puissance: comment interpréter le processus de destruction créatrice", *Revue de philosophie économique* 14, 2013/2.

Laruelle François, *En tant qu'un*, Aubier, 1991.

Laugier Sandra, "Emerson, la voix, le perfectionnisme et la démocratie", in Sandra Laugier (dir.), *La voix et la vertu*, PUF, 2010.

Lee Kuan Yew, *From Third World to First*, Harper, 2000.

M. Malherbe et F. Brugère, *Shaftesbury, philosophie et politesse* (actes du colloque de Nantes, 1996), edited by Champion, Paris, 2000.

Malingrey Anne-Marie, *Philosophia. Étude d'un groupe de mots dans la littérature grecque, des présocratiques au IVᵉ siècle après J.-C.*, coll. « Études et commentaires », Klincksieck, 1961.

Mantoux Paul, *La Révolution industrielle au XVIIIᵉ siècle*, Société nouvelle de librairie et d'édition, 1906.

Marc Aurèle, *Écrits pour lui-même*. Tome I: Introduction générale. Livre I. Translated to French by Pierre Hadot, Les Belles Lettres, 1998.

Marc Aurèle, *Pensées pour moi-même*, VIII.

Marcus Aurelius, *Thoughts for Myself*, VIII.

Martin Roger, "The Virtue Matrix: Calculating the Return on Corporate Responsibility (HBR OnPoint Enhanced Edition)", *Harvard Business Review*, December 1, 2002.

Marx/Engels Selected Works, Vol. 1, Progress Publishers, Moscow, 1969. Translated: Samuel Moore in cooperation with Frederick Engels, 1888; first edition 1848.

Merleau-Ponty Maurice, *Éloge de la philosophie*, inaugural lesson at the Collège de France, Gallimard, 1960.

Merleau-Ponty Maurice, In Praise of Philosophy and Other Essays. Translated to English by John Wil and James Edie, Northwestern University Press.

Michel Foucault, *Dits et écrits II, Gallimard, « Quarto »*, 2001.

Milne A., *Winnie the Pooh*. London: Methuen & Co/Ltd, 1926.

Molinier P., S. Laugier, P. Paperman, *Qu'est-ce que le* care*?, Op. cit.*, p. 35. Joan Tronto, *Caring Democracy: Markets, Equality, and Justice.*: New York University Press, New York, 2013.

Monk Ray, *Ludwig Wittgenstein: The Duty of Genius*, Penguin Books, 1991.
Monk Ray, *Wittgenstein, le devoir de génie*. Translated by Abel Gerschenfeld, Flammarion, 2009.
Montaigne, *The Essays of Montaigne, Complete*. Translated to English by Charles Cotton.
Montaigne, *Essais*, mis en français moderne et présentés par Claude Pinganaud, Arléa, 2002
Moore Geoffrey A., *Crossing the Chasm, Marketing and Selling High-Tech Products to Mainstream Customer*, HarperCollins Publishers, New York, 1991, revised edition 1999.
Moore Geoffrey, *Crossing the Chasm*. HarperCollins Publishers, New York, 1991.
Neuberg Marc, *La Responsabilité: questions philosophiques* de. Presses universitaires de France, 1997.
Nicolescu Basarab, *Manifesto of Transdisciplinarity*, State University of New York Press, 2002.
Nicolescu Basarab, *La transdisciplinarité*, Manifesto, Éditions du Rocher, Monaco, 1996.
Nidumolu R., C.K. Prahalad, and M.R. Rangaswami, "Why Sustainability is Now the Key Driver of Innovation", *Harvard Business Review*, September 2009.
Nietzsche Friedrich, *Thus Spoke Zarathustra*. Translated to English by A. del Caro, ed. A, Del Caro and R. B. Pippin, Cambridge University Press, Cambridge, 2006.
Nietzsche Friedrich, *Fragments posthumes sur l'éternel retour*, Allia, 2003, p. 87. Published in English as *The Will to Power*.
Nietzsche Friedrich, *On the Geneaology of Morals*, III. 14 On the Genealogy of Morality ed. Edited Bykeith Ansell-Pearson. Translated to English by Carol Diethe.
Norbert Alter, "Entreprise: les innovateurs au quotidien", *Futuribles*, January 2002.
Ortega y Gasset José, *The Revolt of the Masses*, 1932 by W. W. Norton & Company, Inc.
Ost François, La *Nature hors la loi*, La Découverte.
Owen Richard, John Bessant, Maggy Heintz *Responsible Innovation: Managing the Responsible Emergence of Science and Innovation in Society*, edited by Wiley, 2013.
Paquet Léonce, *Les Cyniques grecs, fragments et* témoignages, Le Livre de Poche, 1992.
Pavie Xavier, C. Jouanny, D. Carthy and F. Verez, *Le design thinking au service de l'innovation responsable*, Maxima, 2014.
Pavie Xavier, *Exercices spirituels. Leçons de la philosophie antique,* Les Belles Lettres, Paris, 2012.
Pavie Xavier, *Exercices spirituels. Leçons de la philosophie contemporaine*, Les Belles Lettres, Paris, 2013.

Pavie Xavier, *L'innovation responsable, levier stratégique pour les organisa-tions*, Eyrolles, 2012.

Pavie Xavier, Victor Scholten and Daphne Carthy, *Responsible Innovation, from Concept to Practice*, World Scientific, 2014.

Perroux F., *La pensée économique de Joseph Schumpeter: les dynamiques du capitalisme*, Genève, Librairie Droz, 1965.

Perroux François (1935), *La Pensée économique de Joseph Schumpeter*, Presse de Savoie, 1965.

Philippe Gérard, Ost François and Van de Kerchove Michel (eds.), *L'Accélération du temps juridique*, Brussels, Publications des Facultés universitaires, Saint-Louis, 2000.

Pinçon Michel, Monique Pinçon-Charlot, *Voyage en grande bourgeoisie*, PUF, 2005.

Pindare, *Pythian* 2, line 72.

Plato, *Apology of Socrates*, 29d.

Plato, *Ménon*, 77a–78b. Translated to English by Benjamin Jowett.

Plato, *The Banquet*, 204 a-d, trans. Léon Robin, Gallimard, "Bibliothèque de la Pléiade", 1950.

Plato, *The Republic*, 518c.

Plato, *The Republic*. Translated into English by B. Jowett http://www.gutenberg. org/files/1497/1497-h/1497-h.htm.

Plato, *Theætetus*. Translated to English by Benjamin Jowett http://www. gutenberg.org/files/1726/1726-h/1726-h.htm.

Platon, *Alcibiade*, 133c.

Platon, *Apologie de Socrate*, 29d.

Platon, *République*, trad. Léon Robin, *in* Platon, *Œuvres complètes I*, Gallimard, « Bibliothèque de la Pléiade », 1950, IV, 420b.

Platon, *Théétète*, 155d, trad. Léon Robin, Gallimard, "Bibliothèque de la Pléiade", 1950.

Plotin, *Ennéades*, I, VI (1), 9, 13, trad. Émile Bréhier. Plotinus *The Six Enneads*. Translated to English by Stephen Mackenna and B. S. Page http:// www.documentacatholicaomnia.eu/03d/0204-0270,_Plotinus,_The_Six_ Enneads,_EN.pdf.

Plutarch, "Laconic apothegms", in *Plutarch's Morals*, translated by several hands. Corrected and revised by William W. Goodwin with an Introduction by Ralph Waldo Emerson. Boston, Little, Brown and Co. (based on 5th ed. of 1718).

Plutarch, *Moralia On Listening to Lectures*. Translated to English by F. C. Babbitt. (The work appears in pp. 201–259 of Vol. I of the Loeb Classical Library's edition of the *Moralia*, first published in 1927.)

Plutarque, Comment écouter ? in *Œuvres morales*, tome I, 2e partie. Traités 3-9, Trad. R. Klaerr, A. Philippon, J. Sirinelli, Les Belles Lettres, 1989.

Plutarque, *Œuvres morales*, t. III, trad. F. Fuhrmann, Paris, Les Belles Lettres, 1988.

Rabelais François, *Gargantua and Pantagruel, Complete. Five Books of The Lives, Heroic Deeds and Sayings of Gargantua and His Son Pantagruel.* Translated into English by Sir Thomas Urquhart of Cromarty and Peter Antony Motteux https://www.gutenberg.org/files/1200/1200-h/1200-h.htm.

Rahbek Pedersen Esben "Modelling CSR: How managers understand the responsibilities on business toward society", *Journal of Business Ethics* 2010.

Rand Ayn, "The Objectivist Ethics", *The Virtue of Selfishness.*

Rand Ayn, in *Atlas Shrugged*, Random House, New York City, 1957.

Rand Ayn, *La Grève.*, Translated by Sophie Bastide-Foltz, Les Belles Lettres 2011.

Rand Ayn, in *Atlas Shrugged*, Random House, New York City, 1957.

Rand Ayn, "Introduction", *The Virtue of Selfishness.*

Raymond Jonathan, "La Ford Pinto: le contre-exemple américain", *Le Polyscope Le journal de l'École polytechnique de Montréal* 36, 2003.

Reinert H. and E.S. Reinert. 2006. "Creative destruction in Economics", in J. G. Backhaus et W. Drechsler, *Friedrich Nietzsche (1844-1900), Economy and society*, New York, Springer.

Ricoeur Paul, "Le concept de responsabilité. Essai d'analyse sémantique", in *Le Juste 1*, Paris, Seuil 1995, pp. 281–282.

Robert E.B., *Entrepreneurship in High Technology: Lessons from MIT Beyond*, New York, OUP, 1991.

Rousseau, *Discourse on the Origin of Inequality,* Dover Publication 2004.

Rousseau Jean-Jacques, *Discours sur les sciences et les arts*, Garnier-Flammarion, 1992.

Rousseau Jean-Jacques, Discourse on the sciences and the Arts. Translated by Ian Johnston, Richer Resources Publications, 2014.

Rousseau, *Discours sur l'origine et les fondements de l'inégalité parmi les hommes*, Flammarion, 1989.

Rufus Musonius, The Roman Socrates Lectures and Fragments. Translated to English by Cora E. Lutz.

Sahlman W. A., "How to write a great business plan", *Harvard Business Review* 4(75), 1997.

Schumpeter Joseph A., *Théorie de l'évolution économique.* Translated by Jean-Jacques Askett, Dalloz, 1999.

Schumpeter Joseph, *Capitalisme, socialisme, démocratie.* Translated by Gaël Fain, éd. Payot, 1951, p. 40. Joseph Schumpeter, The Theory of Economic Development: An Inquiry into Profits, Capitals, Credits, Interest, and the Business Cycle. Transaction Publishers, 2004,

Schumpeter Joseph, *Theorie der wirtschaftlichen Entwicklung,* revised edition 1925. Translation to English by Redvers Opie, *The theory of economic development: an inquiry into profits, capital, credit, interest, and the business cycle*, New Brunswick, Transaction Books, (1938) 2008.

Schwartz Mark S., "Universal Moral Values for Corporate Codes of Ethics", *Journal of Business Ethics* 2005.

Sen Amartya, "Health in Development", Keynote address to the 52nd World Health Assembly, Geneva, May 18, 1999, in *Bulletin of the World Health Organization* 77, 1999.

Seneca, Ad Lucilium Epistulae Morales, William Heinemann, London; G. P. Putnam's Sons, New York. Translated to English by Richard M. Gummere, https://en.wikisource.org/wiki/Moral_letters_to_Lucilius.

Seneca, *Dialogues and Essays.* Translated by John Davie, Oxford University Press, 2009.

Seneca, Minor Dialogs Together with the Dialog "On Clemency". Translated by Aubrey Stewart, Bohn's Classical Library Edition; London, George Bell and Sons, 1900.

Seneca, *Of Peace of Mind* (1900), Translated to English by Aubrey Stewart.

Sénèque, De la tranquillité de l'âme, II, 6–15, trad. R. Waltz.

Shionoya Y., *Schumpeter and the Idea of Social Sciences*, Cambridge, Cambridge University Press, 1997.

Shusterman Richard, *Vivre la philosophie – Pragmatisme et art de vivre*, trad. Christian Fournier et Jean-Pierre Cometti, Klincksieck, 2001.

Shusterman Richard, *Practicing Philosophy: Pragmatism and the Philosophical Life*, Routledge, New York, 1997.

Smith Adam, *Recherches sur la nature et la cause des richesses des nations* (1776). Translated by G. Granger, Flammarion, Paris, 1991.

Sombart Werner, *Krieg und Kapitalismus,* Munich, Duncker & Humblot, 1913.

Sophocle, *Antigone*, Loeb Classical Library. Translated to English by Hugh Lloyd-Jones.

Sophocle, *Antigone.* Translated by P. Mazon, Les Belles Lettres, 1955.

Stoïciens Les, translated into French by É. Bréhier, Gallimard, "Bibliothèque de la Pléiade", 1962.

Tarde Gabriel, *Les lois de l'imitation*, Paris Seuil, 2001.

Thoreau Henry David, A Week on the Concord and Merrimack Rivers; Walden, or, Life in the Woods; The MaineWoods, Robert F. Sayre (ed.) https://azeitao.files.wordpress.com/2007/05/walden.pdf.

Thoreau Henry David, *L'Esprit commercial des temps modernes et son influence sur le caractère politique, littéraire et moral d'une nation.* French translation by D. Bazy, Le Grand Souffle, 2007.

Thoreau Henry David, The Writings of Henry David Thoreau, Volume VI, Familiar Letters. F. B. Sanbonrn (ed.), Copyright 1865 By Ticknor And Fields, Copyright 1894 and 1906 By Houghton, Mifflin & Co. http://www.gutenberg.org/files/43523/43523-h/43523-h.htm.

Thoreau Henry David, *Walden ou La vie dans les bois.* French translation by L. Fabulet, Gallimard, 2007.

Tronto J., *Moral Boundaries. A Political Argument for an Ethic of Care*, Routledge, New York, 1993.

Tronto Joan, *Caring Democracy: Markets, Equality, and Justice*, New York University Press, New York, 2013.

Truong Jean-Michel, *Totalement inhumaine*, Les empêcheurs de penser en rond, 2003.

Vernant Jean-Pierre, *Mythe et pensée chez les Grecs*, La découverte, 1996.

Vincent Bernard (dir.), *Histoire des États-Unis*, Paris, Flammarion, 1997.

Von Schomberg René, *Prospects for Technology Assessment in a framework of responsible research and innovation*, in Technikfolgen abschaetzen lehren: Bildungspotenziale transdisziplinaerer Methode, Wiesbaden, Springer VS, 2011.

Williams B., L'Éthique et les Limites de la philosophie. Translated by M.-A. Lescourret, Gallimard, 1990.

Xenophon, *Memorabilia*, I, 21–34. Translated to English by H. G. Dakyns.

Xénophon, *Mémorables*, IV, 4, 10, trad. L.-A. Dorion, « Collection des universités de France », Les Belles Lettres, 2003.

Xenophon, *The Memorabilia: Recollections of Socrates*. Translated to English by H. G. Dakyns http://www.gutenberg.org/files/1177/1177-h/1177-h.htm#link2H_4_0006.

Index Nominum

Index